*Suspended Animation*

# SUSPENDED ANIMATION

## Children's Picture Books and the Fairy Tale of Modernity

*Nathalie op de Beeck*

University of Minnesota Press

*Minneapolis*

*London*

This book is published with assistance from the Margaret S. Harding Memorial Endowment honoring the first director of the University of Minnesota Press.

Permission credits for illustrations in this book appear on pages 249–54.

Published by the University of Minnesota Press
111 Third Avenue South, Suite 290
Minneapolis, MN 55401-2520
http://www.upress.umn.edu

Library of Congress Cataloging-in-Publication Data

op de Beeck, Nathalie.
   Suspended animation : children's picture books and the fairy tale of modernity / Nathalie op de Beeck.
     p.  cm.
   Includes bibliographical references and index.
   ISBN 978-0-8166-6573-0 (alk. paper) — ISBN 978-0-8166-6574-7 (pbk. : alk. paper)
    1. Children's literature, American—History and criticism.  2. Picture books for children—United States—History—20th century.  3. Illustrated children's books—United States—History—20th century.  4. Literature and technology—United States—History—20th century.  5. Popular culture and literature—United States—History—20th century.  6. Picture books for children—Publishing—United States—History—20th century.  7. Children—Books and reading—United States—History—20th century.  I. Title.
   PS490.B44    2010
   810.9'9282—dc22

2010031771

Printed in the United States of America on acid-free paper

The University of Minnesota is an equal-opportunity educator and employer.

17 16 15 14 13 12 11 10    10 9 8 7 6 5 4 3 2 1

# Contents

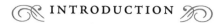

# INTRODUCTION

## *Picture Books in Modern Times*

American readers grow up with picture books. They consider the picture book a fixture of the library or bookstore, the elementary school, and their home bookshelves. The ubiquitous picture book—whether a splashy, award-winning title or a commonplace, scuffed cloth hardcover—is a familiar form of entertainment for children, a site of bemused reverie for parents, and an object of fascination for devoted collectors and critics. It seems always to have been around. Whether adult readers purchase hardbound editions for their kids, borrow well-thumbed and penciled-in library copies, or do the work of soliciting manuscripts and graphic portfolios at publishing houses, they effortlessly read picture books and fondly remember books from their own childhoods. They take pleasure in the poetry and prose styles, humor and seriousness, artistic media, and design strategies of picture-book storytelling. They feel as comfortable scanning a text's sequential words and images as they do reading comics or watching a film, and they expect younger generations of readers to feel (and read) the same way when encountering the visual-verbal text. They might count *The Story of Ferdinand* (1936), *The Story of Babar, the Little Elephant* (1931; U.S., 1933), or *Mike Mulligan and His Steam Shovel* (1939) among their favorite childhood books. They state their allegiance to Dr. Seuss or Margaret Wise Brown, cosmopolitan creators who forged their careers in the modernist crucible of New York in the years between the First and Second World Wars.

In the twenty-first century, readers still enjoy Hans Augusto and Margret Rey's *Curious George* (1941), in a version that no longer berates the title monkey for having "only one fault: he was very curious and always tried to imitate things."[1] They have a choice of *Curious George* commodities, from the 2006 animated film to stuffed animals, cookie jars, cards, clothing, DVDs, and board books, and for these millennial audiences there is no longer any fault in curiosity.[2] Critics, spoiling the fun, argue that *Curious George* reiterates colonial narratives of capture and forcible domestication, or view the book as the Reys' account of the irrepressibility of subjects under fascism, given that the German-Jewish husband-and-wife team fled the Nazi invasion of Paris and came to the United States as refugees in 1940.[3] Another favorite picture book,

Robert McCloskey's *Make Way for Ducklings* (1941), lures readers to visit a commemorative bronze duck family in Boston's Public Garden and the nearby swan boats in the very pond where the ducklings made their home. The charm and all-weather sturdiness of the oversize sculpted ducks produce a warm nostalgia for McCloskey's work, mingled with a flickering glimpse of changing American childhood. McCloskey's beloved story of the guileless ducklings following their determined mother across a bustling city street and protected by a kindly policeman harks back to earlier eras and superficially promises that in childhood we find a safe refuge for whimsy, kindness, and harmless fun. Scholars are quick to point out that the ducklings serve as utopian representatives of fragile nature, flourishing amid urban technologies that squish wildlife and despoil habitats. They accurately contend that McCloskey's visual style "reflect[s] the 'art-for-everyone' attitude that . . . prompted the Federal Art Projects of the nineteen-thirties" and that emerges from McCloskey's artistic practice of 1935–37, when he painted bas-reliefs in his small-town home of Hamilton, Ohio; notably, McCloskey was creating murals for the Lever Brothers Building in Boston when he wrote *Make Way for Ducklings*.[4] Such are the multiple interpretations of picture books, whose paradoxes make them valuable case studies on ideology, childhood, and modernity.

Links between modernity, modernism, and children's literature have gained increasing critical attention since the 1990s. Indispensable work such as Beverly Lyon Clark's *Kiddie Lit: The Cultural Construction of Children's Literature in America* (2003), Juliet Dusinberre's *Alice to the Lighthouse: Children's Books and Radical Experiments in Art* (1999), Katherine Capshaw Smith's *Children's Literature of the Harlem Renaissance* (2004), Philip Nel's *Dr. Seuss: American Icon* (2004), and Leonard Marcus's *Margaret Wise Brown: Awakened by the Moon* (1992) makes salient connections between picture-book practices and modern subjectivity, investigating the children's text and child audiences in a context of modernism and modernity. Barbara Bader's *American Picture Books from "Noah's Ark" to "The Beast Within"* (1976) remains a key resource on picture-book creators and U.S. history. Marcus's *Minders of Make Believe: Idealists, Entrepreneurs, and the Shaping of American Children's Literature* (2008), Jacalyn Eddy's *Bookwomen: Creating an Empire in Children's Publishing* (2006), and the conference proceedings in *Stepping Away from Tradition: Children's Books of the Twenties and Thirties* (1988) call attention to book-industry history and the creative ferment between the wars. Surveys such as Bettina Hurlimann's *Picture-Book World* (*Die Welt im Bilderbuch*, 1965), Jean-Paul Gourevitch's *Images d'enfance: Quatre siècles d'illustration du livre pour enfants* (1994), and Evgeny

Steiner's *Stories for Little Comrades: Revolutionary Artists and the Making of Early Soviet Children's Books* (1999) detail international developments in the twentieth-century picture book. Special editions of scholarly journals focus on picture books and modernity,[5] and trade publications such as *Publishers Weekly* track sales developments with a deep institutional knowledge of reading and marketing picture books. Yet interdisciplinary book-length considerations of the words, pictures, and fabrication of picture books are uncommon, possibly because such investigations span literary criticism, visual studies, and material-culture discourses. David Lewis, who, like Brian Alderson, explores picture-book history, writes, "What we do not have is any kind of social history, a history that puts the picture book within the contexts of its production and its use." He says a fine-art or a canon-centered approach cannot succeed, because "a history informed and guided by a concern for the artistically fine will grant neither time nor space to the popular, the vulgar, the hybrid, and the crude."[6] A combined literary, cultural studies, and art historical approach is necessary to provide critical perspective on the picture book itself, through examples from a range of primary sources, historical accounts, and viewpoints. The picture book—despite its youthful, domestic audience and seeming lack of affiliation to any aesthetic or political movement—has roots in vernacular culture and the avant-garde alike. The picture book's materiality, narrative structures, and topical content develop in parallel with political movements and reflect differing myths of social progress.

## SUSPENDING ANIMATION

*Suspended Animation* situates the American picture book and its visual-verbal sequences in the cultural and critical contexts of modernity and the machine age. This project works within and beyond the field of children's literature to show how the American picture book—a hybrid text shared with the developing modern subject—functions as a sequential visual narrative, a literary work, a mediating object, and a tangible material artifact of U.S. culture. Without wishing to dismiss the historical situatedness of every text, I use the formalist or narratological term "suspended animation" to refer to the way a picture book's words and frames constitute a narrative. Storytellers compose the sequence and audiences forge imaginative connections by reading across the pages, experiencing a sort of extracinematic montage. The idea of suspended animation implies technology and alludes to paused images and texts in sequence over a series of pages, an accumulation of information akin to, but distinct from, comic-strip panels or cinematic cels. Joseph Schwarcz refers to a "cooperation of word and picture" in the picture book: "The combination of the two forms of communication into a common fabric where they complement each other creates conditions of dependence and interdependence.... The full meaning of the illustration can only be revealed in context."[7]

Because of its limited written content, numerous illustrations, and liberal use of open or negative space, the picture book looks easy. With its oversize print and diverting, often caricaturish imagery, it conjures the illusion of simplicity and the expectation of entertainment. Any semiliterate reader can skim a picture book's pages in a matter of moments, then recall the text's plot and give an opinion. The picture book seems a breeze to read, in the sense that it lacks the high word-to-page ratio associated with text-heavy books; a form of modern mass media, it deprivileges the word in favor of balancing words with visual and tactile stimulation, suspending words and pictures in continuous sequence. For example, a nonnarrative pictorial primer such as *What Baby Sees* (1937) merely matches words to images ("sled," "kitten," "mechanical toy," "wooden beads").[8] But the reader must beware of assuming mastery of the text or of claiming genuine literacy after one glib scan. As Perry Nodelman writes, "The idea that words are merely lineal and pictures merely spatial is extremely simplistic. We could not read words if we could not interpret the visual symbols that stand for them on paper; reading is itself an act of vision."[9] Nodelman suggests that "all perception ... including the perception of pictures, might actually be an act of verbalization—a linguistic skill rather than an automatic act."[10] The picture book, far from being automatically understood, requires learned interpretive abilities and the mastery of modern modes of perception. By experiencing and reexperiencing the concise words and pictures of a picture book, relaxing during rereading, and committing a visual-verbal story to memory, a reading subject integrates the tale and the auratic book-object into his or her experience and develops a profound, personal sense of custodianship of this knowledge.[11] Printed words and pictures ostensibly carry the text's message, yet the text's cloth, paper, thread, glue, and ink contribute to the narrative experience as well, given that the text is made to be handled. Besides conveying narrative via interdependent literary and pictorial imagery, the commodity's form itself contributes to the implicit and explicit meanings of a picture book. The reader not only masters visual-verbal reading skills by toying with a picture book but also values that book as a consecrated consumer good. Like a store-bought stuffed animal, the picture book is a mass-produced item with any number of duplicates; its alienated origins are evident in its cardboard-and-paper package. But it is also a special belonging for one person in particular. The alienated labor and cultural ideology behind its manufacture become part of the memory and identity of its young reader. The correspondences produced by the picture book exceed those it is assigned to (or typically expected to) produce.

By no means can one audience (e.g., adults in general) predict exactly how another (e.g., children) will interpret pictorial and written information. In her assessment of the "sugar-coated language"[12] of pious tales as compared to irreverent, secularized texts, Juliet Dusinberre warns, "Children are capable of not noticing aspects of books which would deter adults from reading them," and sometimes "the readability of the books creates the adult's protest against their pernicious influence."[13] There is no guarantee that the child will recognize nuances and biases in ways older creators might intend. The hypocrisies or biases reflected in the picture book inevitably are products of adult beliefs, to be embraced or discarded by younger generations; the site of reading is not a one-way street transmitting adult wisdom to impressionable minds.[14] As Beverly Lyon Clark cautions, "We can start to question some of our kitchy-kitchy koo condescension, some of our temptation to be dismissive by the discourse of infantilization."[15] The picture book is a constellation of textual and peritextual elements that carries a thick concentration of meaning, not exclusively related to plot, words, images, sequence, or materiality. Strict attention to written story, or even visual-verbal expression, fails to register the effects of the text's size, shape, and media—not to mention its referent, given that the child is both subject and object of the modern picture book.

To think about the picture book is to think about the child, for the two share an iconic link. In a negative review of Gertrude Stein and illustrator Clement Hurd's *The World Is Round* (1939), an illustrated book that received accolades from New York Public Library children's specialist Anne Carroll Moore and other child literature proponents, Katharine White wrote, "With a few exceptions, the critics of children's books are remarkably lenient souls. They seem to regard books for children with the same tolerant tenderness with which nearly any adult regards a child. Most of us assume there is something good in every child; the critics go on from this to assume there is something good in every book written for a child. It is not a sound theory."[16] White explains that the living child and inanimate text are associated with one another, to the point that a text receives indulgent treatment. This duality encourages a misrecognition in which the commodity is equated metaphorically with the modern child.

Attention to story over materiality also sidesteps the issue of how the text is produced, by adults and generally for children; in his 2008 book of the same title, Perry Nodelman refers to "the hidden adult" in all children's literature. With typically large, splashy pictures and just a few choice words, the picture book seems to embody the notions that language-and-picture combinations are instantly understood, that pictures are more or less stable in their referents than written language, and that fewer words make reading easier for a novice who will later graduate to pictureless texts (which are, implicitly, superior).[17] Childhood and childhood reading are so much a part of every grown individual that they are assumed to be second nature. If a text implies a connection to the child and the condition of childhood, it seems to be intuitive, totalized, and unified. Yet, of course, the picture book is not as basic as its outward appearance might indicate.

Maurice Sendak writes, "A picture book is not only what most people think it is—an easy thing to read to very small children, with a lot of pictures in it. For me, it is a damned difficult thing to do, very much like a complicated poetic form that requires absolute concentration and control. You have to be on top of the situation all the time to finally achieve something that effortless. A picture book has to have that incredible seamless look to it when it's finished. One stitch showing and you've lost the game."[18] Sendak describes the complex interdependency of visuals, words, and sequence in the skillful picture book. In a well-made picture book, "words are left out—but the picture says it. Pictures are left out—but the word says it."[19] Neither words nor images, nor word-image combinations, carry a complete meaning or provide absolute closure. Reading practice, ever changing, depends on factors including the reader's level of attention, repertoire of knowledge, and situated environment.

In 1930, graphic novelist Lynd Ward recognized this word-image synergy in Ukrainian-born artist Boris Artzybasheff's *The Fairy Shoemaker* (1928), a selection of five poems paired with illustrations. The poems include the title poem along with "The Fairies" by William Allingham, Walter de la Mare's "Sleepyhead" and "Berries," and Matthew Arnold's "The Forsaken Merman." Artzybasheff's high-contrast black-on-white illustrations of elfin men have an opaque, silhouetted, and almost woodcut appearance, and the paper stock feels slick and coated. To contemporary readers, *The Fairy Shoemaker* might seem a run-of-the-mill collection produced using old-fashioned methods, yet to Ward in 1930, the images and text represented fresh achievements in picture-book craft. Ward explained, "The book did not exist even potentially until a series of encounters with verses by various and scattered poets began to form a pattern in Mr. Artzybasheff's mind. The pattern found visual expression in . . . a book medium, and . . . 'The Fairy Shoemaker' was the eventual result. The thing is a unit. You cannot take away the verses or the drawings or the medium without destroying the whole; in that mysterious union the art of book illustration exists."[20] Ward refers to Artzybasheff's picture book as a "unit," a unified assemblage, and this compositional approach was taking hold in the late twenties in a way that was conventionalized just a decade later.

It bears explaining that the picture book differs so significantly from the illustrated book as to be a different mode of production altogether. Illustrated texts are those novels and chapter books that include images but do not rely on them, and in the same article, Ward derides "the stifling practice, for which more than one generation must be indicted, of commissioning a set of pictures to be scattered through the pages of the book a few minutes before binding." Ideally, he says, illustrations are "a part of the flesh of the book in their technical creation, a part of the spirit of the book in the way they have come into being," and the artist should be "a functional being rather than a mere complementary decorator."[21] Too often, illustrated texts are referred to as "decorated," but this is a whimsical notion. No image is pure decoration, for an image provides information in excess of language and establishes a gap between signifier and signified; for instance, N. C. Wyeth's dramatic, memorable oil paintings for twentieth-century editions of Daniel Defoe's *Robinson Crusoe* and Robert Louis Stevenson's *Treasure Island* are not original to the novels, yet some readers associate Wyeth's renderings with the characters and scenarios. Illustrations by Wyeth—or by W. W. Denslow, Jessie Willcox Smith, or Elizabeth MacKinstry—exemplify the power and nondecorative nature of graphics.

Nevertheless, illustrated texts do not conventionalize sequential illustration as picture books do, although by the 1920s, artists in the illustrated newspaper tradition crafted short visual sequences, as E. H. Shepard did in A. A. Milne's *Winnie-the-Pooh* (1926), a British book that received a warm welcome in the United States. In the illustrated text, a picture or sequence is a bonus or surplus. Creators of an illustrated volume—such as writer Rachel Field and illustrator Dorothy Lathrop, who collaborated on the whimsical autobiography of a doll, *Hitty, Her First Hundred Years* (1929)—select what to include and exclude as visual information, aware that pictures conjure characters and set atmosphere yet are not central to the diegesis. The picture-book format demands complementary words and images, revealed in a controlled sequence that exploits "the drama of the turning of the page."[22] In a foundational essay on picture-book codes, William Moebius writes on how a pictorial sequence "compels us forward": "In the picturebook, we read images and texts together as the mutually complementary story of a consciousness. . . . Each page affords what Bader, the pioneer historian of the genre in its American development, has called an 'opening'; implied, of course, is a closing, a deliberate shutting out of what came before, and a constant withholding of what is to come."[23] Page-to-page closure sets the picture book apart from the graphic narrative form of the comic strip, which depends on panel-to-panel exposition. Both the picture book and the comic qualify as species of graphic narrative.

Besides suspending animation in its formal structures, the picture book nods to the development of modern society as a mass-produced commodity and as a dialogic text. Its contents explicitly and implicitly express time-sensitive concepts of class, race, ethnicity, gender, childhood, and nation—unstable categories that essentialist picture-book caricatures and definitions very often seek to stabilize. Although there is no guarantee that a picture book successfully indoctrinates its junior readers in a given ideology, it does provide enduring signs of its times, whether in its representation of gender roles, class, nation, ethnoracial difference, or environment. In particular, this study takes as a concern and a curiosity that picture books occupy schools, libraries, and attics well past their ideological expiration dates. Some favorites remain in print or are readily available, although the readers they interpellate are no longer the readers of the twenties and thirties. The children of the early to mid-twentieth century have become the grandparents and great-grandparents of present-day children, and several generations share the same texts. For instance, writer Marjorie Flack and illustrator Kurt Wiese's *The Story about Ping* no longer speaks to 1933 America, where Chinese immigration was restricted and the presence of people of Chinese heritage was unusual in many communities. Yet *The Story about Ping* still offers a loaded account of traditional river life in China. The picture book fossilizes information about a lived world and projects its belief system, rightly or wrongly, into new eras.[24]

Aging picture books, which stimulate nostalgia and exemplify printing methods and commodity structures of bygone years, help us contextualize the changing concept of the child in national and publishing history. These texts let us reevaluate reductive, exclusively formalist claims for an apolitical, atemporal children's literature. Popular commodities transmitted through families, schools, and libraries may be at once anachronistic and foundational to new generations' individual and collective identities, and their form and content may act as clues to how U.S. culture has changed. These texts indicate how concepts such as nature, the child, technology, and the nation were developing in the early 1900s. Often, they verbally and visually essentialize aspects of gender, ethnicity, race, and class, enabling present-day readers to consider, with the benefit of hindsight, the transmission of ideology to domestic mass audiences. Picture books are consecrated cultural productions, in Pierre Bourdieu's sense, and close study of these texts suggests what information cultural gatekeepers (publishers, teachers, librarians, parents, and finally children themselves) choose to share and what they wish to keep quiet and out of sight.

This project traces the American picture book from the efforts toward juvenile publishing and literacy at the end of the First World War through the 1940s, when American picture-book conventions gradually became established and postwar, late-modernist modes of visual and verbal experimentation were in evidence. Between the wars, American picture-book content and quality ranged broadly, from traditional nursery fare to experimental sequences. This study, a cultural overview rather than a comprehensive survey, estimates what readers found appealing or surprising in the modern picture book. In every case, a picture book's manufacture, modes of storytelling, and nods to the avant-garde and the mass-popular inevitably comment upon modernism and modernity. Circulating among other productions in literature, cinema, the visual arts, and material culture, the picture book upholds middle-class ideals in its subject matter but defies nostalgia in its modern fabrication, reproducibility, and iconography. The picture book constructs the child as an expert consumer of popular culture and commodities, and acknowledges sociopolitical and technological transformations taking place in the late nineteenth- and early twentieth-century United States. Scholars, therefore, can read the words and images in picture books against the grain to understand how literature created for a young audience is produced, consumed, and reproduced in the same ideological, social, and historical contexts as are works of art for a presumed adult mass audience. This challenges the truism that children's literature is timeless or immortal.[25] Although picture books can seem transcendent when read across multiple generations, they are not outside time in their representation of the past and anticipation of the future. Time, in the sense of impermanence, is the picture book's true medium. A meaningful text can bridge a gap between the child and his or her ancestors, connecting discrete instants. Yet claims of timelessness may be used to depoliticize childhood, as if all children belong to an undifferentiated class until the wider world imposes ideological divisions upon them (according to race, ethnicity, gender, etc.).[26] For example, in order for the Romantic child to have primacy in the public mind, children need to be infantilized and distinguished from their adult providers. If the photographic medium that preserved the image of the unspoiled Romantic child enjoying Nature also captured contradictory evidence of the grimy working child in tenements, cotton mills, and coal mines, then something had to be done about everyday child misery. And as long as children are understood as a unified group unto themselves, their hardships need not be deemed analogous to human misery in general—so that, say, child miners' issues stand apart from adult miners' labor concerns. Utopian claims of timelessness mask reactionary concerns.

Further, picture books are a specifically modern form of the sequential pictorial narrative; the picture book developed at a time when avant-garde art movements, sociopolitical climates, and changing technologies called for shifts in perception.[27] Evaluating pictorial texts through a contemporary critical lens—and bearing in mind that the purveyors of these texts tend to represent a dominant Anglo- or European American middle class with specific anxieties around leisure, labor, citizenship, and immigration—gives insight into early twentieth-century tastes, hopes, and fears constellated around cherished, even sacred, notions of childhood and U.S. citizenship.

## THE FAIRY TALE OF MODERNITY

Between the wars, American picture books tell a fairy tale of modernity to an up-and-coming generation. Picture books of any era constitute a site where young readers inherit a qualified version of the past and receive a fairy tale, or promise, of lived reality and the future.[28] Picture books and illustrated texts specific to the early twentieth-century United States inform readers about ways of life in an industrialized environment while referencing a preindustrial past and antiquated modes of production and consumption. These books' interdependent words and pictures give children qualified, hopeful accounts of the United States as traditionalist adults would have it, while at the same time the texts' materiality and fabrication attest to conditions of production in specific times and places. In their thematic form and content, and in their tangible materiality, picture books provide means by which the contemporary subject can understand and inhabit the nation.[29]

Whereas my narratological term "suspended animation" urges close reading of the picture book, "the fairy tale of modernity" indicates the simultaneous necessity of considering a given picture book in its cultural context. The fairy tale of modernity, an early to mid-twentieth century mode, is conceived in the context of modern, industrial, urbanizing life and realized in a commodity form. It celebrates youth or childhood interests in an affirmative manner and provides a dual audience of young and older readers with counsel for negotiating modern life. Whether the goal is simply to make readers laugh, say their ABCs, count from one to ten, eat their broccoli, or keep a bedroom neat, the picture book is "literature as equipment for living," offering pithy proverbs in verbal and visual form, suggesting strategies for succeeding in life, and serving as a sort of folk criticism pitched to an elementary level.[30] Yet, in its coded words, images, and material construction, the picture book also signifies the anxieties and erasures of those who produced it.[31] The fairy tale of modernity can take the outward form of a traditionalist tale, such as Wanda Gág's *Millions of Cats* (1928) or Emma Brock's *The Runaway Sardine* (1929), or it can be housed in an informational book on machinery, such as Wilfred Jones's *How the Derrick Works* (1930) or George E. Bock's *What Makes the Wheels Go Round* (1931). Its content and form are intertwined, a mixture of old and new approaches to writing, illustration, design, and manufacture. The picture book may be the ideal format in which to express the fairy tale of modernity, due to changes in American print culture, the increased ability to mass-produce images in affordable texts via offset lithography, and the development in thinking of the child as a consumer.

Gillian Avery concludes her three-hundred-year critical survey *Behold the Child* (1994) with Carl Sandburg's 1922 *Rootabaga Stories*. She calls Sandburg's collection "a wholly American literary work, the culmination, it could be said, of the indigenous fantasy begun by James Kirk Paulding some ninety years before, which produced authors as various as Hawthorne, Christopher Cranch, Joel Chandler Harris, Frank Stockton and Frank Baum. It also launched America's own golden age, in which it was accepted that literary worth should be the criterion in what was written for children, and that pleasure was as important as moral profit."[32] Avery marks the end of the Progressive Era when she chooses a 1922 stopping point. She notes the combination of pleasure and moral profit, definitely a concern of Sandburg's subtly political "nonsense" stories, which interrogate modernity and evoke longing for a less frantic time—as in, say, a tale of corn fairies who miss the "zigzag rail fences" delineating fields, or another tale in which a rabbit leaps a tall building but never returns. In Sandburg's gauzy, playful stories, flesh-and-blood Nature is in a battle to the death with industrial America. Although Sandburg wrote folktales and not picture books, his ideological concerns pervade the picture books of the 1920s through the 1940s. Whether categorized as "indigenous fantasy" or as fairy tales of modernity, Sandburg's collection germinated in a specific region and culture, and his stories (however unruly and odd) may be contextualized within their time and place. In addition, Sandburg's original work included illustrations by Maud and Miska Petersham, who went on to success as picture-book creators. Avery implies that to carry her study deeper into the 1920s would necessitate a shift of research gears and a change in perspective on multiple media, and thus marks Sandburg's evocative collection as a prudent place to start something new.[33]

The concept of the fairy tale of modernity also borrows from critical work such as *The Arcades Project* and *One-Way Street*, in which Walter Benjamin recognizes a decaying past in the objects and narratives of an ephemeral present moment. For scholars examining nostalgia, time, memory, and the fragile present, few objects of study can match those related to childhood and children's pastimes, and Benjamin himself was an avid collector of children's books. Benjamin recognized that, in their tangibility and storytelling, mass-produced picture books give evidence of human desires that were sustained or became outmoded. Today, anachronistic texts remind readers of obsolete objects, old cultural values that undergird present systems of thought, and antiquated wishes for the future. They provide unsettling perspectives on today's consumer habits and ideological assumptions.

Chapter 1 of this book, "Here-and-Now Fairy Tales," looks at the competing fashions for Old World tradition (including fairy tale retellings) and for the technological modern world in the United States of the 1910s through 1930s; Wanda Gág's work figures prominently in this chapter. Furthermore, publishers' and educators' urge to familiarize children with British and European storytelling traditions paralleled U.S. enthusiasm for global exploration and the commonplace foregrounding of an ethnographic gaze in children's literature. Curiosity about international topics, as described from a white middle- to upper-class American perspective, is the subject of chapter 2, "Picture-Book Ethnography," which investigates the representation of immigrant citizens as children and animals, and the depiction of white and nonwhite subjects on the illustrated page. Chapter 3, "Sentient Machines," details another component of modernity, the anthropomorphism of nonhuman and nonanimal characters. Mechanical contraptions such as locomotives, automobiles, planes, and steam shovels are represented as clever, lively entities, and their operators secondary to the work machines do. This imaginative leap in thinking about consciousness influenced new generations' perceptions of living beings, alienated labor, and nature as the Depression era began. Building upon this popular direction in picture-book storytelling, chapter 4, "Murals in Miniature," examines the overlap of regionalism, nationalism, and urban-rural versions of domesticity in the modern picture book of the 1930s and early 1940s. A Postscript focuses on the fairy tale of modernity after 1942. Twentieth-century picture-book conventions stabilized around the time of World War II, with the advent of series such as the Little Golden Books, the continuation of established careers in the children's book industry, the institution of wartime rationing on publishing supplies, and national mobilization around conflict. A wartime climate and the ideological shifts it brought about in the United States inaugurated a new era of American picture books, decisively detached from the formative years of 1919–41 and the popular fairy tales of modernity from that between-the-wars period. For this reason my study concludes with the year 1942, fully acknowledging the rich potential for further studies of picture-book development related to and deriving from the global conflict and its far-reaching sociopolitical implications.

*Suspended Animation* traces the picture book's emergence in and reflection of the American consciousness in the early twentieth century. Directed at a young audience, the sometimes humble and sometimes surprising picture books of the period detailed changes in the urban and rural landscape; mobility between city and country as highways and skyscrapers were built; altered lifestyles, jobs, and the U.S. economy; social interests and prejudices related to immigration, gender, race, and class; everyday issues such as child employment, schooling, and space for play; art movements, from the reactionary to the avant-garde; and manufacturing, marketing, and distribution by publishers and other businesses selling products to and for children. Picture books attest to the friction between so-called high and low aesthetics; the excitement, anxiety, and fear around burgeoning technologies; the rise of graphic communication via advertising, comics, caricature, and avant-garde forms such as concrete poetry; and the interactive, homespun, and hybrid narrative principles of oral storytelling and folk art.

# Here-and-Now Fairy Tales:
# Old World Tradition and Modern Technology

## ABCS OF MODERNITY

American picture books of the 1920s identified aspects of ideal childhood and described how children grew up around the world, both in history and in the present day. Yet post–World War I picture books often were not the word-image sequences today's readers have come to expect. Instead, their form and content attest to the tensions between Old World traditions and modern technology, and the tensions between graphic narrative and prose, with one or the other side of the equation emphasized depending on the book creators' preferences. Aside from a few picture-book sequences and duotone wordless novels by Lynd Ward and Milt Gross, in the United States, and Frans Masereel and Max Ernst, in Europe (most of them designed for an adult avant-garde rather than a mainstream youth readership), most 1920s picture books are weighty with words and abundant illustrations.[1] By today's standards, these texts can appear cluttered or disadvantageous for children's actual reading. This chapter explores the development of pictorial sequence and the influential dialectics at play among words and pictures, nostalgia and modernity.

Historian Barbara Bader notes that British artist William Nicholson's *Clever Bill* (1926) and *The Pirate Twins* (1929) "supplied a new format and a new literary form that Americans adopted with alacrity."[2] Instead of a wordless sequence or "continuous lengthwise pictures . . . (think scroll—comic strip—motion picture)," Nicholson used a horizontal (landscape) layout and individual frames in a "running text, spare and suggestive, fluid, suspenseful, a form of writing unique to picturebooks. Two results were to follow: the fewer the words, the more each would count; the fewer the words, the more—meaning, not detail—would go into the pictures."[3] In *Clever Bill*, a little girl prepares to visit her aunt and accidentally leaves her soldier doll behind, only to have him pursue her train; in *The Pirate Twins*, a matched pair of black dolls escape their child owner for oceangoing adventures (*Twins* was based on the Nicholson family's Golliwog toys and does not pass muster in these more racially sensitive days). Nicholson handwrote the texts in an imperfect cursive and expected playful readers to fill in the gaps between images and between words and images, exploiting what William Moebius calls a "semic slippage, where word and image seem to send conflicting, perhaps contradictory messages about the 'who' or the 'what' of the story."[4] Tessa Rose Chester agrees that *Clever Bill* and *The Pirate Twins* are among "the earliest picture books of the century to show a real sense of fusion between text and illustration, partly due to Nicholson's pioneering use of offset colour litho and partly because of the handwritten script. The economy of words and shrewd use of the turn of the page to create tension are combined with informal yet consistently balanced designs in bold, broad lines with flashes of bright colour that are the result of an effortlessly controlled craftsmanship and technique."[5]

Nicholson was not the first picture-book artist, although he deserves credit for mid-1920s innovation. His style of word-image montage developed in tandem with comics, cinema, advertising, and other appealing media of the nineteenth century and earlier. Randolph Caldecott updated old nursery rhymes with new visual sequences in the 1880s, and W. W. Denslow produced a picture-book series around popular songs in the early twentieth century. Yet, with the exceptions of comics and gift books, true picture books were uncommon until 1920s improvements in color lithography.

In early twentieth-century children's literature, many creators seemed to think a picture was worth a thousand words, and vice versa. Experimentation was common and conventions were in flux. With age-grading and pigeonholing of children's book categories only nascent in education and library circles, this was a time of exploration across what are now seen as developmental boundaries. Pictorial experiments found inspiration in European printing and art, including the work of Belgian woodcut artist Masereel, who collaborated with satirist Georg Grosz, Dadaist Tristan Tzara, and other antiwar artists. Masereel crafted wordless woodcut sequences, or *romans en images*, such as *Passionate Journey* (*Mein Stundenbuch*, 1922) and *The City* (*Die Stadt*, 1925), that emphasize alienation in the modern metropolis. In a 1926 introduction to *Passionate Journey*, Thomas Mann wrote, "We are dealing here with a creative work of such simplicity that you do not even have to know how to read or write to see it: it is a novel in pictures, a kind of movie which, except for two introductory quotations, needs no other words, captions or sub-titles to explain it. It appeals directly to the eye."[6] Mann does not theorize the verbal-visual interplay, however. Instead, he attempts to contextualize the visual sequence by discussing two epigraphs—from Walt Whitman and Romain Rolland—on generosity and human experience. Masereel's titles and epigraphs set the tone for the "wordless" narrative. Mann then looks at Masereel's printmaking, which he pronounces "traditional, conservative, age-old; it is romantic and turned toward the past. Hence it would not arouse complete confidence were the content not imbued with such immediacy and such sustained modernity that the old and the new, the traditional and the dynamic fuse to inspire human confidence."[7] Mann acknowledges a modern intersection of multiple media and argues that a conventional form—the graphic narrative (or picture book)—blends with avant-garde content. In Masereel, Mann sees "an infusion of the aristocratic spirit of art into the democratic spirit of the cinema."[8] Masereel's sequences do criticize mass labor and the crushing of the creative spirit in the modern urban center. Nevertheless, it can be difficult to see past the surface of the visual text to recognize the play of critique in a picture book's narrative content, just as the signs of modernity may be concealed by its superficial child-centeredness.

American readers of the 1920s had seen much notable sequential work— much of it in illustrated newspapers and comics—both from European creators and from the likes of "Little Nemo" inventor Winsor McCay and E. Boyd Smith, author-illustrator of pictorial books including *The Chicken World* (1910).[9] Yet for all the conventions of the Sunday funnies and the illustrated news, picture-book characteristics had not been standardized, social critique was somewhat unexpected by leisure readers, and a lack of categories and absolutes made for surprising variety in pictorial texts—especially children's books. Writers, illustrators, editors, and readers in America explored their creative options. For instance, graphic artist Peter Newell's ebullient pre–World War I efforts involved paper-engineering features, interactivity, and attention to print materiality. Newell produced advertising illustrations, a syndicated "Polly Sleepyhead" comic, and collections of *Topsys and Turvys*, which required readers to look at a cartoon, read a phrase, then flip the page for the conclusion of the rhyme and a visual punch line (e.g., a walrus head with tusks becomes a horned goat). Newell specialized in jokey picture books based on die-cut or unusually shaped pages, for which he scrupulously patented the designs. *The Hole Book* (1908) charts the progress of a bullet shot from a mischievous boy's gun; the actual hole drilled through the center of each page is smaller than a pencil, but it still prompted 1920s reviewers to praise the bullet's "amazing and startling entrance upon everyday peace."[10] *The Slant Book* (1910) is a highly impractical, effectively dizzying parallelogram-shaped book whose tilt suggests a steep incline. A runaway baby carriage—much to the delight of Bobby, the baby in it—rolls downhill, destroys a fire hydrant and causes a water spout, hits a woman carrying a basket of eggs, trundles through a watermelon patch, and wreaks havoc with a German oompah band ("The Go-cart struck the bass drum square, / And passed completely through it. / The Drummer madly tore his hair / And said, 'Vy did you do it?' ").[11] *The Rocket Book* (1912) traces the path of a rocket shot by "Fritz, the Janitor's bad kid" from a basement through the first to the twentieth floor and on into the attic, where it collides with a barrel of freshly churned ice cream and freezes in place. Among other things, the rocket lights a man's cigarette ("Thanks, awfully," he says) and pierces a potted plant ("I never thought / That plant would shoot so quickly!"), a piano ("It stopped that rag-time like a shot"), the brim of a woman's giant hat (" 'I said that hat was all too loud!' / Her peevish husband muttered"), and a "tattoo" (alarm) clock. The rocket hole is a centimeter-wide oval, indicative of the sort of mass-produced gimmickry one could expect circa 1910, and the stacked apartment setting wryly acknowledges cheek-by-jowl living arrangements in the modern metropolis.

Although the First World War halted the supply of movable picture books from Germany and reduced American artisans' opportunity to mimic the envied Bavarian printing, 1920s U.S. bookmakers continued refining their art. In later decades, Guatemalan-born animator and puppeteer Tony Sarg took up Newell's mantle by creating interactive lift-the-flap games like *Where Is Tommy?* (1932), a book that lets readers peek inside a henhouse, into a sideboard, under a tablecloth, and behind a bed curtain for a sleeping boy. The book's thin paper, doubled for the flap features, was easily torn at its unreinforced folds, yet publishers indulged Sarg's evident playfulness and willingly experimented with technology and resources to advance the picture book as a game with a modern format.

Among the most celebrated picture books of the early twenties came from commercial artist C. B. (Charles Buckles) Falls. Falls's 1923 *ABC Book* is a compendium of stylized images of wild and domestic animals, from Antelope to Zebra (Plates 3 and 4). Falls famously pitched his original idea for the *ABC Book* to fledgling Doubleday editor May Massee, and the resulting four-color picture book is an exemplar of the woodcut-printing craft, a graphic designer's hand at clever composition, and a publishing house's effort to market work for inexperienced readers. "We may well feel proud that an A B C book so admirable in design and in color printing has been produced on this side of the Atlantic," wrote the New York Public Library's Anne Carroll Moore. "The drawings are cut on wood blocks and printed from four-color plates, and the artist personally superintended the reproduction of them. . . . It is high time we set about in earnest the production of American picture books of original character in distinctive form. Our own country needs them and other countries may even come to enjoy them as they now enjoy the best of our children's stories."[12] Moore calls for "genius" in American picture books, applying a distinctly modernist term of approbation to Falls's work.[13]

The *ABC Book*—a formulaic chain of letters, key words, and images—is modern in appearance and manufacture. Nevertheless, its sequence implies a Romantic, nature-oriented concept of childhood. The subject matter conveys a predictable domesticity and nursery exoticism, implying adult expectations of children's easy delight in zoos, circuses, and farms. Predatory animals such as the Bear and Wolf glance away from the audience and prowl without aggression; the rampant Lion is fit for a sculpture or coin; a profile view of a white-feathered Turkey exhibits tameness and calls to mind Thanksgiving feasts. Even the Kangaroo, a dynamic animal, rests on its hind legs, and the calico Cat strolls benignly past a bowl of milk. Falls usually envisions his animal icons in static poses, although the Fox sneaks under a rail fence and the Antelope is in mid-spring. The text's rare surprises include one fantasy animal, the Unicorn, and one Latin designation, "X is for Xiphus," with an image of a swordfish (placidly swimming). The rectangular boundaries of the images, the black outlines of the animal shapes, and the poster-style compositions—each image is suitable for tearing from the book and mounting on the wall—strongly recall Nicholson's *The Square Book of Animals*, created in 1896 and published in 1899. Many critics, including Moore, noticed and applauded the similarity. Falls's Nicholson-esque framing contains and delimits the imagery, lending a stained-glass-window formality to each page. The *ABC Book* deals in nostalgia, alluding to artisanal printmaking and serene animals, at the same time as it highlights the most modern printing methods of twenties publishing.

Seven years later, Falls produced *The Modern ABC* for the John Day Company. This lively book describes modernity in bright lithographic images featuring saturated orange, yellow, teal, and turquoise, with no inky blacks whatsoever (Plates 5 and 6). Where the first *ABC* is shadowy and alludes to Nicholson's turn-of-the-century book of animals, Falls's self-consciously contemporary 1930 ABC ranges from Airplane, Battleship, and Crane to X-ray, Yacht, and Zeppelin. The "J is for Jazz" page acknowledges the latest music (later in the volume, "R is for Radio"), although Falls's rendering of white musicians diverts attention from the Harlem Renaissance and the African American jazz and blues sound; a crisis in the representation of nonwhite subjects may be recognized in Falls's account of modernity, although the sequence seldom pictures people at all. One image, in which a girl photographs a boy outdoors, shows home-use cameras, acknowledges a brand-name becoming part of common speech, and serves as nifty product placement: "K is for Kodak." Where the *ABC Book* pictured a Swan for the letter *S*, here "S is for Skyscraper," depicted from a dizzying bird's-eye view. Although each image is contained within a symmetrically square boundary, the large letter shapes break the confines of the squares and sometimes tilt for an electrified appearance. Even the endpapers imply greater mobility. Where the *ABC Book* endpapers provide the alphabet in an orderly fashion, printed in elegant ochre-on-yellow, *The Modern ABC* endpapers feature antic, overlapping white letters on an ocean-green ground.

In the time between these two abecedaries, Falls and his peers in publishing and bookselling were reimagining childhood and reconsidering what the young reading subject might enjoy. Although a traditional approach to childhood entertainment endured, the 1930 text exemplifies how modernity was conveyed to the youngest readers. With its "B is for Battleship" and "U is for U-boat," *The Modern ABC* allowed child awareness of militarization, and "H is for Harvester" and "I is for Irrigation" (which shared a spread) acknowledged agricultural processes on the landscape as the Depression era began. After 1930, of course, it is possible to weigh the relative merits of both books. Tellingly, although *The Modern ABC* is more kinetic, it is the sedate *ABC Book* that survives in paperback editions. The original text enjoyed greater popularity than its sequel perhaps because of the downturn in luxury book buying during the Depression. But its popularity also implies that the synchronic and conventionalized signs of childhood, seen in Falls's fashionable animal icons, artfully composed four-color designs, and repetitive layouts, maintain their currency and nostalgic significance. The diachronic concept of the modern, no longer characterized by 1930s Jazz, a Newspaper, or a U-boat, remains in flux, like generations of childhood experience.

As the mixed reaction to Falls's nostalgic and modern ABCs implies, the picture book is a commodity with built-in nostalgia. People are conditioned, by educators and the marketplace, to associate the picture book with ephemeral, wonderful childhood. Antique picture books are ideal sites in which to interrogate this sense of longing. Replete with visual and literary references to obsolete ways of life and archaic technologies, older picture books such as Mary Steichen Martin and her father Edward Steichen's *The First Picture Book: Everyday Things for Babies* (1930) illustrate bygone assumptions about growing up, too.[14] *The First Picture Book* consists of a nonnarrative series of black-and-white photographs of household items, and its only words are the author's introductory preface: "When my two children reached the stage of interest in pictures, a search found practically none which could be considered either satisfying to them or in line with modern educational theory. Therefore I set about providing a book of such pictures, not only for my own but for the other children faced with a similar need. The pictures presented here have had the seal of approval of the children of a progressive country nursery school, ranging in age from one and a half years upward."[15] Martin testifies as an experienced parent addressing other parents and educators. She assumes that ordinary children, similar to her own and those "of a progressive country nursery school," arrive at a "stage of interest in pictures." She suggests that her children did not recognize themselves in the available literature, so she set out to create a book to invite them as its implied readers. The First Picture Book contains unlabeled black-and-white photographs of objects including a telephone, a high chair, and an array of toy balls of different sizes. In one photograph, a scattering of books provides a metacommentary on things children should be reading: The First Picture Book is there, open to the photographed toy balls, and so are Falls's ABC Book, Robert Louis Stevenson's A Child's Garden of Verses, and Beatrix Potter's The Tale of Peter Rabbit.

Each spread of The First Picture Book includes a blank white page on the left and a photograph on the right, so the viewer can concentrate on one item at a time (Figure 1.1). Each still life is composed against a plain, often empty background, reducing visual clutter and decontextualizing each object so that, perhaps, it can be imagined in one's own home. The photos bleed to the edge of the page, so that despite the lack of color and shallow depth of field, they visually overlap into the audience's three-dimensional space.[16] Other than the explanatory title and the introduction, the text is entirely wordless, leaving it to the middle-class child of 1930 to name the functional items and modern conveniences. The text prompts the reader to establish a denotative relationship between photo and object, thereby achieving satisfying closure page by page. The book can be reopened later for a repetition of pleasurable, visual reading. Steichen photographs common toys of the time: a wooden tricycle, a pram with a doll inside. He also pictures ephemera that, despite the upbeat preface, convey melancholy and imply that a child is about to arrive or has been there and gone. A tin cup of milk sits on a tablecloth next to a small plate and a cut piece of buttered toast; the same tin cup appears on an empty high chair with a scattering of crumbs and some graham crackers; an apple, banana, and grapes form a basic still-life; and a glass bowl holds a bouquet of daisies. The creators include no images of children, only of children's things.

FIGURE I.I. Familiar household objects such as Falls's first ABC, *A Child's Garden of Verses*, and a telephone are photographed as "everyday things for babies" in *The First Picture Book* (1930) by Mary Steichen Martin, illustrated by Edward Steichen.

A child in a 1930 home surely could name the items from daily experience or point out his or her own similar belongings. Even a child who lacked the items could use the text as a sort of catalog containing images of products whose users are conspicuously absent. Steichen's static image of a riderless tricycle associates the toy with normal childhood (or triggers a sense of longing in a child who wants a tricycle). *The First Picture Book* coaxes young readers to enjoy looking at pictures and turning the pages of a book, but it just as surely acquaints readers with the alienated products of a then-modern home.[17] Today, the black-and-white photos, with their antique phone and glass milk container, signify lost time rather than a typical home; the denotative meanings are the same, but the connotations have changed. This collection of household goods no longer reflects everyday life and never represented all children from all walks of life. *The First Picture Book* demonstrates that although picture books are dialogic and the creative reader makes meaning by engaging with sequential words and pictures, picture books do not have indefinite life spans and do not welcome all readers equally. Like all media, picture books delimit their audiences by their content and context, and unexpected signifiers of difference can interrupt the dialogic play between text and reader (a static that becomes apparent when a twenty-first-century reader sees, for instance, Steichen's photograph of a 1930s telephone).

A sequel, *The Second Picture Book* (1931), appeared a year later using the same wordless format. In Harcourt, Brace's advertisement, a white child holds a teddy bear and sits in a wicker chair, and a caption explains that "babies again see their own familiar world, but with people like themselves in it."[18] In addition to presenting inanimate objects, *The Second Picture Book* introduces white children as the audience and positions the reader's gaze much differently by the addition of the child as a visual object. The photographed child and denotative term "baby" stand in a one-to-one correspondence, so the reading subject may both identify desirable store-bought products and understand who is and is not implied as the interlocutor of the text. The photographs embody reflections for some, yet they also establish an outsider. *The Second Picture Book*'s twenty-four wordless images construct class by what is shown and not shown, and visually indicate the adult buyer's and the junior reader's presumed race.

This is not to suggest that a child becomes pleased or offended at the sight of another child who is superficially like or unlike herself. An actual child might simply point out the pictured baby, as the book's creators seem to expect. He or she might be more interested in the garden background than in the objects, or be too inexperienced to identify the photographed children by any criteria such as class, race, or gender. The stuffed bear in the picture might be likened to any plush toy, homemade or store-bought, and there need not be a value judgment. Nor is this an argument for censorship of such books or an appeal for a wider range of photographs. Instead, this is a description of commonplace texts, among the first communicative devices owned and explored by a preliterate child. Martin and Steichen's photographic books suggest how cultural assumptions influence the production of picture books of any era, position the child's gaze, and establish standards by which people of any background recognize a normative baby. With the benefit of hindsight, we can play spot-the-ideology with older (and more recent) texts, but ultimately we receive an imperfect record of the past at best, a perpetuation of stereotypes or antiquated attitudes at worst. Anne MacLeod comments, "It would certainly not be possible to construct an accurate record of the social, political, or economic developments of this nation [the United States] between 1920 and 1940 from the evidence in children's stories—that one cannot do in any period. Yet the shifts in cultural attitudes are there, recorded in the indirect way in which children's attitudes always document the time, and expressed in the values the books held out to young readers."[19] Modern picture books give insight into a bygone world whose ideological inheritance remains with us, and the texts that became popular (whether informational books or cheap-to-produce reprints of old tales and nursery rhymes) say more about social conditions than they do about real children. MacLeod argues that "children's books change with the slower and deeper currents of their time, rather than as the surface of culture changes. There was little of the flashing glitter of the Roaring Twenties in that decade's children's stories; the literature was still deeply rooted in an earlier era . . . and the recurrent themes were of striving and achieving in a mobile, competitive society."[20]

As MacLeod suggests, modern picture books and illustrated texts present a partial account of middle-class childhood, yet they do suggest the tenor of their times. Their words and images represent current situations for which prior generations are responsible and sanitize the twentieth-century world in ways sanctioned by cultural producers. Gillian Avery notes, "American children's books, and their counterparts in Britain, responded only obliquely to the social and political events of a period that saw the great Depression, the Wall Street crash, the 'roaring 20s,' the New Deal, and Sinclair Lewis' attack on Middle American values in *Main Street* (1920), or H. L. Mencken's *Prejudices*. The image of America in children's books clung on to ideals—notably of family life—that were being eroded."[21] In other words, fairy tales of modernity acknowledge cultural anxieties by buttressing ideals, and their superficial sunniness belies socioeconomic events. When picture books describe a bygone era or show bucolic settings rather than brick and concrete, they acknowledge what has been lost and give consumers a peculiarly modern chance to preserve that past—first by making it available in commodity form, and next by ensconcing a culturally approved version of history in children's collective memories. Modern picture books shed light on commonplace jobs and situations, direct an ethnographic gaze to faraway countries, or glance with longing on eras that still resonate with older individuals. In addition, these texts materially represent the labor of writers and editors, printers and binders, and signify as objects of value to booksellers and to a young audience.

## THE MARKETING OF POSTWAR PICTURE BOOKS

The picture book as we know it now is a precociously modern communicative device, a product of the late nineteenth and early twentieth centuries. It has the relative shape and feel of a book, the images and oversize words of an advertisement, editorial cartoon, or store catalog, and the iconography of nursery songs and stories. It fuses old-fashioned print culture and literary structure with mass-produced novelty. Although the picture book signifies modernity, it did not spring fully formed from American publishing houses to libraries, schools, and bookstores. Like its formal and thematic influences in cinema, avant-garde poetry, and modernist art, the picture book emerged as a cultural artifact only after decades of artistic ferment and technical experimentation.[22]

The picture book grew out of seventeenth- and eighteenth-century chapbooks, broadsheets, and toy books. David Lewis writes, "Just as the chapbook could ingest almost anything that came its way, so the picture book seems to be able to assimilate almost any kind of text," noting similarities in the "folkloric themes" and "brevity" of chapbooks and picture books.[23] Lewis uses metaphors of bodily incorporation: the chapbook "ingests" and the picture book "assimilates." The modern picture book, Lewis emphasizes, is "first and foremost a form for young children," even though older readers love it too. He calls the picture book "inherently heterogeneous, not so much a genre itself but a uniquely flexible, composite kind of text more than capable of adapting itself to changes in the wider culture."[24] In addition to any lesson or message it provides to a given audience, the picture book has myriad associations that complicate its overt content. Shifting incarnations of the picture book, moreover, make it more or less like a toy, a game, or a comic book. Like the wider category children's literature, the picture book is often referred to as a genre. But because it can involve multiple media and audiences, the picture book demands a more inclusive term. I call the picture book a mode of production, dependent on shifting beliefs about childhood, cultural tastes, and standards of judgment. Although picture books are associated with children, critics need not naturalize a link between text and child or assert a stable category of childhood. Text and reader come together by cultural networks related to commerce, public and private education, family dynamics, and structures of modern time; a child inevitably "chooses" a book from a batch preselected by adult gatekeepers. The picture book is not a preordained part of the child's environment or a natural development in media, but a culturally constructed signifier of childhood to which readers adapt.

Studies of English printer Edmund Evans's studio, Lothar Meggendorfer's movable books, Heinrich Hoffmann's *Der Struwwelpeter*, and U.S. toy-book publishing firms such as Elton and Company, McLoughlin Brothers, T. W. Strong, R. Shugg and Company, and Huestis and Cozans attest to the development of the picture book as a large-format black-and-white or chromolithographed text, created from paper alone as a simple primer or bound with board covers as a holiday luxury.[25] "The picturebook was, after Edmund Evans, conceived of as a whole 'product,'" writes Moebius. "Text was 'script' or libretto.... Covers, endpapers, title-page design, all were carefully chosen elements of a whole, an experience wrapped, not without conscious intention, as a gift."[26] Picture books emerged on the American multimedia front in the nineteenth century as an offshoot of modes of production including newspaper comics, illustrated storybooks, musical notation, holiday cards, paper dolls, and decorated nursery rhymes. Initially, U.S. printing and distribution methods were not up to the task of picture-book mass production, beyond the gaudy toy-book series and novelties produced by companies such as McLoughlin Brothers from 1828 until McLoughlin's purchase by Milton Bradley Company, in 1920.[27] Quality color inks and good paper came at a premium cost, and American picture books were compared unfavorably to their European counterparts. A McLoughlin Brothers marketing history from 1928 admits as much and boasts about new standards for children's texts as art:

> "Beauty" is acclaimed the "new tool of industry," and the use of it is
> prominently revealed in the new McLoughlin Line. Not long since,
> most nursery books were atrocities of primitive color appeal, ignoring
> the tenets of art to such an extent that they were corruptive, rather than
> constructive, to the child's color sense; McLoughlin nursery books of
> today—the A B C, Animal Picture, Mother Goose and Child Activ-
> ity books—are on the same artistic plane as the most costly illustrated
> volumes. Colorful in the extreme, but with color intelligently applied,
> each is a first step in true art appreciation for children.[28]

Following World War I, interdependent reforms in technology, the workplace, and public education had begun to alter the affordability and quality of printed matter for young readers. With "beauty" a "tool of industry," well-designed and appealingly illustrated picture books came to be seen as prestige items for a literate, productive, and promising American citizenry.

The American picture book gained popularity in the early twentieth century, as cultural definitions of childhood and the lives of actual children altered substantially across socioeconomic lines. Children went from being nineteenth-century wage earners and shop customers to being twentieth-century consumers, leisure citizens, and not just elementary but secondary school students.[29] Children had of course been familiar with their elders' exchange economy for generations, but in the past many had been family breadwinners themselves.

Now they began collecting allowances from parents and participating in an expanding national and international marketplace, with some holding part-time jobs to make extra money.[30] Viviana Zelizer describes a "radically revised concept of child work" throughout the Progressive Era, in which children made a transition from being economically "useful" to "useless" as financial contributors, treated to special goods and services because of their now "priceless" and even sacred membership in the modern family: "By 1930, most children under fourteen were out of the labor market and into schools. . . . The useful labor of the nineteenth-century child was replaced by educational work for the useless child."[31]

After school, free from their laboring or work-at-home parents, nonworking children loitered in city streets and constituted a large portion of the audience for mass communications, spending their small change on the nickelodeon, the movie theater, comics, snacks, games of chance, and (potentially) more wholesome pursuits such as reading literature that ostensibly could instill proper bourgeois social values.[32] Then, as now, adults voiced concerns about how unsupervised children spent their time and their pennies. Organizations such as the Payne Study and Experiment Fund, which grew out of Frances Bolton's National Committee for the Study of Juvenile Reading (NCJSR), in 1927, formed to warn parents of the dangers of movies and to promote children's interest in other recreation, notably reading.[33]

In this shifting labor and education climate, the American child of the 1910s though the 1940s learned to value store-bought objects and to define his or her identity around personal belongings.[34] Children learned to desire material goods that signified the social levels to which they aspired. The radio broadcast and newsreel influenced the ability to get international information, and the phonograph and telephone became commonplace accoutrements, establishing communicative links between previously dissociated groups. Preliterate children observed their parents' familiarity with the novel and the black-and-white newspaper and got acquainted with color Sunday comics, flashy shop signs, competitive advertisements and billboards, radio serials, and sound film. (They would have children of their own before witnessing the advent of television.) Those who had trouble reading English or conventional printed texts could seek out a variety of inexpensive visual and sound media, including glossy magazines and illustrated texts.[35] Along with newspaper reading and radio listening, habits of book borrowing and ownership signified quality of life, socioeconomic class, and modern subjectivity for a child who read at home with parents, went to libraries that in earlier eras had denied access to the disruptive young, or associated books with a classroom setting or holiday gift. Concurrently, elite cultural producers sought to control the means of education and technological production by providing the sorts of entertainment available to the masses. Not just any popular book or form of amusement would do for the next generation.[36]

Thus, children's education and entertainment became a labor concern, a safety issue, a marketing opportunity, a moral requisite, and a means of nation building. The picture book addressed childhood at every socioeconomic level, as a didactic national item, as a form of amusement, and as a possible means of sparing the child from physical and emotional harm in the modern sphere. This placed critics of children's literature in the awkward position of defending popular print work while disparaging the corruptive influence of nonliterary modes of production. They cheered children's books' aesthetic value, as opposed to the social leveling that reading might make possible. Many critics prescribed rhetorical solutions that still sound familiar today. In a 1919 address to the American Library Association (ALA), Franklin S. Hoyt of Houghton Mifflin Company said, "[Due to the] highly stimulating environment in which they live . . . [children] become accustomed to the sensational, rather highly seasoned, unreflective type of reading presented in juvenile magazines, and represented by the movie plot. The older type of classic literature, therefore, has lost much of its former appeal, and the author and publisher who wish to provide children with books which are both wholesome and attractive have a difficult undertaking."[37] Hoyt worries that magazines and movies overstimulate young people, and wonders how publishers might make the activity of reading not only desirable but "wholesome" again—with the additional benefit of selling more books. Although he esteems his company's classic backlist, he believes canonical work cannot captivate modern youth and charges book professionals with inventing new commodities that might counteract the sensational, shocking effects of magazines and movies.

In 1921, linguist and education reformer Lucy Sprague Mitchell echoed Hoyt's call for a new literature, minus his praise for canons: "I maintain we have never had [a children's author] of the first order. The best books that we have for children are throw-offs from artists primarily concerned with adults,—Kipling and Stevenson stand in this group,—or child versions of adult literature,— from Charles and Mary Lamb down. The world has yet to see a genuinely great creator whose real vision is for children."[38] Like Hoyt, Mitchell hopes for the future of reading as a pastime. But where Hoyt demonizes the mass media with an economic aim, Mitchell criticizes artists' shortcomings and challenges them to express a "real vision . . . for children," whatever their economic mo-tives. She spurs creators toward inventive thinking, even if she elides Kipling's and Stevenson's colonial, masculinist prejudices. She implies that children are a historically and socioeconomically stable demographic and expresses faith that a gifted adult can communicate in ways that suit the changing needs of actual young people.

Hoyt's and Mitchell's comments attest to the postwar sensibility and its at-tendant confusion: old stories no longer sufficed, new fictions had yet to arise, and the book industry was imperiled. These critics, like booksellers, librar-ians, and teachers, limited the discourse around children's literature by their implicit beliefs that the popular was irreconcilable with the literary and that there must be an "adult" literature and subjectivity distinct from that of chil-dren. (Mitchell believed children were reading adult "throw-offs.") Yet their remarks also suggest a wish to cultivate a niche of juvenile readers and dutiful parents, and a means to improve a perceived dwindling reading practice.

The publishing industry took note and worked to respond in a way that kept print culture current. With child labor increasingly regulated, literacy efforts under way, entertainment media reaching a young crowd, and public school required, publishers explored the children's book market.[39] They organized book fairs and promotions through organizations like the Camp Fire Girls and the Boy Scouts of America; catered to libraries, which "represented a body of organized opinion, backed by purchasing power";[40] and coaxed parents to give books as gifts, appealing to the twin concerns of literacy and keeping chil-dren safe in the home. In November 1919, *Publishers Weekly* editor Frederick Melcher, Boy Scouts chief librarian Franklin K. Mathiews, and Anne Carroll Moore organized the first annual Children's Book Week.[41] In 1922, Melcher established the John Newbery Medal for the best children's novel in the United States, which assured consumers of a book's quality and guaranteed sales for the lucky author, publisher, and Newbery Honor runners-up. By 1938, Melcher saw room to establish the Randolph Caldecott Medal for the best picture-book illustrator, with the cooperation of librarians and booksellers. The New-bery and Caldecott medals, named after historic British innovators, canonize newly published titles. But despite their retrospective names and aims, which suggest a continuing and conventional appeal to middle-class audiences, these literary prizes—and annual book-design competitions such as the American Institute for Graphic Art's (AIGA) annual "Fifty Best Books" lists—suggest how design and pictorial communication gained ground in public apprecia-tion between 1922 and 1938. Special new awards, where none existed before, imply how the picture book, comics, and other graphic work destabilized the conventional separation between word and image, how verbal-visual narratives gained prominence from the 1910s through 1930s, and how children's education and entertainment could be marketed to a receptive public.[42]

Publishers also appointed star editors to staff their expanding "juveniles" departments. In 1918, Macmillan created the first children's book department in a major U.S. publishing house, to be headed by Louise H. Seaman; Longmans, Green's, Little, Brown and Company, Coward-McCann, and Frederick A. Stokes soon followed suit with dedicated children's departments. Doubleday, Page Company hired ALA *Booklist* editor May Massee in 1922; E. P. Dutton and Company appointed the New York Public Library's (NYPL) Marion Fiery in 1925; and Harper and Brothers hired Virginia Kirkus in 1926. These influential new editors tended to be middle-class women raised in the prewar Progressive Era, who left librarianships, teaching roles, and sales positions to enter the publishing field. Their presence often was viewed as a chance for motherly types to "nurture" children's books. In a 1928 retrospective, the quarterly *Horn Book Magazine*—founded in 1924 by Bertha E. Mahony and funded by the Women's Educational and Industrial Union—praised the domestic rather than feminist implications of women in editorial roles. Mahony's account envisions the editor's desk, a traditionally male domain, as a site for child rearing by those with an instinct for it:

> In the year 1918 two important and far-reaching events occurred in the publishing of books for young people:—(1) The Macmillan Company created a separate children's department; and (2) the President of that firm, Mr. George P. Brett, one of the ablest and wisest men in the publishing profession, selected the peculiarly right young *woman* as head of the new department.
>
> We do not mean to depreciate or minimize the splendid publishing of books which men have done but we do believe that men (with few exceptions) have been baffled and groping where children's books are concerned and that they have not had the vision to shape their organization so that the right people have had the necessary time for these books. There seems every natural reason why women, properly qualified, should be particularly successful in the selection of children's books to publish and their publishing. When it comes to deciding upon the format of a book, it is more like dressing a little girl than anything else. One chooses every detail of her wardrobe in harmony with herself. So

with a book, its size, type, style of printing, cover material and color of cover, book paper and jacket, manner of illustration—all should be selected to express the book itself. To this delightful task women would seem to bring particular interest and ability.[43]

Mahony saw women leaving their customary roles as booksellers and educators, and becoming editors with a controlling interest in what got published. Women vetted promising manuscripts, supervised the production process, and critiqued finished works. They occupied a central place as mediators and altered the course of publishing. Meanwhile, according to Mahony, accomplished women filled a maternal gap in editing, and the children's book was analogous to a little girl who could not dress herself without assistance. The picture book reified a notion of childhood, and childhood in turn required some maternal origin or midwife rather than a "baffled" man. By this logic, the feminized children's text and the feminized editor landed squarely in the nursery.

Yet the commodity circulates in the public, popular arena. The picture book interpenetrates public and private, outside and domestic, and the woman-as-editor—or as author-illustrator—does the same. Although protofeminists' efforts did not counteract the most overt misogyny and inequity in the old-school publishing business (women lacked equal pay and advancement opportunities relative to men), women did change publishing by inaugurating an influential commodity, the picture book. As these editors chose or commissioned manuscripts, they operated within an established field of discourse and published texts based on consensus among other professionals, but at the same time they subverted established formats for language-heavy, minimally illustrated texts. This blurring of boundaries characterizes the postwar period in the United States, when material goods, contradictory opinions, and shifting representations circulated as never before, destabilizing certainties about subject identity and the world order. The picture book stood in counterpoint to realist literary forms and brought marginal individuals into the male-dominated marketplace.

Numerous women book critics likewise operated in a restrictive field of discourse and committed themselves to picture-book production. These women were dispatched by male magazine and newspaper editors to judge the persuasiveness and marketability of American children's texts. "Standards of appraisal consistently applied to the consideration of children's books as holding a place in contemporary criticism were unknown in 1918 when I was invited to contribute a general article on the children's books of that year to the *Bookman,*" recalled the NYPL's Moore. After this debut publication, "the knowledge that my review had given this book [W. H. Hudson's *A Little Boy Lost*] a place in literature for children rather than as a mere juvenile—that it also had direct sales value, gradually dawned on me. . . . I had found a practical way of helping in a more discriminating selection of children's books for publication."[44] Moore lends equal weight to "standards of appraisal" and "sales value," and sees it as her duty to discriminate among the children's books on the market. Her triumphant reaction to reviewing *A Little Boy Lost* suggests she overturned the norms of major publications. She wanted a noteworthy book to gain critical attention rather than be dismissed "as a mere juvenile." In 1924, the year Mahony transformed her Boston *Bookshop for Boys and Girls* newsletter into the *Horn Book Magazine*, Moore began contributing a weekly children's book column to the *New York Herald Tribune*. By 1930, the *Saturday Review of Literature* had a "Children's Bookshop" section, and the *New York Times*, the *Nation*, and the *New Republic* covered the preholiday children's book marketing blitz. Critical voices appealed to connoisseurs and defended children's literature against naysayers who considered the popular picture book (or any text with young people as its likely audience) antiliterary.

The picture book found ardent supporters in the business and education communities and came into its own as part of the U.S. book industry. Cost-effective printing and distribution brought down the price, making books affordable to public libraries and schools (less so to middle- and working-class shoppers). Bibliographies such as *Realms of Gold in Children's Books* (1929) list prices ranging from $0.50 to $0.75 cents for a mass-produced toy book, $1.75 to $2.50 for an illustrated story collection, and $2.50 to $4.00 for an imported edition.[45] Mass production and widespread distribution to libraries, schools, churches, and youth organizations helped ensure that conventional literacy, through child- and age-specific books in English, remained a crucial part of growing up in white America.

Publishers not only promoted a dominant discourse and targeted avid shoppers, they also constructed a definition of childhood that remains prevalent today. Ultimately, children were redefined as market groups distinct from adult readers, with books scientifically calibrated to their age-related needs. For example, from the turn of the century through the 1930s, publishers such as M. A. Donohue and Company of Chicago, G. W. Dillingham Company of New York, and Charles E. Graham and Company of New York created "indestructible" books of felt, muslin, or linenette for inexperienced readers. Muslin books were color printed and washable, with floppy pages; stiff-paged linenette books, printed on thick and inflexible cloth material, could be wiped with a damp towel. Saalfield Publishing Company of Akron, Ohio, had an "Ever Wear—Never Tear" motto, and some volumes included an advertising jingle on the back cover: "They may be washed / And the colors will not run, / A child can chew them / And have lots of fun." By comparison, Dean's Rag Book Company of London advertised cloth books as "Quite Indestructible"; Dean's company logo pictured two muscular dogs playing a vicious tug-of-war with a cloth book.[46] The indestructible books had ancestors in the toy books and instructive hornbooks of the past, and the fragility and expense of color-printed paper were obvious considerations. Children's books were meant to serve an educational, entertaining purpose, but children themselves were not a gentle audience, and parents were presumed reluctant to shop for a nondurable good. Publishers attempted to make long-lasting, quality objects that provided a pleasant sensory experience.[47]

Indestructible books exemplify cultural producers' efforts to design and print work for children at different stages of development. Texts were declared physically and psychologically suited to children of a particular age or grade. In some cases, books originally marketed to a general readership were recategorized as juveniles. In one of her midcentury lists of American best sellers, Alice Payne Hackett wrote,

> Many [best-selling] titles listed as juveniles were originally published as adult books, but changing taste has now definitely placed them in the category of juvenile reading, and they are so indicated in accordance with modern standards. . . . Juvenile fiction has a disconcerting habit of changing its audience. Some of the best sellers like *Freckles* [by Gene Stratton Porter, 1904] and *Penrod* [by Booth Tarkington, 1914] started their careers as adult fiction. Others were launched as juveniles and have since added an adult audience, like the A. A. Milne books.[48]

Among other top sellers, Hackett notes the affordable Little Golden Books series, which debuted in 1942, and individual picture texts including *Little Black Sambo* (1899), *The Tale of Peter Rabbit* (1903), *The Little Engine That Could* (1930), and *Pat the Bunny* (1940). Hackett also attributes enormous sales figures to "captive audiences" in organizations such as the Boy and Girl Scouts, and emphasizes that many book sales took place in nonliterary venues: "The 10-cent to one dollar stores, department stores, and newsstands are the chief outlets for . . . coloring books, cut-out books, and paper-doll books, for example, as well as versions of the classics and juvenile fiction."[49] Varied audiences, from middle-class white shoppers to lower-income, ethnically diverse families, had ready access to inexpensive classics and dime-store texts.

As public schooling was mandated and library visits increased, publishers and educators increasingly found it advantageous to construct stages in child development and to market books to distinct demographics. Bertha Mahony and Elinor Whitney's bibliographical *Realms of Gold* and *Five Years of Children's Books* (1936) recommended texts by age. The editors admitted ambivalence:"Books certain to interest children from four to eight years old have been selected [for a section on picture books] from nearly every subject represented in children's books. But many mothers will want to choose also from [sections on early readers and illustrated novels]. It is impossible and uninteresting to make any hard-and-fast age divisions for books. Seven-year-olds are often ready for [Charles] Kingsley's *Heroes* and [Padraic] Colum's *Adventures of Odysseus*. Grown-ups enjoy *Winnie-the-Pooh*. And so it goes."[50] Thus, specific consumer groups, based on age and school grade, were established within the wider categories of childhood and adolescence. Within a few decades, age classification came to the fore, and the marketing of juvenile modes of narrative came to parallel the diversification of childhood away from the similarly artificial category of adulthood, into more and more stages, more and more child-specified interests.[51] Publishers, booksellers, librarians, and teachers labeled certain books and subject matter as age appropriate, and specified audiences for select books, the better to construct the modern citizen. J. H. Plumb writes,"Precision of age is a remarkably modern phenomenon; most societies until modern times simply grouped the young into blocks—infants, noninitiate boys and girls, and the like—in which age was irrelevant."[52] Age divisions, practical for grouping children at similar levels of emotional and physical development, provide an outwardly neutral way of isolating readerships by socioeconomic class, putting cultural differences under erasure, determining what sort of texts might be suitable (or not) for children of diverse backgrounds, and constructing children's desires. What appears to be an empirical calculation of age appropriateness, based on actual children's developmental needs, is also a system for instilling a social order and consumerism. The late nineteenth- and early twentieth-century shift toward classification has repercussions for critics who perceive childhood as a catch-all class. If one group comprises all children, everywhere and of every heritage, then all children are subject to middle-class hegemonic control in the form of reading material, school lessons, store-bought "children's" consumer goods, and so on.[53] The establishment of reading grades and age-appropriate children's literature enables a tidy, outwardly nonideological co-optation of childhood and the actual child and guarantees the stability of middle-class conventions of literary and visual representation across generations. Educators and publishers of the era tried to articulate general developmental stages and assign reading material for certain groups of children, with marketing motives, disciplinary intent, and middle-class interests at heart.

Further, although modern picture books often represented rural or mystical scenes and domestic comforts, these texts arose from urban centers. Then, as now, East Coast cities usually were the sites of publishing companies, distribution hubs, major booksellers, and promotional festivals. The majority of the American population lived outside cities, yet texts produced and marketed in urban centers ended up in small-town libraries, stores, and traveling book fairs (such as the Boston Bookshop's Book Caravan, a truck that plied the beach towns of New England from July to October 1920, making for good promotion despite poor sales).[54] These urban texts purvey the concerns of the well-to-do middle-class editor, publisher, and author-illustrator trickling down to a more diverse audience of young readers and parents. Brandished by teachers and librarians, the picture book served as a material site for literacy and social inclusion, including cultural assimilation. Sold by booksellers to parents, it signified a domestic concern for little citizens' future productivity in the workforce and military. Soon after the war, the Boy Scouts' Mathiews compared the thirst for reading among soldiers during World War I with reading interests among the U.S. population of boys aged ten to sixteen, the next generation of military recruits.[55]

Citizenship and national defense, indeed, were on Americans' minds. In an era when picture books increasingly became popular, communication was too swift and people too cynical to invent postwar myths of innocence, and actual children's experiences were changing in terms of family life, education, urbanization, and cultural diversity. Humphrey Carpenter notes the difficulty of peddling golden-age illusions in Britain after World War I: "It must have been harder to dream up River Banks and Never Never Lands after the experience of the Somme."[56] Although golden ages are notoriously subject to debate, this argument has merit in the postwar United States as well. Although throwback arcadian fare such as A. A. Milne's *When We Were Very Young* and *Winnie-the-Pooh* caused a transatlantic sensation among children and their anxious guardians, many readers deplored such books as overly sentimental.

The common English language enabled the easy transatlantic exchange of texts, including older picture books by Beatrix Potter and L. Leslie Brooke, books of newer vintage by William Nicholson and Cecil Aldin (*The White Puppy Book*, 1917), and longer fiction by British-born Hugh Lofting (*The Story of Doctor Dolittle*, 1920). But in Britain, "the far-reaching social and economic effects of the [First World War] caused drastic cut-backs in book production in general and in the de luxe editions and the family periodical in particular. Publishers were therefore forced to find alternatives to these in cheaper forms of reading," and British innovation in children's literature changed course out of socioeconomic necessity.[57]

American experimentation in picture books and illustration, however, went into full swing. The United States had a unique combination of technical resources, quickening commodity culture, immigrant influx, and dislocated longing that lent itself to the idealistic reinvention of childhood in pictorial literature. At a time of expanding capitalism and collective destabilization, when a combination of artistry and mechanical technology established the grounds for a reimagination of the social, the mass-produced form of the picture book gained currency and helped define the concept of childhood. But if U.S. cultural producers appropriated the fanciful material of arcadian literature for the modern text, they still lacked a suitable fairy tale of modernity to assist subjects in negotiating the joys and crises of contemporary life. Much ado was made of what Gertrude Stein dubbed the "lost generation" of American novelists, born at the turn of the century and struggling to convey their experience in print, and most picture-book producers of the era belong to this "broad confraternity." Malcolm Cowley writes, "They were seceding from the old and yet could adhere to nothing new; they groped their way toward another scheme of life, as yet undefined; in the midst of their doubt and uneasy gestures of defiance they felt homesick for the certainties of childhood. It was not by accident that their early books were almost all nostalgic, full of the wish to recapture some remembered thing."[58] Cowley believes that when children in this generation attended elementary school in the prewar years (prior to federal enforcement of child-labor laws, educational reform, women's suffrage, and other reforms), they did not recognize social conditions locally or abroad: "Since their playmates were also middle-class they had the illusion of belonging to a great classless society. All but a handful were pupils in the public schools, where they studied the same textbooks, sang the same songs, and revolted rather tamely against the same restrictions. At the colleges they attended, usually some distance from their homes, they were divested of their local peculiarities, taught to speak a standardized American English and introduced to the world of international learning."[59] Cowley summarizes the ideological indoctrination not only of Hemingway and Fitzgerald but also of those who grew up to produce the picture books, illustrated literature, comics, and animation of the 1920s and after. Picture-book producers, in particular, recast the past and present for an audience that was not yet in a position of doubt, thereby creating the fairy tale of modernity. To create a semblance of certainty against loss, adults reinterpreted modernity and distracted children with commodities that told a reassuring story. Children participated in this desperate reiteration of the past and invention of the present, by becoming the objects and the consumers of the new texts, which nostalgically recuperated folkloric structures, esteemed a pastoral ideal, and reified tradition.

The picture book, itself emerging from the lost generation, provided a means of conveying representational information. It established icons for beginning readers to decode and a disciplinary means of describing the emergent (or preemergent) structures of feeling of modernity.[60] It provided a space for whimsy, yet it also offered an outlet for middle-class ideologies that were under threat due to immigration and labor unrest. The picture book, arriving on the American scene at a moment of international disillusionment, signified a hope for sustaining, or at least commemorating, a fading vision of childhood.

## "THE GREAT FAIRY TALE DEBATE": FANTASY, REALISM, AND MODERN LIVING

Depending on the storyteller, old and new models of childhood competed in mass-produced picture books and illustrated texts. Familiar stories and narrative formulas, altered by literary and material allusions to contemporary life, were retold in combinations of words and pictures. Some picture-book creators embraced the modern and the avant-garde; others treated children's books as repositories for a mythical golden-age childhood, despite their up-to-date manufacture and distribution. Challenges to idealism met with considerable opposition, because collective illusions and fears depended upon the preservation of childhood innocence. Americans needed narratives for modernity, and for want of a sufficient account of postwar shock they revisited myths, preindustrial craft, and folk artifacts.[61] National anxieties could be seen in the 1920s boom in folk-art collecting and exhibition; in an increased preservation of heirlooms, songs, folk stories, and oral histories using new recording technologies; and in a stated (if not always enacted) belief in the sanctity of childhood and a new generation's worldly inheritance, implied in the anti-child-labor movement and the proliferation of children's books about bygone or mythic times.

The editors of *Realms of Gold* included long lists of folk- and fairy tale collections, and confidently declared,

> In The [Boston] Bookshop we often suggest that fairy tales be included with the geographical study of a country. They are full of descriptions of the land as well as of the customs and life of the people. . . .
>
> These stories "should remind you that children all the world over, whether tanned by the hot sun to a deep brown or black, or bleached by cloudy skies to pallor and flaxen hair, share with you a love for tales. Perhaps these very tales which you are now reading in English are being told to-day to other children in Breton or Hungarian or Russian or Japanese or whatever their native tongue may be."[62]

As nostalgic narratives and works of art amused the child and soothed the parent alike, a debate arose around whether children's development benefited more from heroic visions of distant lands and colorful times or from stories and images representing some current interpretation of reality. One or the other kind of narrative—the first deemed metaphysical and creative, the second practical and realistic—was purported to be more conducive to children's aesthetics and psychological well-being. As a result, self-contradictory arguments fueled what Bader calls "the Great Fairy Tale Debate that raged between 1929 and 1931."[63] Repetitious rhymes and narratives about machines, domestic animals, and the sounds of urban life, known as "here and now stories" to education reformer Lucy Sprague Mitchell and her followers at her Bank Street School in Manhattan, were opposed to teleological myths and derivative tales of brownies, fairies, and legendary heroes.[64] Mitchell (whose philosophies influenced a young Bank Street School teacher, Margaret Wise Brown) believed that children should not only read naturalistic material about cities and machines but also physically imitate things in the natural world in order to develop their motor skills. She demanded stories in which children could hear about everyday urban environments while making corresponding movements and sounds. Mitchell bookended the time of the fairy tale debate, such as it was, with her *Here and Now Story Book* (1921) and *Another Here and Now Story Book* (1937), which demonstrated her methods for encouraging visceral experience and demystifying metropolitan life, and which charted child development according to age. In the first anthology, empirically tested on Bank Street pupils, Mitchell took "children's first-hand experiences as a starting point" for poems and stories, on the belief that the child "cannot yet experiment easily in the world of the intangible." Her introduction challenged purveyors of fantasy literature:

> It is only the blind eye of the adult that finds the familiar uninteresting. The attempt to amuse children by presenting them with the strange, the bizarre, the unreal, is the unhappy result of this adult blindness. Children do not find the unusual piquant until they are firmly acquainted with the usual; they do not find the preposterous humorous until they have intimate knowledge of ordinary behavior; they do not get the point of alien environments until they are securely oriented in their own. Too often we mistake excitement for genuine interest and give the children stimulus instead of food. The fairy story, the circus, novelty hunting, delight the sophisticated adult; they excite and confuse the child.[65]

Mitchell endorses the immediate experience and everyday wonder to be found in city streets. Her opinions came to be reflected in children's books about modern industry, including her poetry-and-photography collaboration with Elsa Herzfeld Naumburg and Clara Lambert, SKYSCRAPER (1933); informational material such as Maud and Miska Petersham's popular Story Book series; and Margaret Wise Brown and Leonard Weisgard's onomatopoeic *The Noisy Book* (1939), which describes the sounds perceived by a blindfolded dog. Notably, in *Another Here and Now Story Book*, which she calls a "supplement" to its predecessor, Mitchell softens her stance and strives for "a safe middle ground between the purposely new and the purposely traditional," although she continues her empirical research. She suggests that overseriousness can be as damaging as too loose a hold on modern reality, and says her stories and sketches might "help the adult reader over his greatest handicap—his adultness!"[66]

The so-called fairy tale debate sets up an untenable binary opposition between imaginative literature and realist formalism that has less to do with children than with cultural concerns in the States. The fairy tale debate encompasses arguments around audience-appropriate reading material; gendered understandings of popular and intellectual literature; class struggles and cultural hegemony as they are exerted through dominant narratives; literary and artistic modes of production (with traditionalist versus upstart designers); and the idealization of childhood in a time of historical crisis. Such a debate rehearses the antagonism among supporters of realist fiction (perceived as the domain of white males), fantasy and escapist fiction (supposedly for middle-class women and children), and popular literary forms such as the serial or dime novel, calculated to please the masses. This polarization ensures that the burgeoning field of children's literature remains a subset of literature in general, at once inviting a mass readership and instituting prior gender, class, and race boundaries. Beverly Lyon Clark attributes these boundaries to an "anxiety of immaturity," a too-close association with maternity and feminized domesticity that began delimiting the readership and criticism of children's literature in the mid- to late nineteenth century.[67] Literature once thought suitable as family reading began to be dismissed as jejune and unworthy of the masculine canon: "The view that children's reading should overlap with adults' reading is frequently urged in the *Atlantic* and elsewhere toward the close of the nineteenth century, at a time when the two readerships were, in fact, diverging," Clark writes.[68] By the early twentieth century, this split was taken for granted despite the mobility of creators and purveyors in the publishing industry, particularly women such as Massee and Louise Seaman, who took plum editing jobs; Domino Press copublishers Esther Averill and Lila Stanley, who provided transatlantic connections among children's literature specialists from their Paris base; Mahony, who dominated Boston children's bookselling; and librarians such as Moore, Alice M. Jordan, and Frances Jenkins Olcott, who exerted influence far beyond the stacks. "The boundaries separating editing, publishing, education, and library work for children were startlingly fluid in the early twentieth century, but the boundary between literature for children and literature for adults was much less so," Clark explains.[69] For those committed to protecting the fairy realm, the desire was to deepen this perceived rift, separating children's from adults' material so that children might receive counsel from tried-and-true nursery rhymes and fairy tales rather than from new tales concocted in a modern context. The here-and-now faction believed there could be no formal separation of child from modern experience and therefore recommended immersion in modern sensation.

Influential critics of children's literature countered the industrial world and the mass popular by recommending texts that glorified preindustrial days or went on flights of fancy. Pro–fairy tale Moore favored *The Poppy Seed Cakes* and longingly described "Auntie Katushka, fresh from the old country in the brightest of shawls"; she also offered qualified admiration for C. B. Falls's *Mother Goose* (1924), whose "rhymes have been well selected from authentic sources."[70] Although Moore did praise tales involving modern machinery, she preferred not ordinary machines but enchanted ones, such as the engine in Cornelia Meigs and Berta and Elmer Hader's dreamlike *The Wonderful*

*Locomotive* (1928) and the self-sacrificing female train that rescues a crowd of toys in Watty Piper's *The Little Engine That Could* (1930). Moore, in a dig at Bank Street, contended,

> Didacticism and pedagogy staked early and stultifying claims in the realistic field and reared a long succession of commonplace writ-ers extending from the school of Dr. [John] Aikin and Mrs. [Anna Laetitia] Barbauld, anathemized by Charles Lamb, to present-day experimenters in educational theory and practice who regard the writ-ing of children's stories in terms of their day's work and look to books whose content should be purely recreational and inspiriting to carry on cherished methods of education outside the classroom. Propagan-da in this form, as in any other, however attractively set forth, is fore-doomed to pass into oblivion. Nothing survives in a children's story save character and atmosphere, and these are usually least considered by the writer with an axe to grind.[71]

Moore shifts the blame of purity from the aesthetes to the reformers, but she does not indicate how recreational reading equates to propaganda or how her own dogma leaves her without "an axe to grind." Quoting Hughes Mearns, Moore writes that "'children are in the main still artists while adults have too often ceased to be,'" and agitates for both imaginative *and* realistic narrative, so that children and adults alike have recourse to childhood pleasures via fantasy: "Children are, even as grown-ups, both realists and romanticists."[72]

Like Moore, other modern-era critics cheered stories of imaginary worlds that encouraged creative thinking and an appreciation for a quality of beauty. Writing in the *Horn Book Magazine*, a venue whose title advertises its alle-giance to traditional wisdom, Marguerite MacKellar Mitchell quoted French critic Maximilien Vox on childhood: "Vox [in 'Avenir du Livre,' *Le Crapouillet*, December 1929] prophesied that because the book, as pure diversion, had been abandoned by the masses in favor of the mechanical pleasures of the radio and cinema, it was entirely possible that we might now have a chance to return to the creating of books that satisfy the desire for beauty of execution."[73] Here, aesthetic diversion counteracts the "mechanical pleasures" of the masses. Vox proposed an aestheticization of the book-object and its verbal-visual narrative, which led to a reinscription of the book as something for appreciation by a cultural elite that shunned (or at least knew how to question) the allure of mass entertainment such as radio and cinema. Mitchell continues:

In the past few years the important young beings, half saint, half
savage, that inhabit the nursery, have been analyzed, exploited, and
invited to taste the heady cup of self-expression. They look at their
picture books with a new sense of adventure. If we want to share
their exuberant experiences we must make ourselves and our books as
beautiful and as gay as possible, for the day of the dull book and the
didactic grown-up is done. The contemporary child has a tendency to
challenge historic delusions: the infallibility of the parent, the indis-
pensability of routine, the superiority of the human over animals. The
unexpectedness of his point of view often startles us.[74]

The *Horn Book Magazine* writer acknowledges the unknowability of the modern child and suggests that this "half saint, half savage" beast might be awed,
and its imagination safely liberated, by the enjoyment of a gorgeous book. As an
example of such a liberating and beautiful narrative, Mitchell chooses Wanda
Gág's *The ABC Bunny* (1933), lingering on an opening sequence that introduces
the dozing rabbit ("A for Apple, big and red / B for Bunny snug a-bed") and
startles it with the falling apple ("C for Crash! / D for Dash! / E for Elsewhere in a flash") (Figure 1.2). Mitchell writes, "Here is a book that should be
placed—by stealth—on the desk of every harassed business man. The song,
the end papers, the text—what fun Wanda Gág has given us and how skillfully
her bunny has scampered through the alphabet. The secret of all literature lies
in the E, for is it not the mission of every book to get us 'elsewhere in a flash'?"[75]
The reviewer yearns for "elsewhere" and implies an escape for the white-collar
worker who needs a reprieve. Like the opening and closing of a camera shutter,
the turning of the page seals off one instant and captures another in sequence,
miming a journey. But this escape can happen only if the man accepts the reified object of childhood, the picture book that signifies a happy-go-lucky child
reader with free time to play. The picture book, with its promise of fun, reaches
the man's desk only "by stealth," and it is up to him to do the rest. This modern working stiff of the 1930s (as opposed to a true hedonist, or a child) has
recourse to literary and visual play, but only on a lunch hour or sick day, and
only when no one is watching. Gág even provides instruction on getting back
to work with her XYZ sequence: "X for exit—off, away! / That's enough for
us today. / Y for You, take one last look / Z for Zero—close the book!" Gág
achieves a youthful liveliness, but the review implies that modern men suffer
for their lack of nursery rhymes and diversions such as the "ABC Song" that
decorates *The ABC Bunny*'s endpapers. Mitchell's review evidences the modern

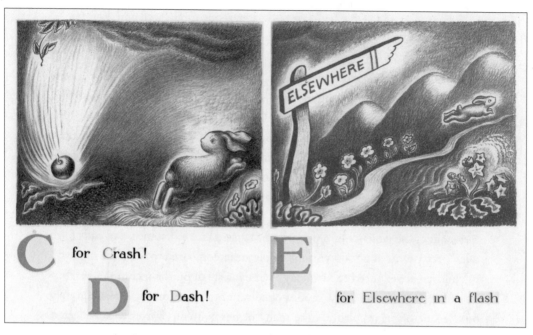

FIGURE I.2. A falling apple startles a rabbit and initiates the left-to-right momentum in Wanda Gág's 1933 escapade *The ABC Bunny*.

era's belief in the separation between the serious-minded male adult, the giddy child, and even the feminized reader (and writer) of the children's book review, who still has access to whimsy.

Gág herself was very much aware of the tensions between traditional storytelling and here-and-now concerns, and she added her critical opinion to the discussion. In a 1939 essay titled "I Like Fairy Tales," Gág makes a case for retelling old stories in an industrialized and potentially violent age. She celebrates a vanishing and ostensibly magical past in books that simulate an ephemeral condition known as childhood:

> Ten years ago, when I first began to take an active part in the creating of children's books, it dawned on me that there was such a thing as a fairy tale controversy. . . . One of the most frequent remarks I heard was, "But children aren't interested in imaginary stories nowadays. They live in an age of machinery, electricity, aeroplanes and so on. They want to read about practical things." . . . In fact, I believe it is *just* the modern children who need it [their "rightful heritage of Fairyland"], since their lives are already overbalanced on the side of steel

and stone and machinery—and nowadays, one might well add, bombs, gas masks and machine guns.[76]

Gág reports that children watch movie scenes of "horrible tortures" (some viewers "look frightened; others seem already hardened to it"), listen to violent radio dramas, receive toy guns for Christmas, and read newspapers ("One looks at the lurid 'funnies,' another ponders over pictures of the latest trunk murder or love-nest scandal"). She contrasts these modern commonplaces with fairy tales "in which, l-o-n-g, l-o-n-g ago, a fabulous dragon was brought to his well-deserved end; or where 'once upon a time' a giant's head was cut off, without blood, without mess—much like a log being chopped in two." Gág rationalizes the violence of old stories because it is at a distance, and calls fairy tales "pretty tame, if not downright wholesome, compared to what the majority of children are exposed to nowadays!" She insists upon the incommensurability of familiar tales and new modes of communication, coming down squarely on the side of print culture. Like many of her contemporaries who collected folktales and imagery from other cultures, Gág calls for a folk revival without noting how the tales might adapt to new publication methods or how fairy tales represent multicultural Americans far removed from, say, the Grimms' nineteenth-century Germany.

Detractors argued that fantasy and old-fangled storytelling could not prepare children for everyday life and were not sufficient to hold the attention of the child distracted by mass media. They proposed attention to the modern landscape, altered technologies, and the human being's physical—not just individual and intellectual—engagement with the world. Yet, like their opponents, these champions of modernity too often fail to discriminate between an unrevised myth, which may not have counsel for the present day, and the practice of storytelling as a strategic response to a situation.

Today, both the fantasy collections and the here-and-now accounts have been all but swallowed into the overall category of the fairy tale of modernity. Critics sometimes miss the modern aspects of texts that would have caused a fuss in the twenties and thirties, when new print and artistic media (including picture books) and impressive large-scale technologies wooed young readers away from conventional texts. Book collector Harold Darling argues that in the 1920s, "children's books seem to exist in isolation from the intellectual and artistic crosscurrents of their time. As people try to isolate children from unpleasant realities, so children's books usually reflect dreams, ideals, and fantasy."[77] However, Darling's pictured examples include Frank King's *Skeezix at the Circus*

(1926), derived from serial comic strips, as well as Elsa Beskow's *Pelle's New Suit* and a McLoughlin Brothers' informational book called *The Story of the Ship*. In saying that children's books do not resonate with modernity, Darling overlooks the fusion of visual content and materiality. Although written narratives may direct attention away from "unpleasant realities," allusions to comics or modes of travel such as steamer ships are specific to modernity.

Since the turn of the century, educators and librarians had fretted over comics' dismal influence on young minds and crusaded against such lowbrow modern abstractions. In 1934, Moore complained of her misbegotten early attempts to damn cheap pictorial literature and especially the comic strip, which smacked of modernity. "I well remember the rapture with which my 'warnings' in connection with pictures were hailed by visitors who chanced to have a preview of them in the children's room of the Pratt Institute Free Library [in 1900]," Moore told a gathering of the American Library Association. "I was to have a similar experience three or four years later when a collection of picture books I had gathered for the purpose of making a graphic presentment of the comic strip, in contrast to a selection of books designed and illustrated for children, proved irresistible to the librarians assembled for a New York State meeting at Lake Placid. They blissfully pored over my 'warnings' by the hour to the utter neglect of books chosen for their values of idea, line, and color."[78] By 1934, Moore could joke about her uphill slog against the shock of the new, given that all her "warnings" against pictorial illustration and comics had fallen on the deaf ears of curious librarians, who were modern and numbered themselves among the loitering crowd.[79] The printed format and contemporary design of even the most nostalgic text exemplified the futility of an antimodernist stance.

In the end, both camps in the fairy tale debate were guilty of blinkered vision, one retreating to an illusory, treacly fairy past and one wholeheartedly embracing engines-and-concrete progress, to the point that neither provided a workable model for childhood in modernity. On the surface, the fairy tale debate appears to pit Romanticists against strict Enlightenment rationalists, or perhaps wild, mystic classicists against stern, puritanical moderns. But the liberatory rhetoric of each side is complicated by the cultural nostalgia for childhood and the violence of recent historical events. Fairy tale admirers purport to infuse the urbanized world with ruralism and imagination, and here-and-now proponents seemingly pursue a socially conservative project. Yet the former unapologetically use the tools of the latter (printing and distribution facilities, resources such as color ink, and the picture-book format itself) to make their case, ignoring their nontraditional and paradoxical methods. For instance, Moore celebrates fairy tales in a daily newspaper that reaches thousands of readers. The here-and-now moderns, meanwhile, close off rich avenues for storytelling by rejecting fairy tales and myths out of hand.

## "WHAT COULD BE MORE SUBSTANTIAL THAN A PEASANT?" WANDA GÁG'S FOLK VISION

As an essayist, picture-book artist, and translator, whose *Snow White and the Seven Dwarfs* (1938) was meant as a rebuke to Walt Disney's 1937 film, Wanda Gág exemplified the early twentieth-century tendency to borrow from folk handicraft and the oral tradition while profiting from an expertise in new media. Her characteristic work blends the endlessly flexible folk- or fairy tale and a novelty mode of modern production, and shows the way to other author-illustrators who recognized the picture book as a viable art form. Ruth Hill Viguers writes that in the 1920s, American picture-book artists felt confident enough to break stylistically from "Old World traditions and the constraints of European prestige." These artists explored new graphic and storytelling techniques, which involved "not only pictures interpretive of the text, but an understanding of design and typography and physical make-up of the book and an ability to integrate perfectly all these elements." The 1920s artist, Viguers notes, attended to the pleasure of materiality when planning a book. Further, she writes, "the republication of old favorites with new illustrations and unusual format became typical of this period of experimentation, and . . . this reissue of books in attractive new forms brought a fresh interest and vitality to many titles."[80] In familiar stories and structures, U.S. author-illustrators found a basis for imaginative play and a means to navigate present experience. American creators had the technical proficiency and economic wherewithal to depart from European models yet still resorted to Old World subject matter for their experiments. This adaptation of oldies-but-goodies not only created "fresh interest" in previous generations' tales but also meant that new commodities acquainted an up-and-coming generation with dominant traditions. Throughout the 1920s, illustrated texts and picture books combined the latest artistic media and production techniques with structural conventions (e.g., the "once upon a time" inauguration and "happily ever after" closure), generic features (e.g., the peasant family, rustic cottage, and enchanted animal or tool), and didactic discourse. Occasionally, contemporary subject matter such as urban life and mass transit were added to the mix, as in Mary Liddell (Wehle)'s picture book *Little*

*Machinery* (1926) or Angelo Patri's picaresque update of Carlo Collodi, *Pinoc-chio in America* (1928, illustrated by Liddell). In these books, modern technol-ogy and fashionable motifs met conventional fairy tale structures.[81]

In 1928, Gág worked with Coward-McCann editor Ernestine Evans to cre-ate her most recognized book, *Millions of Cats*.[82] This picture book indicates a design sensibility on a par with that of Nicholson, whose *Clever Bill* had debuted two years earlier. Like *Clever Bill*, which starts in a middle-class Brit-ish home and pictures the amenities of modern life (a typewriter, a train trip), the watershed *Millions of Cats* celebrates domesticity in its narrative content while its material form represents developments in mass production. *Millions of Cats* presents an Old World setting, nursery rhyme repetition, and memo-rable black-and-white graphics that resemble casual sketchbook doodles with a German expressionist edge. It alludes to oral storytelling conventions and con-temporary visual sequence alike. *Millions of Cats* earned Gág a Newbery Honor and was exhibited among the AIGA's fifty best books of 1928 (Figure 1.3).[83]

Written in prose with a rhyming refrain, *Millions of Cats* takes place "once upon a time" amid rolling pastureland. It opens on a stone cottage surrounded by a picket fence, tended by a "very old man" with a long beard and pipe, and a "very old woman" wearing a head scarf, apron, and ankle-length dress. No machines are in evidence, and when the country folk decide to get a cat to keep them company, the very old man goes on foot to find one. His journey takes him all the way across the spread. On the left-hand page, at the man's back, his own tiny cottage, two small farms, and a church occupy wooded valleys and hillsides, and there are few signs of human habitation and no industrial equip-ment.[84] Eventually, the man comes upon an enormous herd of cats, occasioning a catchy refrain: "Cats here, cats there, / Cats and kittens everywhere, / Hun-dreds of cats, / Thousands of cats, / Millions and billions of trillions of cats." Not supernaturally but nonetheless bizarrely, the millions of cats follow him home, devouring all the grass and drinking all the water along the way. When the very old man and his wife cannot choose from among the many pets, they ask the cats to select the "prettiest" one. This instigates a huge fight, and when the dust clears, only a "thin and scraggly" kitten remains: "'Oh, I'm just a very homely little cat,' said the kitten, 'So when you asked who was the prettiest, I didn't say anything. So nobody bothered about me.'" In a happy ending remi-niscent of Hans Christian Andersen's "The Ugly Duckling," the peasants raise the humble cat, which grows "nice and plump" in a series of time-lapse images that suggest a clock face, the phases of the sun, or the curve of a smile.[85] The account focuses on satisfied longing, in the form of the peasants' realized desire,

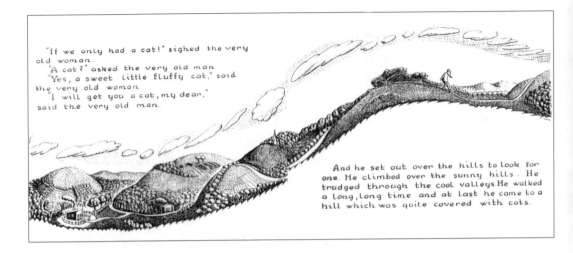

"If we only had a cat!" sighed the very old woman.
"A cat?" asked the very old man.
"Yes, a sweet little fluffy cat," said the very old woman.
"I will get you a cat, my dear," said the very old man.

And he set out over the hills to look for one. He climbed over the sunny hills. He trudged through the cool valleys. He walked a long, long time and at last he came to a hill which was quite covered with cats.

Cats here, cats there,
Cats and kittens everywhere,
Hundreds of cats,
Thousands of cats,
Millions and billions and trillions of cats

FIGURE 1.3. In *Millions of Cats* (1928), Wanda Gág uses a landscape-oriented spread to create a sense of distance as the "very old man" goes in search of a pet. Her folksy refrain accompanies his surprise at "millions and billions and trillions of cats."

the worthy kitten, and the formation of a family. Gág concludes with an image of the couple in rocking chairs, the woman knitting and the man smoking his pipe. They sit under their old wedding portraits, in the light cast by an oil lamp, while the kitten plays with a ball of yarn. This nostalgic tableau, like a natural history exhibit behind museum glass, crystallizes artisanal culture in modern memory.

Gág's compact illustrations of humble folklife, with their left-to-right momentum and firm black lines, make graceful transitions from page to page. Each carefully composed spread balances the hand-lettered text with illustrations of an expansive countryside. This meticulous balancing of words and pictures reveals Gág's and her publishers' familiarity with verbal-visual story-telling, developed in the picture stories of the nineteenth century and evident in turn-of-the-century comic strips and early animation. Gág's images have been called "halfway steps between academic realism and the European avant-garde, like so much of American art of this era."[86] The high-contrast black-on-white imagery, twisting shapes, and acute angles reference modernist cinema and art, at a time when brooding films such as director Robert Wiene's *The Cabinet of Dr. Caligari* (1920; U.S., 1921), F. W. Murnau's *Sunrise: A Song of Two Humans* (1927) and *Nosferatu* (1922; U.S., 1929), and Fritz Lang's *Metropolis* (1927) were appearing on American movie screens and demonstrating innovation in set design and subtitling. In *Metropolis*, a strange inner-city farmhouse might belong to Gág's own oeuvre, in which the residue of the archaic countryside lingers among the shiny artifacts of urban space.[87] The off-kilter village sets for *The Cabinet of Dr. Caligari* resemble Gág's tilting backgrounds, which seem to dance with the refrain of her picture book; *Caligari's* spiky, hand-drawn intertitles have the immediacy (but not the softness) of the round, unaggressive hand lettering in *Millions of Cats*. Gág's written narrative was hand lettered by her brother Howard Gág, and the thickness of his lettering matches that of the illustrative line, visually unifying words and illustrations. The Gágs rejected the modern convenience of mechanical type and enhanced the book's homespun quality with slightly uneven calligraphy suggestive of a needlepoint sampler or homemade greeting card.

Sunrise, which describes transitions between an insular country village and a cosmopolitan center, also provides insight into the attitudes shaping 1920s texts. In *Sunrise*, the "leading characters . . . are noted only as 'The Woman from the City', 'The Man', and 'The Wife'—labels which emphasize their broad, universal qualities."[88] Like Murnau, Gág uses fixed iconography to stabilize the identities of "the very old man" and "the very old woman." Gág's peasants are uncomplicated folk who solve grievances with simple ease. Their counterparts may be seen in earlier cinema melodrama, which traded in stock types.[89] Short comedies such as *The Country Man and the Cinematograph* (Great Britain, 1901), which influenced American shorts including *Uncle Josh at the Moving Picture Show* (United States, 1903), constructed stereotypes of a rural oaf unfamiliar with newfangled equipment. Films about Uncle Josh show a generic bumpkin, complete with overalls and beard, becoming confused by a projected, moving image and clumsily pulling down the cinema screen to spoil the illusion. Karal Ann Marling observes a corresponding trend in 1930s hometown murals that picture rustic types:

The rural stereotypes purveyed by movies, cartoons, fiction, drama, photographs, and the press provided important clues to the Regionalist. . . . Whether a given cultural stereotype of the day—a ragged sharecropper or a prim farm matron—could be corroborated by a given factual example was beside the point. What was relevant was the capacity of the operative stereotype—the Ozark shanty or the white clapboard farmhouse—to communicate shared and current ideas in familiar terms to a small-town audience which, thanks to the media, was a participant in a new, mass culture.[90]

Peasants are one-dimensional and predictable. They follow set narratives, unlike actual human friends and neighbors of the twentieth century. By ensuring that representations of such folk (if not the folk themselves) existed, filmmakers and visual artists reified a preindustrial past in the postindustrial present. Picture-book artists reinforced this imagery to a young readership.

Gág's pictorial narrative esteems bucolic isolation and keeps the complexities of city life at bay, and her folktale form and thematic content convey a yearning for the past and for cozy domesticity. Yet *Millions of Cats*'s technological production and wide distribution are the results of technological improvements and an expanding children's book industry. A picture book is the product of an industrial hive, and Gág's swoony black-and-white imagery and serial illustrations show her awareness of montage and commodity culture. This conflict between rural bliss and machine-culture individualism expresses itself in the plot and storytelling too. The old man's search for the perfect pet is like a shopping trip gone awry, with a consumer confronting an overwhelming array of commodities. The book's mythic countryside, uncorrupted by evidence of city life, becomes the setting for warlike violence when the greedy cats battle to be best: "They bit and scratched and clawed each other and made such a great noise that the very old man and the very old woman ran into the house as fast as they could." Silence falls, and the man and woman peek out the window. "They could not see a single cat! / 'I think they must have eaten each other all up,' said the very old woman. 'It's too bad!' " The woman expresses an ambiguous regret, yet the cats' disappearance reestablishes harmony. The millions conveniently vanish, leaving the couple with all they need: one pet, and peace and quiet.

Cynical readers might compare the climax of *Millions of Cats* to Filippo Tommaso Marinetti's 1909 Futurist Manifesto, which proclaimed war the "world's only hygiene."[91] Gág's repetitive folktale builds to a breaking point and finds its resolution in a violent civil war. The argumentative cats destroy each other, and the meekest reaps the benefits. Afterward, rural tranquility is restored, albeit for only three out of millions. In this respect, *Millions of Cats* reflects its postwar context at a geographical though not a temporal remove from European disillusionment and economic depression. One might say that the book solves its problem by wiping out dissent. Then again, despite being a popular reproducible text, *Millions of Cats* rejects the new and suggests a visceral hostility toward modern life. Gág and her peers in 1920s Manhattan belonged to a dynamic tradition influenced by Italian futurist nihilism, Wyndham Lewis's noisy English vorticists (evident in 1913–14's *BLAST* magazines), the absurdist aesthetics of Tristan Tzara's Dada (1916–24), and post-Dada modernism such as the surrealism of André Breton and Louis Aragon.

Thus, *Millions of Cats* highlights peasant life but also carries traces of the avant-garde. Gág's undulating, organic landscapes and ominous, jagged black clouds echo prints and paintings by Wassily Kandinsky's German expressionist group, Der Blaue Reiter, and the somber prints and sculptures of the German artist Käthe Kollwitz in the 1920s. Moreover, every image in *Millions of Cats* is reproduced crisply enough that Gág's handwritten name or initials are visible on the pages. The author's signature stakes a legal claim and signals a tension in the work. If the picture book truly is a single unit—a sequence like an animated short or a comic strip—there is no need to sign individual pieces. Gág, like other illustrators of her era, treats each page or spread singly, raising issues of authorship and suggesting that the original creator retains some control over her alienated product. Gág's signature is a surplus, even though the illustrations operate as a unified composition.[92]

Gág's use of negative space and material resources is significant, too. Prior to the 1920s, few widely available texts made flagrant use of negative space, because it required (not to say wasted) a great deal of paper. Gág's picture book, which looks unspectacular to twenty-first-century eyes accustomed to fine-tuned color, deluxe paper stocks, and digital art, was unusual in its day. In 1928, American readers familiar with nursery-rhyme reprints, illustrated storybooks, and serial novels were still wowed by editions that combined words and pictures, often in color. In 1927, for example, a librarian marveled at Margery Williams Bianco's *The Adventures of Andy*: "Its distinctive feature is its riotous illustrations by Léon Underwood. What an orgy of fantastic colors, of splashes of green and black and yellow!"[93] In Underwood's black-and-white inset drawings and tipped-in color figures, a stylish, slender doll named Andromeda—Andy for short—falls off a city fire escape where her incautious owner has placed her, speaks with a sparrow about losing her "job" as a toy, gets captured by a terrier and a poodle, and is carried off by a crow (à la Rachel Field's *Hitty*, two years later). These escapades, painted in strokes of blue, peach, brown, red, and green ink, no longer call to mind the word "orgy." Yet this book and others like it were produced for the children of 1927, who were born into a world of comics, moving pictures, and recorded sound. Such texts confounded those who defined real books as thick, squarish, and black and white. Although the illustrated storybook, with glossy and staid tipped-in illustrations, still met traditional expectations of the book form, picture books like *Millions of Cats* and illustrated texts like *The Adventures of Andy* redefined visual and verbal storytelling conventions for children's literature.

Gág's contemporaries nevertheless pointed out her books' pastoralism, taking for granted the technological profusion of the work's subtext. Moore wrote, "Wanda Gág sees everything as a child sees and she draws with a strength and beauty far removed from the commercialized art which is flooding the market with flashy picture books in crude colors. . . . Wanda Gág has something special to say, something to share, in this first picture book of hers which is so sure of a place among early American children's books of the future. . . . One marvels at the vigorous technique and the fertility and variety of an imagination which could give birth to such an old world picture story book in present-day New York."[94] Moore rightly predicts that Gág's work will endure because it mimes a child's vision and rejects "commercialized art." Moore does not consider the child a part of "flashy," "crude" commercial culture and credits Gág's work with an organic "fertility" that more approximates the condition of childhood. In a utopian double move, Moore places Gág's work with "early American children's books of the future," simultaneously admiring the text as an object of nostalgia and projecting it into the unknown future (where, indeed, it is available in a paperback edition). The glowing review ends by calling *Millions of Cats* "a book of universal interest to children living anywhere in the world."[95] Moore alleges a universal child subject fascinated by "old world" imagery, and suggests a potential for global harmony via an embrace of Western folk culture. Moore's response indicates an idealized Western model for childhood that was, and remains, in effect. Moore sees Gág as providing relief from cultural anxieties and suggests that Gág's books are here-and-now fairy tales for the twentieth century.

*Millions of Cats* made Gág a sought-after children's author, an artist of nostalgia and humor. *The Funny Thing* (1929), about a gnomish man's encounter with a deer-sized, dinosaurlike monster who likes to eat "little children's dolls," and *Snippy and Snappy* (1931), a story of sister and brother field mice who unwisely enter a human house in search of cheese, repeated the narrow page height and wide horizontal format of *Millions of Cats*, as well as its quaint outdoor settings, complementary hand-lettered text, and rippling, rolling compositions that stretched the width of the spreads. *Snippy and Snappy* includes memorable singsong chants reminiscent of "millions and billions and trillions of cats" as the mice play with a ball of knitting yarn in their hilly landscape: "They rolled it up, they rolled it down, / They rolled it up and up and down. / They rolled it up and DOWN and down, / They rolled it UP AND DOWN." Although *The ABC Bunny* (1933) departs from this format in its tall portrait layout, grainy oversize lithographs, and deliberate alphabetic sequence, it, too, highlights Gág's ability to craft pleasing rhyme and to establish visual momentum from frame to frame. *Nothing at All* (1941), about "three little orphan dogs"—one of which is invisible and is thus the book's namesake—returns to *Millions of Cats*'s landscape format and hand lettering despite being more text-heavy than the prior picture books. From a jackdaw bird, the invisible Nothing-at-all learns "that he who is Nothingy, yet wishes to be Somethingy, must get up at sunrise and whirl around and around and around. While whirling thus, he must say this magic chant: I'm busy / Getting dizzy." By performing this incantation nine days in a row, Nothing-at-all becomes visible and a worthy pet like his brothers. Gág illustrates the book in papaya orange, lichen green, and mossy brown (Nothing-at-all appears as a spherical bubble of white space on the pages), and she resolves the dog's dilemma with a folk ritual.

Besides being known for picture-book innovation, Gág held strong opinions on the translation and telling of folktales. Her publishing success gave her an influential voice in library circles, where oral, communal modes of storytelling were viewed as necessary components to an educational system threatened by mass-media entertainment. Gág's *Gone Is Gone; or, The Story of a Man Who Wanted to Do Housework* (1935), *Snow White and the Seven Dwarfs* (1938), and *Three Gay Tales from Grimm* (1943) retold or revised märchen from her childhood. In an introduction to her translated collection *Tales from Grimm* (1936), whose sixteen tales are liberally sprinkled with her homespun black-and-white imagery, Gág connected the Grimms' rustic setting with the modern realm: "The fairy tale world in these stories, though properly weird and strange, has a convincing, three-dimensional character. There is magic, wonder, sorcery, but no vague airy-fairyness about it. . . . The story of the spindle, shuttle, and needle is more airy than most, but even here the supernatural agents are not ballet-skirted fairies with wands, but three plain workaday objects. Aside from this, many of the stories are folktales rather than fairy stories—and what could be more substantial than a peasant?"[96] Gág takes pains to identify the sturdy ancestors and solid objects that underpin tales of the past. She allows that the Grimms provide a "properly weird and strange" fantasy component, but she also insists on the tangible presence of the folk milieu. She dismisses metaphysical characters in favor of earthy types and aggressively notes how "plain workaday objects" may play a "supernatural" role; for instance, a spindle, shuttle, and needle operate themselves, ghost-in-the-machine style, suggesting the automation and assembly-line operations of Gág's day. When Gág asks, "What could be more substantial than a peasant?" she denies that these literary characters are in any way ethereal or unreal. Her argument echoes Freud's own remark on the fairy tale and the absence of the uncanny in that form of litera-ture: "Fairy tales quite frankly adopt the animistic standpoint of the omnipo-tence of thoughts and wishes, and yet I cannot think of any genuine fairy story which has anything uncanny about it. We have heard that it is in the highest degree uncanny when an inanimate object—a picture or a doll—comes to life; nevertheless in Hans Andersen's stories the household utensils, furniture and tin soldiers are alive, yet nothing could well be more remote from the uncanny. And we should hardly call it uncanny when Pygmalion's beautiful statue comes to life."[97] Whereas the living doll or machine is defamiliarized (made *unheim-liche*, or uncanny), the vivified fairy-tale object retains—or used to retain—a homely (*heimlich*) status. Yet one might ask whether, in the modern world, the antique object begins taking on an uncanny quality because it signifies a bygone past. In an environment filled with conveniences, an old spindle pos-sesses an auratic magic to the point where it becomes not a functional item but a collectible that stimulates nostalgic reverie. Similarly, the contemporized fairy tale is housed in a mass-produced storybook and takes on a mechanical life in the industrialized world. Whether or not the fairy tale's standard content changes, its mode of production and material existence were anachronistic in the capitalist twentieth century.

Gág, with her critical concern for careless modern progress, suggests that an ordinary-looking but extraordinarily powerful spindle, shuttle, and needle have enduring value. They are not just fanciful props or useful hand tools but items that link discrete moments of Then and Now. Yet Gág still wishes for the comforting embodiment of the peasant, in an era when folk rhetoric in Ger-many was employed with fascist objectives and the alluring Communism of the Soviet Union increasingly came under American political scrutiny. Gág, work-ing from a decidedly leftist position, attempts to invest folk culture with be-nign modern meaning via her reproduction and reillustration of German fairy tales for a young audience.[98] In a decade of disillusionment, Gág undertakes a redemptive project, while mourning tradition and lost community in her fine-art work and in the illustrations she did for the leftist publications the *Liberator* and *New Masses*.

Gág reified the objects of nostalgia in the mass-produced artifacts she created. She kept well-loved tales in print and recuperated a fading way of life through storytelling a century after the Grimms' 1806–57 efforts to collect and inscribe oral tales.[99] The anthology *Tales from Grimm*, updated with fresh illustrations and a modern format, became the archive for new generations. Gág reconfigured the folktale so that it had a chance of survival in an era of speedy reproducibility and rapid changes of fashion. She repackaged old tales as modern consumer items, with the paradoxical impulse to interrupt consumerism and put children in touch with a vanishing past.

In her non-picture-book art too, Gág conjured images of folk heritage. She created lithographs and ink drawings of the changing New York metropolitan area and her native Minnesota. These quiet images of decaying farm equipment, dilapidated wooden shacks, sagging trees, and country-house doorways imply the passing of time and the things that fall out of use in modernity. In the humble scenes she creates, cobwebs grow and dust gathers, doors seem to creak on their hinges and bang in the breeze, and yellowing autumn trees look ready to drop their leaves. In a *New Yorker* review of Gág's 1930 print exhibition at Weyhe Gallery in Manhattan, Murray Pemberton wrote, "What Lankes is to Robert Frost, Miss Gág is to Carl Sandburg. She is only faintly bitter, and her worst philippics have a certain kindly, childlike quality. We think of her, somehow, in terms of . . . one-hundred-per-cent iron."[100] Pemberton alludes to Sandburg, whose *Rootabaga Stories* (1922) preceded Gág's contributions and whose children's book *Abe Lincoln Grows Up* (1928), a condensed version of his Pulitzer Prize–winning Lincoln biography, helped cement his reputation as a home-grown, all-ages American prose poet. Pemberton discerns a "kindly, childlike quality" in the politically charged rusticity that Gág, like Sandburg, evoked. Gág's non-children's-book artwork, picture books, and illustrated books demonstrate an attachment to the quaint and a cynical attitude toward progress.

Although critical of progress, Gág was part of progress too. All her texts bind allusions to ruralism and modernity in tempting commodity packages. As an art student in New York, she worked at designing children's products for the marketplace, including the Happiwork product line of folding boxes decorated with illustrated children's stories. Her fine-art prints were available by subscription as well, attesting to an entrepreneurship she shared with her art-world contemporaries.[101] If Gág's representations of folklife and obsolete technology seem a reactionary effort to stifle the new, her professional acumen provides a counterweight. Gág certainly hoped her children's books would finance her fine-art endeavors. Audur Helgadottir Winnan writes that "when the Depression put works of art into the class of super-luxuries, she had to turn her efforts to something more saleable, juvenile books. . . . She had intended to write books only as needed to earn a living," yet these became the work for which she is remembered.[102] Gág's paradoxical picture books never venerate urban reality, yet they emerged in a context of mass production, rapid transience, and economic need.

## READY-MADE ANTIQUES:
## OLD WORLD CRAFTS AND NEW WORLD COMMODITIES

Like the fairy tale, the material picture book possesses both functional and mythological capacities, occupying immediate and immanent time. According to Jean Baudrillard, "There is a whole range of objects—including unique, baroque, folkloric, exotic and antique objects—that . . . appear to run counter to the requirements of functional calculation, and answer to other kinds of demands such as witness, memory, nostalgia or escapism." These liminal artifacts nevertheless exist "in modernity, and that is what gives them a double meaning." Antiques mediate between Now and Then, and "serve less as possessions than as symbolic intercessors. . . . They are a way of escaping from everyday life, and no escape is more radical than escape in time, none so thoroughgoing as escape into one's childhood."[103] Baudrillard describes objects acquired by collectors years after their original production. Yet picture books, even of recent vintage, reproduce and also simulate antique qualities due to multiple layers of signification. If picture books last long enough to become genuine antiques, they effectively complete a self-fulfilling prophecy.

Margery Williams Bianco's Little Wooden Doll waits years in an attic to be discovered by any child owner. Rachel Field's century-old Hitty (who boasts of being carved from mountain-ash wood) returns to her first home to find she has outlived her original family, only to be sold for a lofty price at an estate sale. Like these hardy fictional picture-book toys, the picture book itself can enjoy a multigenerational longevity, one in which its meaning changes. Ready-made to serve a practical purpose, the picture book can last long enough to become an antique, even if its paper, cloth, and cardboard are not as sturdy as mountain ash. Then, outgrown by its owner, the picture book supplies a connection to the past and a realization of the future fulfilled by the reader's growth.[104] Because picture books are associated with an ephemeral period of life, these eminently modern commodities automatically suggest a bygone age. Eventually they are abandoned in favor of new texts, but they may be reencountered years later by their reader, now a literate subject who can reflect upon childhood and its playthings or objects. The picture book imitates, and one day may become, a repository for memory and dream.

Due to their sensitivity to the present time and their persistent association with the past and memory, picture books—the fairy tales of modernity—qualify as ready-made antiques. Every picture book is a ready-made antique, because its significance encompasses past, present, and future. Picture books are not only material goods for immediate enjoyment; they function also as manufactured antiques with nostalgia and sentiment built in. As a pseudo-antique, the picture book corresponds to other inventions of modernity: Marcel Duchamp's found objects (*objets trouvés*), such as the bottle rack and urinal; Dada and surrealism's jarring juxtapositions of primitivism and machine culture; and material artifacts valued for their longevity versus objects of convenience for instant gratification. André Breton and his fellow surrealists haunted flea markets hoping for an epiphany, an encounter with an object that triggered their dreams. Among the secondhand items on display, they sought catalytic objects that would link their moment to instants in the past. Eventually, they chose to construct "found" objects rather than wait for these things to appear in flea-market detritus. The surrealists used familiar junk to produce the effect of chance, to harness the revelatory power of involuntary memory, and to stimulate childlike reverie. They also rejected the deadening aspects of modernism by recovering the tangible past.[105] A similar process takes place when the author-illustrator sets to the hopeful task of creating a text that represents childhood, when a reader opens the material picture book for a story, or when the secondhand-store or library browser happens upon a previously forgotten picture book. It is not by coincidence that the creative and technical heyday of the American picture book corresponds to the surrealist movement and the popularization of psychoanalysis, both concerned with mediation between Now and Then.

In addition, the picture book satisfies a modern interest in the collectible.[106] As changing consumer habits displace handicraft, the value and rarity of an authentic handicraft correspondingly increase. This transition applies to the simultaneously old-fashioned and mass-produced picture book. Many picture books of the twenties and thirties celebrate the mechanical despite holding

domestic life and oral storytelling in high regard, partly because of their makers' personal experience with the decline of community as a consequence of
modernity. For example, Dorothy Kunhardt is known for the perennial best
seller *Pat the Bunny* (1940), an interactive beginner book of textures, including
fuzzy cloth to represent rabbit fur. Yet her earlier books, *Junket Is Nice* (1933)
and *Now Open the Box* (1934), reveal her long-standing interest in reader participation and in a thirties avant-gardism. *Junket Is Nice* and *Now Open the
Box*, printed on a horizontal landscape format and hand-lettered in careful
but uneven lowercase, look amateurish and homemade, even more like domestic crafts than Gág's picture books do. Yet the books are not as naive as they
appear. Kunhardt's repetition and long, unpunctuated sentences glance back
at Lucy Sprague Mitchell's here-and-now stories, resemble Gertrude Stein's
wordplay, and anticipate the mature work of Margaret Wise Brown.

*Junket Is Nice*, printed exclusively in gradations of red and black on white
pages, concerns "an old old man" with a bald head, a gray tuxedo jacket, and a
voluminous curly, red beard, dipping a serving spoon into a tall, wide mixing
bowl full of junket (a sweetened milk custard set with rennet, never defined
in the narrative).[107] A narrow red frame runs around the page border, unifying the loosely drawn illustrations (Figure 1.4). Commas, quotation marks,
and question marks are missing from Kunhardt's punctuation repertoire, in
the very year Stein's *The Autobiography of Alice B. Toklas* explained, "Gertrude
Stein said commas are unnecessary, the sense should be intrinsic and not have
to be explained by commas and otherwise commas were only a sign that one
should pause and take breath but one should know of oneself when one wanted to pause and take breath."[108] Kunhardt revels in run-on sentences and linguistic excess: "The old man ate and ate and ate. More junket and more junket
and more junket and more junket until at last people began to be very much
surprised at how much junket he was eating and they began to tell their friends
about him because he seemed to be such a very hungry old man." Kunhardt
pictures a gathering crowd of small red and black stick figures ("all the people in
the world") full of astonishment at the man's appetite. The man stops eating to
ask, "People why don't you try and guess what I am thinking about all the time
I am eating my junket and if you guess right I will give you something nice." He
reveals he is "NOT thinking about" three animal-related things, pictured one
by one on separate spreads and including "a walrus with an apple on his back."
The people begin hazarding bizarre guesses, visualized in Kunhardt's clumsy
line drawings ("a kangaroo jumping over a glass of orange juice so as not to spill
it"; "a daddy-long-legs holding up his foot for the sun to warm it"; "a vulture

looking all around the rocks for five lumps of sugar but I suppose he's forgotten about the one on the top of his head"; "a bear climbing a ladder because his toenails are too long for walking on the ground"). The call-and-response resembles a surrealist game of exquisite corpse, each addition patently absurd and cumulatively hilarious. The audience's silly responses might be described as childlike, yet the correct answer is supplied by an actual child. A boy logically says, "JUNKET," and these six giant letters fill a complete spread. As a reward, the old man invites the boy to lick the bowl and the boy in return gives the man a ride home on the back of his tricycle (a pedophilic suggestion that would appear even more grotesque in a picture book of recent vintage).

*Now Open the Box*, lettered in the same informal lowercase and printed exclusively in red, black, and yellow, describes the denizens of a circus and especially the contents of the ringmaster's mysterious box: "the teeniest weeniest teeny teeny teeny weeny weeny weeny little dog in all the world and he was dear little Peewee the circus dog" (Figure 1.5). Again, Kunhardt builds her narrative on lists and repetition, naming and picturing each circus performer and adding each time, "He [or she] loved little Peewee." All is well until Peewee grows: soon, "poor little Peewee the circus dog was just the same size as any other plain dog that you would see anywhere if you were looking at any plain dog and how could a circus man keep just a plain dog in his circus." Everyone weeps to think the now-normal Peewee must go, until he starts to grow again. He becomes "the hugest most enormous dog in the whole world" and once again causes a spectacle when the ringmaster opens the box. (Peewee could be an ancestor of Norman Bridwell's 1962 *Clifford the Big Red Dog*.) Kunhardt's early books, awkwardly sketched but revelatory in their comic, experimental

FIGURE 1.4. Dorothy Kunhardt's offbeat *Junket Is Nice* (1933) concludes with a man and boy celebrating their favorite dessert and pedaling away on a tricycle.

FIGURE 1.5. In Dorothy Kunhardt's naively drawn *Now Open the Box* (1934), performers weep when tiny Peewee the dog grows too large to be in the circus.

sentences and outsider artistry, unmistakably blend children's entertainment and a lighthearted avant-garde sensibility. *Junket Is Nice* and *Now Open the Box* have a spontaneous, ready-made quality, like communal games suspended in a bound book format.

In *The Little Book about God* (1934), crafted to resemble a tiny illuminated manuscript, author-illustrator Lauren Ford likewise mimes a handmade look, but to much different effect (Plates 1 and 2). Ford borrows the hand-lettered style of French books by Françoise (Seignobosc), including *Images à colorier* (1929) and *Les paysans de France* (1931). Ford pens the words in black, red, and blue, and her pages are tinted a papyrus wheat-blond that requires folded and gathered sheets rather than single sheets of paper. For every four pages, one piece of paper is folded in quarters; what usually would be eight pages when cut turns out to be only four, with the untinted side of the paper folded in. Doubleday's artisanal printers made concessions so that Ford's book could have its golden, aged color.[109] Ford's tiny (4 × 6 inch), noteworthy book, which received critical accolades, suggests the predominantly white, middle-class, Protestant audience for children's literature, despite (or perhaps because of) the immigrant influx, religion-based schools, and particular influence of Judaism. Ford covers mostly Old Testament material—opening with Adam and Eve and progressing briskly to the story of Noah and the Ark—but concludes with the birth of Christ. Despite her allusions to an illuminated manuscript, however, Ford takes a conversational tone, noting that "lazy people" and "stupid people" are at fault for war and hatred, and "little ones," or children, are kind and not to blame for the global population's idiocy. In the years of the Depression, with its large-scale homelessness, hunger, and parental desertion of children, Ford incorporates a modern story of the angel Gabriel rescuing a starving child and reuniting her with her missing parents, placing biblical stories in line with current events.

Developments in mass media and fine arts in the United States, along with nostalgia for self-sufficiency and better economic times, influenced the publishing of illustrated texts whose sequential imagery either suggested old-fashioned modes such as illuminated manuscripts and homemade scrapbooks or celebrated novelties like kinetic motion, time-lapse photography, and cinematic montage. Throughout the 1920s, improvements in photolithography meant that consumers became familiar with illustrated variations on the conventional pictureless text or books with tipped-in images on coated paper. Stylized systems of representation, adapted from established media including comic strips, advertisements, animation, and illustrated storybooks, found their way into picture books and became picture-book conventions, types of visual or verbal shorthand for the reader to interpret. Most texts passed muster as picture books so long as they seemed to enable reading at the level of the word, although some early picture books were criticized for being oddly shaped and easy to shoplift, and others—notably Maud and Miska Petersham's influential *Miki* (1929), measuring ten inches on its vertical edge—were thought too tall for bookshelves. Esther Averill and Feodor Rojankovsky's oversize Domino Press edition of *Daniel Boone: Historic Adventures of an American Hunter among the Indians* (1931), 14½ inches high and 11½ inches wide, must have seemed enormous and utterly impractical.[110]

*Daniel Boone*, with its text printed in English and French editions by Robert Coulouma of Argenteuil and its lithographed illustrations printed by Mourlot Frères of Paris, was a true artists' book; the lithographs were printed in a limited edition, without text, on fine-quality paper. Created in France by the expatriate American Averill and the Russian émigré Rojankovsky, this modernist book defies naturalism, featuring stencil-like imagery in saturated, grainy black, yellow, green, red, and blue. Crediting Rojankovsky's love of the theater, Averill called the slim, sixteen-page "album of *Daniel Boone* . . . a dramatic sequence, with stage sets."[111] With its borderless maps of the Americas from Canada to Mexico; blocky, emphatic, multicolored words to describe its hero ("pathfinder / scout / hunter / soldier / backwoodsman / pioneer"); stylized images of North American wildlife; and orderly arrangements of informational words and woodland imagery, *Daniel Boone* lacks narrative momentum but generates visual excitement through its integration of color pictures and shaped blocks of text. It styles a 1734–78 frontier epic, set mostly in "Kentucky—the

Hunter's Paradise" and depicting white settlers' and traders' battles with villainous "Redskins," as an avant-garde production, mythologizing Boone and bringing his bloody wilderness ethos into the industrial twentieth century.

A comparatively peaceful book, Margery Clark's *The Poppy Seed Cakes* (1924), illustrated by the Petershams, beautifully demonstrates additional artistic possibilities in the early twentieth century (Figure 1.6). This chapter book, decorated with patterned, color borders and folksy icons on every page, introduces two energetic children: Andrewshek, whose parents "brought him from the old country when he was a tiny baby"; and his next-door neighbor Erminka, likewise a daughter of immigrants. Andrewshek gets a visit from his Auntie Katushka, who comes from overseas on his fourth birthday; Katushka totes a bag filled with "a fine feather bed and a bright shawl and five pounds of poppy seeds" so she can make poppy seed cakes for her nephew every Saturday. The delicious cakes attract mischievous animals, including a goose and goat, whose antics get Andrewshek in trouble. Similarly, Erminka receives a visit from her Uncle Anton, who brings her "a set of wooden dolls" and her brother "a pair of red-topped boots" from the generalized Old Country; Erminka does not care for the dolls but covets the boots.[112] The written narrative, in which Erminka's father sails home to see his family, cheerfully implies the cultural exchanges possible in the 1920s while otherwise telling mild stories of two four-year-olds in an unidentified village.

In *The Poppy Seed Cakes*, the Petershams contribute patterns evocative of Eastern European handicraft, printed in yellow frames around each page of text. Their work often alludes to Hungarian-born Miska's heritage (Miska Petersham being a somewhat Americanized form of his given name, Mihaly Petrezselyen). Serigraph-style full-page images, printed either in four colors or in black, depict the cotton head scarves and tunics of the immigrant family members, along with colorfully painted wooden interiors and fanciful vegetable gardens. The small, squarish book packs a visual punch with its tomato red, marigold yellow, loden green, and turquoise palette, as well as Hungarian-inspired images neatly framed in its petite pages.

Cloth toy books, self-consciously avant-garde picture books like *Daniel Boone*, storybooks with special illustrations like *Poppy Seed Cakes*, and folktale collections like Ida Zeitlin and Theodore Nadejen's *Skazki: Tales and Legends of Old Russia* (1926) demonstrate how editors began thinking in terms of harmonious sequences of words and pictures. Twentieth-century people had developed habits of looking and seeing in terms of the camera eye, the dynamic movement of the crowd, the architecture of the city, and the visions of

AUNTIE KATUSHKA BROUGHT A HUGE BAG FILLED WITH PRESENTS

The
Poppy Seed
Cakes

By Margery Clark

Illustrated by
Maud & Miska Petersham

Garden City, New York
Doubleday & Company, Inc.

She wore the red topped boots.

"I must show my red topped boots to those tomato plants at the end of the garden," Erminka said to her mother. "The red tomatoes and the red tops on my boots are just the same color."

She ran down the path in a great hurry.

"See!" she called to the tomato

"MY RED-TOPPED BOOTS AND YOUR RED TOMATOES ARE THE SAME COLOR"

FIGURE I.6. Maud and Miska Petersham's illustrations for Margery Clark's *The Poppy Seed Cakes* (1924), printed in spicy paprika and mustard hues, celebrate immigrants' travels.

individuals new to the American landscape. According to book designer Abe Lerner,

> The revolutionary changes in painting, sculpture, and printmaking
> that had been taking place since the time of the Impressionists were
> affecting the minor arts. . . . Some of the Europeans [including Feodor
> Rojankovsky, Kurt Wiese, and Boris Artzybasheff] emigrated to these
> shores and played an active role, becoming, eventually, important con-
> tributors to our modern heritage in children's books. Under the pressure
> of their needs, we began to develop the platemaking and printmaking
> techniques needed for reproducing their artwork more accurately and
> inexpensively.[113]

In the years after World War I, publishers found many affordable options for creative book composition and sought to increase the appeal of books through the use of improved production methods. Lerner explains the combined crea-tive and technical opportunities newly available to U.S. artists and designers: "Offset platemakers and printers were learning how to print halftones on antique-finish papers. Improvements in machine-made book papers enabled us to reproduce pencil and crayon drawings, and watercolors, with a higher degree of fidelity, without using the unpleasant surfaces of coated sheets."[114]

In a 1936 article, Grace W. Allen looked back on two decades of rapid change in color printing. She explains the impacts of increased production speed and reliable, inexpensive color inks; the merits of smooth, coated paper versus rough stock; and the relative ease of wood engraving, photoengraving, and lithography processes. Allen notes production experts' sensitivity to the book's sensory appeal as an object, for instance by considering the visual, tactile, and olfactory appeal of "highly glazed paper" for those who grow up with it: "Children do not mind this smooth, shining paper because they are sensitive to the 'feel' of things and always associate these cool, smooth papers and the faint odor peculiar to them with the colored pictures they love." As examples, she mentions "all the Beatrix Potter books," the frontispiece of Field and Lathrop's *Hitty*, and tipped-in color images by Arthur Rackham; where Lerner recalls how he loathed coated stock, Allen finds it familiar and comforting. None-theless, Allen details the advantages of heavier, softer paper in legibility and weight, noting how "the hard, cold sheen of the [shiny] paper makes reflected lights that not only hinder reading but are injurious to the eyes."[115]

Allen also acknowledges publishers' and printers' practical needs. In her discussion of direct and offset lithography, which were popular overseas but not widely employed in the United States until the 1930s, she acknowledges,

> It may at first seem surprising that this method of lithographic print-ing from stone has not been in common use in America. In this coun-try, however, we have been more interested in mass production and speed and in the development of precision machinery, etc., than in the use of a printing process that is not adapted to the printing of great quantities of books at once and that requires a great deal of hand work that is not always accurate. . . . We have been quick to take advantage of a new development in this process. Thin sheets of zinc or aluminum have largely taken the place of stones. . . . They can be fixed around the cylinder of a rotary machine which produces at least three times as many impressions in a given time as those used for stone printing.[116]

An ability to provide consumer pleasure is not the only requirement for effec-tive work. Allen recognizes an American need for speed and affordability that until the early twentieth century had not been met by available printing meth-ods, and she notes the decline of artisanal practice in favor of efficiency and ac-curacy. She concludes with the thought that "another five years will completely overcome the age-old difficulties that lie in the way of making thousands of exact reproductions of one beautiful original. It is to be hoped that if our grasp does achieve this aim, the work of the artist may be worthy of this dissemina-tion."[117] Allen questions the artist's talents but does not question the merits of reproducibility. By her estimation, technical processes have triumphed and the age of the unique or auratic original is over. Where an earlier generation fondly recalled pulp pages and tipped-in pictures, children of the present would as-sociate youth with books of a different sheen, surface, and odor. Inevitably, a new generation of children would take these technical changes, and the picture book, for granted.

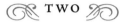

## TWO

# Picture-Book Ethnography:
# Representing the Other

### FOREIGN OBJECTS AND NORMATIVE SUBJECTS

In the American publishing industry, the expansion of children's book departments and the mass production of picture books coincided with the end of World War I and a destabilized social order. Modernization provided the technical and labor conditions to make picture books and other consumer goods available; publishers and printers could draw on a pool of laborers, a structured workday, mechanization, and improved resources such as paper and ink.[1] Simultaneously, American citizens' command of the spoken and written English language, control of the younger generation, and a dominant middle-class Anglocentrism were in question. Political participation by expatriates, military or government families, and immigrant citizens who were bilingual or were not native English speakers, as well as Northern migration by African Americans and low-income white Americans, and cross-country travel by rail, bus, and car, brought both excitement and unpredictability.[2] This chapter examines some of the cultural realities and anxieties that influenced the written and pictorial sequences shared with a young, diversifying, and educated U.S. readership.

Early twentieth-century subjects were willing world travelers, enduring long-distance travel and family separations in search of gainful employment. Consequently, all people were likely to see individuals outside their customary cultural groups, to hear international languages and regional accents, and to encounter texts that foregrounded controversial race, ethnicity, and class issues. Novels, poems, plays, and essays by Langston Hughes (*The Weary Blues*, 1926; *The Dream Keeper and Other Poems*, 1932), James T. Farrell (the Studs Lonigan trilogy, 1932–35), John Dos Passos (*Manhattan Transfer*, 1925; *U.S.A.*, 1930–36), and journalist–fiction writers Josephine Herbst, Tillie Olsen, Muriel Rukeyser, and Sanora Babb; revolutionary images by painter Jacob Lawrence and muralist Diego Rivera; performance pieces and cinema by Orson Welles; and little magazines published by radical critics like Jack Conroy (*The Disinherited*, 1933) brought social consciousness to Popular Front culture. Picture books were part of this intellectual ferment, with popular creators such as Wanda Gág and Theodor (Dr. Seuss) Geisel publishing political illustrations, and developing artists crossing paths at the Art Students League of New York.[3]

Naturalized American citizens of "nationality groups," as ethnicities often were known in the 1930s, gave U.S. urban centers a multicultural character, as popular reading materials and media of the time confirm. The March 11, 1926, issue of *Life* magazine (a *Life* magazine published prior to the photo journal) includes a full-page duotone cartoon captioned "St. Patrick's Day in New York."[4] In the center of the drawing, an Asian man dances a jig with a white-bearded man in a fez. Behind the dancers, someone hoists a placard reading "Armenian Sons of Patrick," and Chinese and Russian shop signs hang from buildings. Three hefty men play a trombone, clarinet, and tuba; their suits, brass instruments, and wide girth suggest stereotypical Germans. An African American man in a top hat and worker's apron looks in from the left margin. And a mustached man in a cap and vest stands waving a flag with a harp on it; his clothing and horse cart suggest an Italian street vendor. This entire issue, or "Saint Patrick's Number," of *Life*, whose green cover presents a cartoon of two Irish men in a fistfight, contains broad, bad jokes about Irish drinking, Catholicism, and literary figures. The national magazine lends credence to the affirmative assertion that migrant and immigrant communities could express allegiance to their adoptive and original homes alike, and could even find common cross-cultural ground. People of many heritages could qualify as American. But the cartoon's implications depend upon context and audience. An elite corporate boss and a first-generation Irish Catholic immigrant would perceive different meanings in this comic picture of multiethnic revelry. As this chapter will argue, picture-book sequences likewise could signify in opposing ways, alternately reinforcing cross-cultural acceptance and increasing suspicion in regard to ethnoracial difference.

Picture books were part of a mainstream culture that often assumed fixed social boundaries based on ethnic and racial stereotypes. An obvious example comes from vaudeville theater, which (unlike burlesque) was touted as an all-ages or even a family-friendly amusement. Vaudeville depended on a nineteenth-century music hall tradition of minstrelsy, white actors in blackface, and skits that played up spectators' superficial and ethnic differences. Cinema replaced vaudeville in the early part of the century, but film historians attest that slapstick comedies and melodramas reproduced vaudeville norms: "Shuffling, stammering blacks, raucous Irish, knife-wielding Italians and sly, hand-rubbing Jews frequented the Victorian stage, particularly the music halls, popular fiction and even Edison cylinders.... Early films absorbed the racial and ethnic stereotypes. Such old movies provide curious artifacts in evidence of national taste and values, if we remember, too, that many were produced, and responded to, by immigrants."[5] Cinematic forms find their parallels in children's artifacts, which emerged from the selfsame culture and comedy traditions.

Theatrical and cinematic caricatures accustomed spectators to various essentialisms. Stereotypes could be drawn in broad strokes, and icons like the Chinese peasant's conical hat and queue, the babushka, and the hayseed's overalls identified the figure of fun—just as they did in pictorial literature for a growing readership. Performers often mocked audience members' backgrounds (e.g., the Jewish and Italian clichés performed on stage and screen by Eddie Cantor or the Marx brothers), exaggerating the types with costumes, masks, and subtitled or printed vernacular. Likewise, early animation won audiences by prompting recognition of simplified caricatures, flirting with social boundaries, and providing scopic pleasure. Film historian Donald Crafton describes how, in the short film *Lightning Sketches* (1907), J. Stuart Blackton uses a chalkboard and trick photography to make "caricatures of a Jew and a black from the words 'Cohen' and 'Coon'—an embarrassment to modern audiences, but a reminder of the many 'Coon, Cohen, and Kelly' jokes familiar to turn-of-the-century vaudeville audiences."[6] Crafton notes the lightning sketcher's sleight-of-hand, which played on word association, visual transformation, and a confidence that ethnic humor would get laughs. Crafton also describes the importance of the theatrical tableau, which, as Miriam Hansen notes, involves a "frontality and uniformity of viewpoint [that] is clearly the mark of a *presentational*— as opposed to representational—conception of space and address."[7] *Lightning Sketches* exemplifies what cinema critic Tom Gunning has termed the "cinema of attraction," in which the spectator participates in the illusion by taking up a particular viewpoint, responding to cues in the framing and camera angle.[8] The denotative words and pictures prompt the recognition of an ideological viewpoint, and a knowing audience anticipates cinematic illusions and allusions. The film plays to insiders who grasp its broad humor and who inhabit its social milieu.

*Lightning Sketches* brings attention to naming practices and equates Jewish and black identities on a derisive level; the hand-printed signifiers "Cohen" and "Coon," written in chalk, appear alongside easy-to-draw visual signifieds, elementary icons of ethnic and racial others. These verbal symbols and visual icons were not necessarily shocking or particularly hilarious even then; the words and images of *Lightning Sketches*, which for twenty-first-century viewers traffic in ugly social taboos, were meant to provide their original spectators with light amusement and a sense of trick cinema's potentials. In addition, Hansen suggests that the movie theater constitutes a parallel public sphere and that the cinema of attractions "allows for a more centrifugal, less textually predetermined reception of filmic images" that appealed to "groups like the new immigrants who encountered the impact of industrialization, urbanization and commodification in an accelerated, telescoped form. . . . If the cinema helped immigrants organize their experience on their own terms . . . it also offered a collective forum for the production of fantasy, the capability of envisioning a different future."[9] Hansen's remarks suggest that immigrants and other outsiders to the industrial environment used filmic information to help them negotiate their new culture. Viewers gained an appreciation for modes of communication (writing, drawing, camerawork) at the same time they became aware of a written and visual shorthand for signs of cultural difference. By watching for these signs, they could gauge their own places in a diverse society. This word-image shorthand proved ideal for picture books and illustrated books, in the sense that these texts concurrently operate as modes of popular material production, methods of communication between individuals presumed to be alike or unlike, and ideological narratives tuned to prevailing cultural attitudes.

Although the still-picture sequence of a children's book deals in suspended animation, it, too, participates in ideologies carried over from slapstick and melodramatic theater and cinema. Picture-book caricature and sequence certainly parallel the rise of animation as a popular early-century medium. In the teens, twenties, and after, the animation industry flourished alongside other strands in the multimedia fabric, such as children's publishing, glossy magazine publishing, and advertising. Animation is of particular interest in comparison with picture books, due to its reliance on mimesis, sequential motion, and limited words; its production through both creative and repetitive labor; and its fantastic or absurd subject matter, which comes to be associated with immaturity, playfulness, and popularity (when the masses are implicitly analogous to children) rather than with elite spectators of a realist (ostensibly serious, adult) bent. Diverse, multilingual audiences could take pleasure—albeit unmeasurable, unequal pleasure—in these texts' comic content and in the sensory experience they provided. Animators themselves sought to please viewers of all ages and in countries outside the United States, as a survey of cartoon censorship reports:

It appears the [Max and Dave] Fleischer studio [which produced films distributed by Paramount Pictures] went out of its way to avoid offending people with its films by 1935. [Animator] Myron Waldman says that when they made *A Language All My Own* (1935) with Betty Boop performing on stage in Japan, they consulted with Japanese college students in the United States to make sure none of her hand gestures were offensive to Asians. In the cartoon she flies to Japan to perform her act. Waldman mentioned that the cartoon was popular in Japan and says he never heard any complaints about it. He adds that years later he saw the cartoon and was astonished that it included offensive images of buck-toothed Asian men in the audience.[10]

The animator claims not to have noticed a stereotype that surprises him now; conversely, he might now take for granted the animation process or the mechanized projection apparatus. In any event, he never again can read the animated film as he did before. The signification of the racial and ethnic caricatures, and of the medium itself, changes with time, as does the audience's reading or spectatorial strategy. The text is unaltered materially, but its historically situated markers of nation, race, ethnicity, and class have new connotations: the iconic "buck-toothed Asian" man recalls vaudeville, World War II propaganda, tabloid cartoons, and other out-of-fashion forms, depending on its present-day observer. For additional proof, one has only to look at Theodor Geisel's World War II editorial cartoons for the left-leaning *PM* magazine, or his "Private SNAFU" series of animated shorts for the U.S. Army, which caricature the Germans and Japanese.[11] His debut children's picture book as Dr. Seuss, *And to Think That I Saw It on Mulberry Street* (1937), originally included a line about a "Chinaman who eats with sticks." In reprints, the language was altered to reference a "Chinese man who eats with sticks," and the illustration was changed to remove the man's pigtail and render his yellow skin blank—that is, "white" like the page. Formally, the rhyming, ludic *Mulberry Street* offers a revolutionary first-person address, character development, verbal-visual sequence, and advertising aesthetic. Yet, in terms of content, it deploys outdated, exoticized caricature (including an Indian raja riding an elephant). Geisel's interventions in the book—examples of author-approved censorship—suggest the consensus necessary to a picture book's continued production. In addition, a contemporary reading of *Mulberry Street* demonstrates how formal excellence meets between-the-wars context, with the result that readers ought not overlook the discomfiting content.

Such texts inscribe a societal division that was ordinary, if unsettling in many cases, to audiences of the past. But the viewing subject's sudden perception that something is lacking (or is ugly, or has been misread) indicates that the division has crumbled or is in the process of breaking down. The audience refuses the boundaries that the popular text indicates are in place, and this failed communication produces a revelatory moment of confusion. A third layer of meaning destabilizes word and image, and a perceptible gap opens in the system.[12] A misinterpretation, or, more correctly, an against-the-grain reading of a coded text, becomes not only possible but likely—and censors sometimes arrive to alter the offending passage and impose their own generation's values on the text.

Hybrid visual-verbal communication, like Sergei Eisenstein's dialectical montage as a catalyst for revolutionary thinking, allows the possibility of *correspondance* through art, even as the chance encounter is averted or censored in the fragmented space of the new metropolis. Popular texts depend on a collective recognition of social commonplaces, including attitudes toward diversity, yet these social commonplaces are notoriously unstable. The troubling gaps in any text indicate cultural shifts, and the potential for shock emerges as we recognize these gaps, as in the 1907 *Lightning Sketches*, the 1926 "St. Patrick's Day in New York," the 1937 *And to Think That I Saw It on Mulberry Street*, and other illustrated texts and picture books for the young readers of the early twentieth century.

Any popular mode, including pictorial texts expected to instruct and delight young readers, anticipates people's culturally determined abilities to match words to images to objects; to associate signifiers and signifieds; and to make meaning—whether that meaning evolves from an optical illusion in a Georges Méliès short, a battered hat to denote a hobo, or the match between the letter *A* and a pictured airplane. Visual images cosignify with verbal information including slogans, captions, titles, and intertitles. But word- and image-based texts are unreliable systems of signification, because as the technology for producing, distributing, and reading them changes, so does everyday experience and a population's habits of looking and knowing. Popular texts signify a place and time in their mode of production, form, and content, and active rereading increasingly provides awareness of gaps between textual representation and lived experience. To notice those gaps in suspended animation and the fairy tale of modernity—that is, in modes of production that require readers to interpret word-image narrative—is to notice the crisis of representation simmering in the United States between the world wars.

The American picture book, addressed to a young audience, metaphorizes and often essentializes the racial, ethnic, and class tensions of the 1920s and the

Depression era. Diverse groups neither assimilated nor resolved their differences in this period, and picture books reflect this ambivalence. For example, immigration was a powder-keg issue, and immigration restrictions focused negative national attention on the influx of specific racial, ethnic, and religious groups; immigration acts applied to China (1882) and to southern and eastern Europe (1924), significantly restricting Chinese and Jewish immigration.[13] Picture books reflect such attention on race, nation, class, and religion by positing overseas locations for their international characters. Such texts may have an affirmative voice and colorful imagery, yet they restrict potential immigrants to countries of origin. Similarly, reflecting the infamous separate-but-equal doctrine inscribed by *Plessy v. Ferguson* (1896), societal divisions between African American and white children were maintained, with one result being that African American children seldom appear in picture books of the teens through thirties, although plenty of African and Caribbean children do.

In addition, private and parochial schools prevented other kinds of cultural, religious, and socioeconomic "dilution" of allegedly pure groups by keeping out members of unwanted factions. Such educational practices kept children from interacting with those deemed different and instilled hierarchies that could be rehearsed in jokes and in conflicts on the way home from school that would resonate for years afterward. Pedagogical guides such as *Intercultural Education in American Schools* (1943) proposed practical ways to counteract institutionalized segregation and other forms of cultural exclusion, although proposals for "intercultural" activities (e.g., pupils "turn their classroom into a Mexican village, dress up in Mexican clothes and 'play Mexican' in the same fashion . . . that they 'play Indian'") designated a white middle-class dominant culture.[14]

Segregation in schools, workplaces, public spaces, and housing—reiterated in children's literature—prevented one-to-one interaction and negated chances for improved communication across ethnic, racial, and class lines. Young readers grew up in this social climate receiving mixed messages about American equality and cultural privilege. Children's reading material made reference to volatile political issues from the point of view of upper- and middle-class cultural producers. As the entertaining images and language of mass-cultural forms such as movies, theater, and advertising found their way into picture books and illustrated texts, children's literature became an ambiguous source of information about U.S. culture.

In the 1925 film *Little Annie Rooney*, set in a tenement neighborhood worthy of Jacob Riis's *How the Other Half Lives* or Lewis Hine's photodocumentaries on working-class children, director William Beaudine presents an international group of children in some surprising ways. The film opens with a brawl among two opposing child gangs, one led by Annie Rooney (played by Mary Pickford, then in her thirties, in one of her customary child roles) and the other led by Mickey Kelly (played by Joe Butterworth).[15] The fight starts when Mickey draws a chalk caricature of Annie on a wall, and Annie's group arises from behind a fence to attack him and his friends. The children are hellions in the Stephen Crane mold.[16] They lob bricks, bottles, shoes, and whatever comes to hand at one another, and Annie wrestles with Mickey and the boys who challenge her. Annie is the only girl in the fight, and practically the only girl in the movie.

Wide camera angles show viewers the breadth of the melee, which occupies a vast dirt yard amid tenement buildings. Middle-distance shots and bird's-eye views survey the chaos. In one intertitle a child calls, "Cheesit de cop!" and everyone pauses until the law is out of hearing range. Given this cooperation and the lengthy duration of the fight, spectators understand that this is rough entertainment rather than serious violence, or that only serious violence entertains street kids. The only child not participating is Annie's close friend Abie Levy (played by Spec O'Donnell), who watches wistfully from a fire escape and is "not allowed to fight" because it is "a holiday." Later, Abie is released to enjoy his favorite pastime: an intertitle says that his "weakness" is junk collecting, to reinforce Jewish stereotypes.

No adults get angry during the battle (they just duck to avoid airborne bricks) until the children frighten a carthorse and cause the loss of five dollars' worth of vegetables and produce. This occasions what an intertitle calls an "international conference." Immigrant parents drag their misbehaving children to the apartment of officer Timothy Rooney, Annie's father, and hold an impromptu meeting to decide on the children's punishment. This scene implies the commonalities among parents, regardless of ethnicity or social position. It also allows for some creative intertitles and peritextual shots of written words, which highlight adult-child roles and heritage. When Officer Rooney calls Annie into the main room to meet the other parents and children, his voice in consecutive intertitles appears in larger and larger type, and Annie's response is printed in meek, tiny letters, to indicate her unwillingness to admit to the fight. One mother berates her child in Greek and in English, assigning ethnicity to her family and setting up later intertitles where others make remarks exclusively in Greek. A Chinese man in a silk hat and jacket brings his son into the Rooneys' apartment, too, and when the children sign a petition vowing to repay the vegetable merchant five dollars, the camera closes in on the paper so that the audience can watch the Chinese child sign his name George Washington Leeng (or, perhaps, Lung). The doubling of the Chinese child's all-American first name and non-English surname is played as a joke, but not unkindly; the boy plays a positive role later in the film. Thus, intertitles and other peritextual details acknowledge the intersections of urban people from different backgrounds, and the use of text relies on print culture and basic literacy (including the understanding that silent-film screening environments were notoriously noisy, a clamor of music, speakers onstage, and vociferous audiences). The emphatic stretching and shrinking of letters on the intertitle cards mirrors the innovative typography in books, magazines, and comics of the period, thanks to global transmission of art and design styles.

The filmmakers signal the children's ethnicities in ways that are humorous but more playful than mean-spirited. Contemporary audiences might be made uncomfortable, yet this is postvaudeville mass humor directed at a young cinema audience from diverse backgrounds. If most ethnicity is treated generously, however, African Americans are singled out for troubling jokes. Bothersome exceptions to the all-in-good-fun humor include the sole African American child, played by Eugene Jackson, who appeared as Pineapple in the "Our Gang" serials. Jackson's character goes by the unlikely name of Humidor, has a heap of unkempt hair, and speaks in garbled intertitles, as does his mother. Humidor performs a hula-style "shimmy dance" (Jackson's claim to fame) when the children stage a theatrical revue to try to raise the money they owe; his enthusiastic dance entertains the crowd of children, although today's audiences will cringe. Similarly, in one scene Abie's Jewish family invites Annie to dinner and serves her a plate of ham to make her feel welcome. Abie and his younger brother put on yarmulkes before eating and say a prayer, and Annie makes the sign of the cross but otherwise does as they do. The scene urges mutual understanding rather than offense. The inevitable punch line arrives when Annie offers Abie a bite of her ham, he enjoys it, and his kosher father drags him from the room. Abie is a sympathetic character and is present throughout the film as a close associate of Annie, although Annie falls in love with Mickey's elder brother, Joe Kelly.

Although the children's diversity is depicted lightheartedly, the adults fight more viciously. Officer Rooney ultimately gets shot and killed in a brawl at the Prohibition-flouting Sullivan Club. He is shot by a Greek man, who tosses away the gun in an alley and tries to pin the murder on Joe Kelly, who is Irish. The disposal of the gun, though, is witnessed by the Chinese father of George Washington Leeng, who mentions it to a friend after seeing a photo of the late Officer Rooney in a Chinese-language newspaper. Leeng overhears the Chinese conversation and puts the information together with Tony's identity. Meanwhile, an unnamed Greek boy hears Tony admitting to the crime in Greek (printed in an intertitle so that the audience knows that translation is going on), and the Greek boy contributes his knowledge in solving the crime. The street children, because of their multiple ethnicities and ability to share information across languages, work as a unit to catch the murderer. *Little Annie Rooney*—which predates James T. Farrell's Studs Lonigan trilogy (1932–35), Henry Roth's *Call It Sleep* (1934), and Mike Gold's *Jews without Money* (1934), all classic American novels on youth—sends mixed messages on ethnicity and childhood. The film implies that immigrant adults may well be dangerous but suggests that immigrants' children have the potential to cooperate, at least when they are not fighting in earnest.

American publishers of the twenties and thirties—especially Macmillan, which published widely on global subject matter—were eager to capitalize on the representation of diverse cultures and different countries in American children's literature, often with the incentive to entertain and inform a multicultural young crowd. And if accented-English speakers, foreign and domestic, already provided fodder for vaudeville skits (and the short films that rapidly replaced live performance), these immigrant citizens and regional representatives also were the audiences and creators of modern American media. "The world was making its way to America and, through picturebooks, American children were to see and know the world," Bader says.[17] For Joseph Schwarcz, the illustrated book for children is "meta-national" and "international," because of the global circulation of art; in the twentieth century and beyond, "children everywhere are face to face with books originating in different countries."[18] An enthusiasm for heritage and global connectedness shows in a proliferation of texts about world travel, magazine advertisements for tourism, and child-centered bibliographies. Brochures of the mid-1930s, including *Children's Books and International Good Will*, *Children's Books from Twelve Countries*, and the *Bibliography of English Translations of Foreign Children's Books*, target librarians and educators wanting to promote inclusiveness and reflect audience heritage in their children's collections.[19] Old World tropes saw immense popularity. The year after *Millions of Cats*, Maud and Miska Petersham published *Miki* (1929), in which an American boy—modeled after their own son and alluding to Miska's immigration—magically visits his father's native Budapest (Figure 2.1, Plate 7). May Massee called *Miki* " 'the first of the international picture books,' . . . and in fact it was roundly welcomed for its depiction of 'everyday

FIGURE 2.1. Maud and Miska Petersham romanticize Budapest in *Miki* (1929), their tale of a modern American boy's travels to his heritage country.

life in a picture book country'" in the late 1920s.[20] Massee and other prominent children's editors thus differentiated between American lived reality and life in a quaint tourist attraction such as Budapest, representing such "picture book countries" as pleasurable and educational escapes for young dreamers and armchair travelers.

*Miki's* travel narrative and richly colorful artwork influenced numerous other immigrant creations: Ingri and Edgar Parin d'Aulaire's *Ola* (1932) introduces a towheaded Norwegian boy modeled on the d'Aulaires' son; their *Children of the Northlights* (1935) and *Ola and Blakken and Line, Sine, Trine* (1936) follow in this Scandinavian mode.[21] Marian King and Elizabeth Enright's festive *Kees and Kleintje* (1934), following in the visual footsteps of *The Poppy Seed Cakes*, *Miki*, and *Ola*, describes a boy and his pet duck in a picturesque Holland (Figure 2.2), and Elsa Beskow's *Pelle's New Suit* (1930, translated by Siri Andrews) follows raw wool as it is dyed, sewn, and turned into a boy's handmade clothing. Wanda Gág's fellow Minnesotan Emma Brock created a folk story set in an Old World fishing village and illustrated in charcoaly lithographs, *The Runaway Sardine* (1929). These fervent celebrations of Old World quaintness present a pristine countryside and mimic folksy storytelling forms but nevertheless view folklife through a modernist filter. Even thirty years afterward, early twentieth-century diversity in picture books received praise: Henry C. Pitz notes the variety of backgrounds implied in names like "du Bois, McCloskey . . . Weisgard . . . Daugherty, Hader, Lenski, Gramatky. . . . These are just names I picked at random, but they call up a wealth of racial and cultural background. Out of this diversity must come something multicolored and exciting."[22]

Exciting, perhaps; multicolored, less so. For all the excitement around diversity, classic and favorite children's books of the period fail to respect nonwhite and non-U.S. individuals. British author Helen Bannerman was persuaded to publish *Sambo and the Twins: A New Adventure of Little Black Sambo* (1936) as a sequel to her best-selling *Little Black Sambo* (1899). Joel Chandler Harris's nineteenth-century Uncle Remus tales still attracted a wide audience, too. In the detailed, if not comprehensive, bibliography *Realms of Gold*, Harris's collections provide almost the only entries under the category "Folklore of the American Negro." After four pages on Harris, the only other book cited is James Weldon Johnson's *The Book of American Negro Spirituals*.[23] Johnson's scathing critique *The Autobiography of an Ex-Colored Man* (1912) is cited among other youth readings in a section titled "The South after the War," along with work by Mary White Ovington and Booker T. Washington's 1901 autobiography, *Up from Slavery*. Unfortunately, these are listed side by side with Thomas Nelson Page's *In Ole Virginia*, which is loaded with vernacular writing and plantation-life stories. Juxtapositions of serious autobiographies with nonwhite comic types, all of which were included among unambiguously positive biographies of white American heroes such as Abe Lincoln and Daniel Boone, constructed a loaded semiotics of childhood, the nation, and the Western world. Despite ethnoracial variety between the wars, American picture books and illustrated texts dealt in the signifiers of cultural difference and upheld an atomized society.

While novels and illustrated texts represent racial, ethnic, and national difference selectively in written language, picture books show and tell difference on every page. As the technical means of producing picture books and illustrated texts developed from the late nineteenth century, especially with improvements in offset lithography and color printing, this showing and telling led to an enhanced visibility of social and cultural diversity. The most xenophobic cultural producers could not deny the existence of, say, an urban Chinatown, the African American clientele of local businesses, or the heritages of the eastern Europeans, Irish, and Scandinavians on a work crew. Yet the same cultural producers

What a gay sight met them!

FIGURE 2.2. Holland's marketplaces and canals, colorfully rendered in national hues of orange and blue, set the stage for 1934's *Kees and Kleintje*, the adventures of a boy and his duck.

could erase a racial or ethnic group from the texts of childhood or romanticize the group in words and pictures. Members of the marginalized group could expect to find literary and/or visual images of themselves as animals, as naive and unthreatening children, as buffoons, or as objects of anthropological scrutiny for an implied dominant spectator. Although immigrants and nonwhite people were a favorite topic of the mainstream mid-1930s photo journals *Life* and *Look*,[24] American-based editors, authors, and illustrators—many of them immigrants or second-generation themselves—persisted in representing cultural difference as happening only outside U.S. national borders, a strategy that enforced white hegemony while giving cultural others qualified visibility. An ethnographic gaze prevailed over an integrationist approach, and a class bias emerged in collaborations between East Coast editors and globe-trotting author-illustrators including Armstrong Sperry, René de Harnoncourt, and Jean Charlot.

Walter Cole's *The ABC Book of People* (1932), a round-the-world view of male types, exemplifies the thrills and shortcomings of a popular enthusiasm for identifiable difference, ethnoracial identity, and national costume (Plates 8 and 9). After a dedication "to George and Richard," illustrated by a sunlit image of a man walking with two boys, Cole creates an Arab-to-Zulu listing of global folk. Each essentialized type gets a full-page description and a facing-page illustration in brilliant color. The illustrations are self-conscious imitations of Falls's 1923 and 1930 ABC books and Nicholson's turn-of-the-century picture books and poster graphics. Every named culture is represented with a single picture of a lone man, although women are sometimes mentioned in the text, and the iconic abstraction—one man serves for all—dismisses cultural complexity. Most groups are described using present-tense verbs, but several groups are defined in the past tense: "the Norseman" wears full Viking regalia and "the Indian," or Native American, is shown as an idealized chief with his arms crossed in front of his chest; the Indian wears an ostentatious floor-length headdress and buckskins, and a war party rides past him in the deep background. "When Columbus discovered America," Cole writes, "he found a savage, red skinned race of people living on the land. . . . The Indians lived mostly by hunting and fishing. They shot or trapped animals and sold the skins and furs. They lived in tents." The Indian is the only resident of the United States in the book, yet his time and location are implicitly past. The letter *I*, which could as easily have stood for Indonesian or Icelander, makes a fairy tale of the Sitting Bull type for the young audience of modernity, a quaint, long-ago figure analogous to the extinct Norseman.

For *The ABC Book of People*'s endpapers, Cole provides a world map with dots to show the locations of each colorful type included in the book. There are two dots on all of South America and three on North America (the Quaker, the past-tense Indian, and the Eskimo in what would become the state of Alaska). Central America's representative is the Yucatecan, and the Caribbean type is filed under *W* for the West Indian. No fewer than fourteen dots adorn eastern and western Europe, Scandinavia, and Russia. Just five dots mark the rest of the planet (China, Japan, and Kashmir among them). South Asia, the Philippines, Indonesia, Australia, and New Zealand go unrepresented, along with other nations.

Cole's matter-of-fact definitions and generalizations astonish a twenty-first-century reader, yet his brisk treatment of his subject matter reveals assumptions about world politics of the 1930s. Allusions are made to chronological time and change in entries on colonies and colonial powers. For example, to accompany an illustration of the West Indian man, who carries a bunch of bananas on his head, Cole provides a quick summary of subjugation:

> Great Britain, Holland, France and the United States own many of [the islands known as the West Indies]; others are independent. Very few of the original Indians, of the Carib and Arawak tribes are left, as the Spaniards mistreated them cruelly.
>
> Thousands of negroes were brought in as slaves to work on the large sugar plantations. Now slavery is no longer in existence and in Haiti the negroes have their own republic.

Cole neglects to mention the 1915–34 U.S. occupation of Haiti, chronicled by 1930s critics and artists such as C. L. R. James, Langston Hughes, and Jacob Lawrence. Nor does he situate the pictured laborer on any island in particular. The West Indian man is actively working, and his national costume includes rolled white cotton pants and a red shirt—nothing like the elaborate outfits worn by the other types, and one that places him in a current time and place. By contrast, the Zulu man is pictured in full-on war regalia, carrying a spear and shield and dancing to the beat of two drums being played in the far distance. Cole explains: "The Zulu lives in South Africa. He fought for years to save his country from the British who settled there. Other African tribes were content to become colonials but not the Zulu." The entry concludes by quoting Rudyard Kipling's 1890 ballad "Fuzzy-Wuzzy," written in Kipling's "barrack-room" soldier's voice and describing a warrior at his "'ome in the Soudan; / You're a pore benighted 'eathen but a first-class fightin' man." Besides Cole's claim that some Africans "were content to become colonials," which contradicts the long list of anticolonial African groups Kipling mentions in his poem, the entry other-wise conflates the Anglo–Zulu War, begun in 1879, with the conflicts between the British and Mahdists in the Sudan in 1884–85; and with the Beja people of the Sudan, known to British as "fuzzy-wuzzies" because they teased out their long hair. Cole misrepresents the Zulu in the boys'-adventure style of impe-rialist writers like H. Rider Haggard, unconcerned that the long and bloody colonial history of Africa be recalled factually for twentieth-century readers.

Throughout the text, Cole indulges colonial practice. Letter *D*, the Dutch-man, pictures a working canal-boat driver in wooden shoes, yet the text notes that the Dutch occupied territory: "The Netherlands has many colonies, in the East Indies particularly, and the [Dutch] people are clever and successful." A segment on the Briton celebrates survival-of-the-fittest conquest for weeding the weak from the strong:

> A great many years ago the Britons were savages who lived in huts and dressed in the skins of wild animals. These tribes were eventually killed or forced into slavery.
>
> The Briton today is a mixture of many races, the Saxon, the Norman, the Celt. Perhaps this is the reason their country is such a powerful nation. Great Britain ... has possessions all over the world. There is a saying "The sun never sets on British soil."

Cole uses the term "race" to designate heritage groups and argues that the combination of these groups contributes to British might. He maintains his affirmative tone despite a postwar depression in Great Britain and the dwin-dling of British global influence. With similar lack of attention to detail, Cole summarizes another empire in describing the Ottoman: "[Historically,] women lived in harems and wore veils whenever they appeared in public. Now all this is changed. Women are free and the picturesque Turkish costume with the wide trousers and fez like the one in the picture is rarely seen." Whereas the Briton exists in the contemporary world (although the formal Beefeater attire that Cole pictures is suitable mostly for the Tower of London), the Ottoman as de-scribed and pictured "is rarely seen." An orientalist vision of a seated man smok-ing a hookah was evidently deemed most picturesque for the full-page image. Likewise, the Arab is represented in breathtakingly generalized, swashbuckling terms, pictured astride a rearing brown steed: "[The Arabs] are a strange, wild, adventurous people and they call themselves Bedouins. They live in tents made of camel's hair and wool and wear flowing white robes with white head-dresses. At one time their nation was strong. . . . The Arab and his horse are inseparable. He is a fearless rider as you can see from the picture." Cole's blatant inaccuracies ("The Japanese belong to the yellow race") and concern for ethnoracial distinctions ("Half the [Uruguayan] population is white, of Spanish and Italian stock. The rest are Indians called 'Charrua.' . . . Many of the people are a mixture of Indian and White") imply eugenicist sentiments, and the term "stock" connotes animal breeding. Even Cole's affirmative statements imply judgments based on race, ethnicity, and nation, with pale skin deemed more desirable than dark: "Many Kashmirians are very handsome. Their skin is a lighter brown than in the south of India and they are tall, straight and have regular features." A remark on indigenous Mexican people is offensive on many levels, notably in the claim that their ancestors' features have been eradicated, and Cole concludes with an effusive, backhanded compliment: "[The Yucatecan] bears no trace of that ancient [Mayan] civilization except for his erect and superb carriage and his exceptional good looks." *The ABC Book of People* is beyond doubt a problematic yet deeply engrossing text, with stunning generalizations and racialized judgments positioned alongside iconic imagery in crisp color. Like Falls's *Modern ABC*, *The ABC Book of People* is designed for maximum visual impact, using the latest color printing technologies, and Cole assumes the persuasiveness of these word-image representations.

Such pictorial primers piqued modern readers' curiosity about distant lands at a time when photojournalism, newsreel reportage, and faster travel made overseas destinations accessible to a range of travelers. Meanwhile, black-and-white and full-color printing capabilities necessitated that picture-book creators rethink strategies of representation, including racial and ethnic representation, and devise creative strategies for communicating with likely readerships. In visual sequences, representatives of a racial or ethnic background deemed unlike that of the implied reader could be pictured in their supposed country of origin and posed to enable inspection of their faces and apparel. In *The ABC Book of People*, twenty-six men stand for inspection, posed in native dress and engaged in native activities; for the letter *E*, the Eskimo goes spearfishing in a furry parka as a dogsled passes; the letter-*L* Lapp skis near a reindeer; and a Venetian gondolier strums the mandolin. Each pictured individual is coded by costume and skin color; in a duotone book, skin could be represented as the color of the page—conveying whiteness as an absent presence—ambiguously shaded in black or gray, or darkened to silhouette black. A crisis of representation, resulting from changes in technology and storytelling, and depending upon international politics and social formations, influenced the conventional ways in which the cultural other and the implied reader were constructed in (and by) narrative and pictures. This crisis of representation, as it played out in pictorial texts shared with young readers during the early twentieth century and afterward, has had profound implications even for the present day. It continues to influence the coded ways marginal and mainstream figures are written and pictured.

## INTERNATIONAL INFLUENCES ON U.S. PICTURE BOOKS

"In the 1920's," bookseller Bertha Mahony recalled in 1947, "book-buyers could find at Brentano's foreign department, at F. A. O. Schwarz, at Bonnier's, at French and German bookstores, and with Czech and Russian importers, many fine and stimulating volumes. During the latter part of that decade, Esther Averill, in Paris, and Frances MacIntosh Schwandt, in Berlin, bought foreign picture books for the Bookshop for Boys and Girls."[25] The post–World War I atmosphere brought increased concern for informing young Americans about global matters. Numerous globe-trotting book specialists (Averill of the Domino Press among them) gathered books that might fill that niche, and librarians and publishers were keen to endorse (and to capitalize upon) international connections, accounts of peaceful coexistence, and stories signaling national populations' shared heritage.

These concerns inspired a nostalgic 1933 exhibition organized by the Metropolitan Museum of Art and the New York Public Library. "Children's Books of Yesterday," a selection of roughly five hundred books, represented a variety of international publications recalled by adults, with a special focus on European texts including first editions of Charles Perrault's fairy tales (1697); Heinrich Hoffmann's *Der Struwwelpeter* (1845); Wilhelm Busch's *Max und Moritz* (1865); selections from Maurice Boutet de Monvel, including *Jeanne d'Arc* (1897); and books by Swedish favorite Elsa Beskow, Russian artist Ivan Bilibin, German artist Elsa Eisgruber, and Czech artist Rudolph Mates. Such an availability of international texts lured European tourists and American guests to the NYPL's Children's Room, Maria Cimino reported in the 1940s:

European visitors were delighted to find on its shelves familiar books from their countries so closely associated with those of other countries. They were attracted by what they called a new idea in education—this bringing before children picture books from many lands—and marveled at the resources of this children's library made so immediately accessible to children and adults. . . .

To many Americans who had given little or no thought to the idea, it opened new perspectives, awakened a consciousness and appreciation of the culture of countries hitherto unknown to them. Not only did it include the best representative European picture books for children in its collection, but on its staff, as its first interpreter, was a gifted Norwegian with several languages at her command. The first picture books were in the French, German, Russian, Swedish and Norwegian languages, with a selection of illustrated books in Czech borrowed from the large Czech collection in a branch library.[26]

Cimino describes a welcoming environment, especially for those people of European or Scandinavian descent whose idealized childhoods were most evidently represented in the texts. She details a generous exchange in which artists recommend worthy books and international visitors send books from their home countries as donations to the collection. International picture books came into demand for inclusion in further exhibitions, including a Polish folk arts show NYPL arranged in 1940, in protest of the Nazi occupation of Poland.[27] Cimino adds that the NYPL's expanding collection enabled cultural transmission among emigrants and their native-born American children, too: "Children accompanied by parents who remember the books from their own childhood in Europe spend long hours with old favorites. Other children drawn to the books by their pictures will follow the thread of the story through the drawings."[28] Cimino's comments call to mind a modernity saturated with longing, in which parents remember and reinforce aspects of their overseas childhoods by sharing books in English and in heritage languages, and children themselves receive highly mediated versions of heritage by which they may form limited cultural associations.

Unfortunately, Cimino's ostensibly global list collected nothing from the Middle East, Asia, or Africa, even though *Illustrators of Children's Books* (1947) named a few contributors to the field, such as Chiang Yee, a writer and painter who left China for Oxford and wrote *A Chinese Childhood* (1940). The Middle East, for instance, was more likely to be represented in picture books by a tongue-in-cheek outside observer, as happened with Russian author-illustrator Boris Artzybasheff's *Poor Shaydullah* (1931), a pictorial folktale about a lazy Moroccan fool, punished by Allah and eaten by a canny lion for his naïveté; or Caroline Singer and Cyrus LeRoy Baldridge's collaborative *Ali Lives in Iran,* an illustrated and ethnographically informed story of an Iranian boy. Mexico, along with American Indian subject matter, was chronicled by the likes of Grace and Carl Moon.[29]

Upon a first reading of a text—or looking at a text in an unfamiliar language—children of the 1920s and 1930s would have had little advance knowledge to enable them to recognize verbal and visual allusions to a remote location or people. But old-fashioned and newly minted international books, fondly embraced by their parents, would have acquainted them with signifiers of national identity, ethnicity, race, class, and gender roles. Subtle choices by the texts' artists and designers—a French typeface, Egyptian hieroglyphic motif, silhouette flourish, or nationalistic color scheme—would have stimulated the memories of older readers while communicating ideologically loaded information to a young audience. Such design and illustration elements could familiarize beginning readers with rhetorical and semiotic systems, and, thanks to cultural transmission through shared books, these elements could remain representational conventions in decades to come. Because layers of signification would obscure the historical development of those representational conventions, visual styles—and corresponding stereotypes—might seem commonsensical and utterly natural.

Abe Lerner suggests how significant typefaces, layouts, and varieties of paper and ink conveyed the cultural diversity of twenties and thirties America. At Viking, Lerner was assigned to design William Pène du Bois's *The Three Policemen* (1938), which he felt "called for an unobtrusive French touch in the typography.... The display lines in the chapter headings, and especially the single line of the name of the book on the title page, were set in faces called Nicholas Cochin and Le Mercure, beautiful typefaces from France which are now [late in the twentieth century] almost impossible to find at any shop."[30] Lerner's meticulous mimickry of antique French typography evidences the western European influence on American children's pictorial texts at a time when German and French printers themselves had begun to imitate eastern European and Russian pictorial work.[31] Although Lerner does not mention the Russian influence on French, German, and eventually American and British picture books and illustrated texts, he acknowledges the American affinity for France, where Pène du Bois grew up, and strives to maintain a nationalized quality even in a text designated for a U.S. readership.[32] Francophiles would recognize his typographic allusions to nineteenth-century French typography, and these adult readers might be persuaded to purchase or borrow such books on that basis, in the hope of instilling their own European aesthetic in their progeny. Meanwhile, design and visual conventions were shifting because of new artists' migration from Russia and eastern Europe.

The Russian influence was strong on European book illustration and design, and consequently on American examples, in the 1920s and thereafter. Russian and Soviet history specialist A. L. de Saint-Rat credits "the large-scale exodus of Russia's cultured classes and their arrival in Western Europe" after the October Revolution with a vitality in European pictorial work that soon caught on in America. "Until 1924 Berlin was, indeed, the capital of Russian publishing in exile," he writes. "The economic crisis of 1923 and subsequent political instability led to the demise of Russian and Russian-German publishers. The scene was now to shift to Paris, and France was to benefit greatly from the influx of Russian talent."[33] Saint-Rat emphasizes the visible Russian influence on French series books, including the *albums du* Père Castor. Of ninety Père Castor books published by Flammarion between 1931 and 1940, forty-nine were illustrated by Russian artists, bringing a postrevolution visual sensibility and lithographic approach to children's reading material in fashionable western Europe. For example, although understood as a quintessentially French production, Jean de Brunhoff's *The Story of Babar, the Little Elephant*, published in France in 1931 and translated for enthusiastic U.S. audiences in 1933, emulates the fashionable sketchbook style of French artists like Henri Matisse as well as the Russian visual style. *Babar* blends French postimpressionism and the Russian avant-garde in its imprecise and flattened perspectives, antirealist and mock-clumsy aesthetic, and original hand-lettered type in visual harmony with the pictorial compositions. Similarly, Cimino notes how the design of the Midgets and Puffin series in Great Britain derived from the stimulating Russian influence, and the trend quickly made the transatlantic journey, where it was picked up by savvy American author-illustrators. In the United States, editor May Massee wrote that *Miki* creators Maud and Miska Petersham "were very much attracted to the Russian educational picture books that showed various phases of Soviet life in revealing and, at the same time, imaginative color lithographs.... From the Petershams' interest in those books grew a whole series of picture books of the arts and industries [such as *The Story Book of Trains* (1935), *The Story Book of Iron and Steel* (1935), and *The Story Book of Wheat* (1936)].... The pictures show their mastery of the lithographer's craft. No one surpasses Miska in his color and in his use of beautiful gray."[34] American information books of the 1930s took their cue from Soviet texts, altering a socialist agenda to celebrate national American ingenuity and capitalist production.

Cimino notes a similar change in Latin American picture-book publishing

following the mid- to late 1930s exodus from Europe and from Spain in particular. She writes, "The upheaval and turmoil of Europe at war brought the publication of children's books to a standstill. Here in the Western Hemisphere,
removed from physical contact with war, it continued to flourish and give
opportunity to many new ventures. With the removal to Mexico and South
America of some Spanish book firms, a few interesting books for children have
begun to come from Latin America."[35] She damns with faint praise the book
industries of Mexico, Central America, and South America, and her international bibliography is brief in this regard; she focuses mostly on the French
expatriates Jean Charlot and René d'Harnoncourt, who were fascinated with
things Mexican but were not Mexican themselves. Yet Harnoncourt, for example, had been interested in Mexican heritage for years.[36] He organized the
Metropolitan Museum's 1930 exhibition of native Mexican art and later illustrated Elizabeth Morrow's Mexican tale *The Painted Pig: A Mexican Picture
Book* (1930), an oversize book about a girl, Pita, who seeks a painted pig toy
for her younger brother, Pedro, at their village market. Harnoncourt's stylized
artwork, in *papel picado* shades of green, yellow, red, and blue, pictures doe-
eyed children and occasionally takes off in magical realist flights, as when Pita
fantasizes riding on a giant yellow-painted pig. Morrow herself was the wife
of a U.S. ambassador to Mexico, Dwight Morrow, which explains her own
confidence in representing the culture; she dedicates the book to "Constance,
who helped me buy a painted pig at the market in Cuernavaca." (She and her
husband were parents to Anne Morrow Lindbergh.) Barbara Bader, writing on
the thirties, calls Mexico "the new magnet for Americans. Here was a foreign
country close at hand and ripe for picturing; there was no influx [in children's
publishing] of Mexican books or talent," so Americans and other international
travelers gladly took it upon themselves to create picture books and illustrated
books representing their ideas of Mexico.[37] All the same, the 1930s were the
decade of a vibrant Mexican muralist movement that brought Diego Rivera,
Frida Kahlo, and José Clemente Orozco to the United States and exerted a
graphic influence on sequential picture-book art that is unrelated to childhood amusement. Picture-book artists, despite their likely audiences, did not
concentrate solely on childhood in their careers—Harnoncourt, as curator and
illustrator, makes an ideal example. Picture-book creators participated in the
globalizing avant-garde and art movements by traveling, exhibiting, and attending gallery events, and their attention to international matters resulted in
their urge to represent international people.

   Lucy Herndon Crockett's *Lucio and His Nuong: A Tale of the Philippines*

(1939) likewise represents an international work from the perspective of an American artist. It is a comical picture book about a tiny but tough-minded young boy who uses kindness to easily tame a stubborn *nuong* or *carabao*, a large water buffalo feared by Lucio's fellow villagers for its irritable temper and long horns (Plate 10). When Lucio reaches age six, he is pronounced "of an age to work," and his family ponders what tasks he should do. His aunt recommends that he be master of the *nuong*, and despite their surprise, Lucio's family members honor her request. Lucio proves to be up to the task, coaxing the animal out of the muddy river where it loves to rest and getting it to plough and pull a cart. When Lucio leaves the *nuong* alone at a marketplace, gets a stalk of sugarcane and leans against a wall to sleep, the temperamental beast also chooses to nap, in a shopkeeper's doorway. Lucio's anxious father, afraid to waken the *nuong*, needs his young son for the task, and the gathered crowd is amazed and amused by little Lucio's talent.

Crockett pictures the tropical setting and Filipinos in a limited palette of greens, browns, reds, and a dark blue-gray for outlines, hair color, and clothing, framing the pages with leafy motifs. As in many pictorial books of the period, her lengthy text crowds the images off some pages, but these are balanced by wordless and near-wordless spreads picturing the river setting and the lively, crowded marketplace. Crockett's narrative is jocular, if at times unnecessarily sexist (Lucio's two sisters are described as "not important in his life, being but girl-children," and Lucio's uncle fears that Lucio will be born "another pretty, useless little girl-child") and unnecessarily prideful of English over other languages (Lucio's father attempts to command the *nuong* first "in the language of the people of that province," then "in Spanish, which was the language of some of the people who were more than commonly clever," and finally in English, "a language spoken by only a few people in the Barrio who were very clever indeed"). Reinforcing stereotypes of nonwhite Others for an implied white, English-speaking audience, she also places emphasis on the region's somnolence, from her description of the location ("the sleepy province of Pangasinan on the Island of Luzon") to her comments on Lucio's idle brother Mario, who "did nothing but lie in the sun through the long hot days, dreaming of going to the fine big city of Manila." Even the *nuong*, "so lazy and so fierce that nobody dares to disturb it, let alone try to get it to do any useful work," whiles away the days with just its back protruding above the river surface. Yet Lucio, alone among the villagers, remains alert and attentive to nature—excepting, at last, the scene where he irresponsibly falls asleep at the market and the shopkeeper cannot budge the dozing *nuong*.

If the narrative has its shortcomings, the oversize text has abundant visual appeal. The spacious portrait-layout pages measure almost nine by twelve inches, creating room for Crockett's loose crowd scenes. In these amiable depictions of Filipino people, everyone is doing his or her own thing, wandering among vendors and selling chickens, fish, fruit, and items of clothing. These spreads suggest folk-art cartooning as well as the large-scale wall art of the New Deal 1930s. The endpapers, styled as maps decorated with parrots, lizards, plantains, straw hats, sacks of sugar and rice, and curlicued, hand-lettered captions, give an exceptionally blithe overview of the Philippines and Philippine occupation by Spain, Britain (in Manila), and the United States. The captions start with "1521—Magellan discovered the Islands" and end with "1898—After the Spanish-American War, the United States acquired the Philippine Islands," never mentioning indigenous populations or the Philippines' Commonwealth status after 1935. Notably, Crockett left high school at age seventeen, around 1931, "to enjoy life as the daughter of an Army colonel in the Philippine Islands," and in 1936 went to New York for art courses. Her connection to the U.S. Army provided the privilege of visiting outposts remote to most Americans, along with an imperialist vision of the Philippines that competes with an otherwise affectionate depiction of farm and market life there.[38] Thus, modern picture-book content and production heavily favor a Eurocentric or Anglocentric view but derive from a spectrum of artistic influences including Russian, Eastern European, Latin American, and East Asian.

## FULL COLOR OR NEGATIVE SPACE?
## REPRESENTING NONWHITE CHARACTERS

Encountered by child readers with certain economic and educational privileges, picture books convey ideological values and provide introductory lessons in cultural hegemony. Thus, it is important to observe how non-U.S. residents, immigrants, and people of color—as well as Native Americans, with indigenous status—have been coded as outsiders in popular, aesthetically pleasing texts for child readers. Whether or not a reader readily articulates that a picture book's words and images depict U.S. residents or a locale perceived as foreign to an American audience, material qualities and imagery influence the way readers interpret and remember representations of the Other. Elizabeth MacKinstry's gorgeously printed, thoroughly orientalist *Aladdin and the Wonderful Lamp* (1935) is a case in point (Figure 2.3, Plate 11).[39] Printed in the United States by New York's Isaac Goldmann Company, *Aladdin* evinces a rare delicacy of line, subtle range of color, and smooth selection of paper stock for an American picture book. Louise Seaman praised its "superbly good lithography": "MacKinstry tried various methods, finally coming back to the old-fashioned one, but here done with black first printing, then with four or five other color printings." MacKinstry's work reminds Seaman "of the big Walter Crane picture books."[40] Decades later, *Aladdin's* imagery remains striking, if bewildering in its catch-all exoticism. Its nominal setting, Cathay, borrows from Persia, Africa, and China. Among its visual wonders, a wordless full-color spread depicts an African or Asian genie, and Aladdin appears Chinese with his shaved head, long queue of black hair, and conical straw hat. A "wicked Magician in Persia" sends Aladdin on perilous missions. For his brave feats, Aladdin is invited to meet a Chinese monarch, "the Emperor of Cathay," who lives in a pagodalike castle with an attractive and unmarried daughter. On the closing page, three white children stand in what looks to be an attic, next to a steamer trunk labeled "Cairo." One of the children, a black-haired boy, has just rubbed a lamp, from which emerges a dark-gold-skinned, bald male genie in a halo of flames. The text is a carnival of global types, materially influenced by the vogues for orientalist themes, international tourism, and deluxe European printing.

MacKinstry's unexamined representations of Asian and African people in an Arabian Nights tale suggest an easy assumption that such representations will be welcome and attractive to an implied readership. Other author-illustrators are more self-reflexive, which is equally problematic. Evidence of a modern crisis of representation may be seen in the self-conscious drawings of married picture book creators Berta and Elmer Hader. In their picture books for Macmillan, the Haders emphasize their authorial presence in the text and cast themselves as gawky global tourists. They often make light of their observational, subjective point of view by including copyright-page caricatures of themselves doing field research. No photographs verify the Haders' likenesses and no captions call attention to the inside jokes. But several texts—notably *Working Together* (1937), their firsthand account of making a picture book—establish what the popular pair "looks like," and insistently call upon readers to acknowledge their authority.

In the Haders' *The Story of Pancho and the Bull with the Crooked Tail* (1942), a poor Mexican potter's son captures a renegade bull and earns money to buy his father a car and his mother a dress. On *Pancho's* copyright page and in an autographed copy of the book complete with a caricature for the recipient, the Haders picture themselves with uncharacteristic dark skin (Figure 2.4). Tall, skinny Elmer rides a burro that is much too little for him. He smokes a cigar

# ALADDIN AND THE WONDERFUL LAMP

*ILLUSTRATED BY E. MACKINSTRY*

THE MACMILLAN COMPANY          NEW YORK ~ MCMXXXV

FIGURE 2.3. Orientalist tropes prevail in Elizabeth MacKinstry's *Aladdin and the Wonderful Lamp* (1935).

and wears a huge sombrero. Berta, wearing a white dress and a Southwestern shawl, walks barefoot behind the donkey and carries an earthenware pot on her head. In effect, the white creators picture themselves trying on the signifiers of an alternative culture. The caricature points out their attempt and slapstick failure to pass as members of another culture and ethnic group, even as it inscribes the dominant culture as one free to make bold presumptions. The Haders' implied reader is American and not Mexican, yet the darkened caricature mildly ridicules a white interloper's privilege and perspective. The Haders again try on the clothing of a marginalized group in *The Mighty Hunter* (1943), the story of a Native American boy who plays at using the bow and arrow of his forebears before running off to a one-room schoolhouse to get a more modern education (itself a parody of the forcible removal of Native Americans to U.S. government schools). On the copyright page, the authors picture themselves wrapped in woven blankets and wearing feathers. Berta's skin is dark and she wears a decorative headband. Similarly, in the black-and-white line drawing that accompanies the illustrated text *Jamaica Johnny* (1935), the Haders wear pith helmets and khaki explorers' gear for a Caribbean tour. Elmer holds a camera at his waist and Berta sketches busily as a Jamaican woman and her baby ride past them on a burro (Figure 2.5).

*Jamaica Johnny's* ethnographic illustration implies that firsthand observation has produced the narrative about eight-year-old Johnny Morgan, a Jamaican boy whose "Uncle Solomon often reminded him that his father's ancestors had served the great Henry Morgan" (9). The nature of this service is summarized by a white American visitor later in the book, who explains, "His [Johnny's] uncle is Solomon O'Connor, the best cutter on the plantation. Johnny's mother was an O'Connor. Long before all the slaves were freed Old Michael O'Connor had freed his own on his plantation. That was a saying of his, 'Every O'Connor is a king'" (66). This passage implies the practice by which masters named slaves. Young readers may deduce that the relationships between the dark-skinned Jamaican boy Johnny, modern American children (implicitly white), and ex-slaveholder Michael O'Connor mirror the privileges and hierarchies set up between the pictured Jamaican mother and the Haders on the copyright page. Many race-sensitive interactions are explored in the text. For example, Johnny's friend Boswell makes a living by selling carved gourds to American travelers, who need a translator to comprehend Boswell's sales pitch: "'It is hard to understand at first,' said Edwards [the tourists' black chauffeur], 'for he speaks so fast and it sounds so strange. But it *is* English'" (24). Johnny outdoes the illiterate Boswell by learning to read a book, *The Story of Tommy, a Little Black Boy of*

all good wishes
Will Johnson
from
Berta and Elmer Hader

FIGURE 2.4. Berta and Elmer Hader picture themselves as mock Mexicans in *Pancho and the Bull with the Crooked Tail* (1942), as well as in an autograph from the period.

*Jamaica* (described as "a stepping stone to good fortune" [90]). He later cements his success by saving Elizabeth Clarkson, a white American girl, from a runaway horse. Elizabeth's grateful parents invite Johnny to live in the servants' quarters on their banana plantation and take reading lessons. When Johnny saves the adventurous girl again (she and her brother get stranded on a reef), the white benefactors give him a "scholarship in the parish school" (90). Each act of heroism buys Johnny a little more education and distinguishes him ever so slightly from his peers. A closing image pictures Johnny in a white coat, shorts, and shoes, his back to the reader as he watches a line of barefoot Jamaican women carrying bananas to a huge cruise ship; by his clothing and his deference to his white educators, Johnny is differentiated from the working people of his country, and the magnificent cruise ship implies something of his destiny, which might be a managerial role among Jamaicans (Figure 2.6). Whatever happens, the young entrepreneur seems fated to remain in Jamaica, where he can be a hero without posing a threat to the American hierarchies, represented by the Haders and the fictional white owners of the banana plantation.

FIGURE 2.5. The Haders envision themselves as ethnographers in the Caribbean in this caricature from *Jamaica Johnny* (1935), with Elmer as a Groucho Marx–Captain Spaulding look-alike.

In their *Green and Gold: The Story of the Banana* (1936), Berta and Elmer Hader once again cast themselves as inquisitive colonists. This time, in a crayon-like color image on the copyright page, the woman and man tip their heads back as they sketch a tall banana tree. They wear yellow straw hats and brown jackets, he in off-white pants and she in an off-white skirt (Figure 2.7). Their expeditionary attire reflects that of the white-suited white man and children

FIGURE 2.6. *Jamaica Johnny*'s title character, dressed in a school uniform made possible by his plantation-managing benefactors, watches an American ship amid the commerce of a Jamaican dock.

on the title page, who admire stalks of bananas as their birthright (Figure 2.8); the endpapers picture a line of nonwhite men harvesting the crop. In this story, blond twins Jack and Jill visit their uncle Amos on his banana plantation in Guatemala. Uncle Amos relates the history of banana growing and its relation to slavery in Africa and Central America, and a pleasant, dark-skinned man named Pedro takes them all on a driving tour of the plantation grounds. Both *Jamaica Johnny* and *Green and Gold* address servitude in their writing

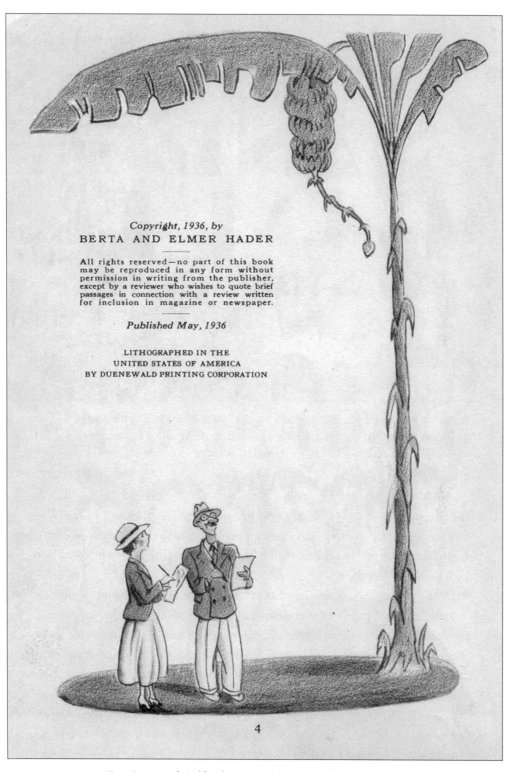

4

FIGURE 2.7. For *Green and Gold: The Story of the Banana* (1936), the Haders take on
the roles of itinerant botanists, dressed for the tropics in matching linen ensembles.

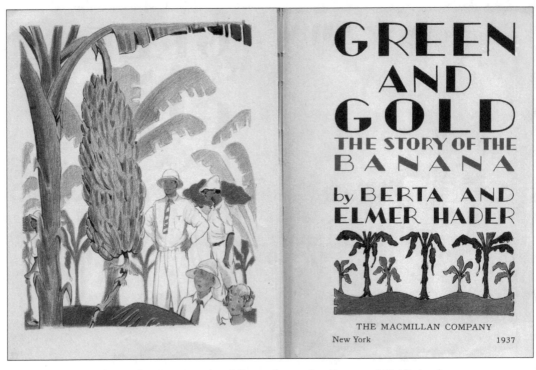

FIGURE 2.8. In the foreground and facing the reader, *Green and Gold's* Anglo-American children and plantation manager gaze at the ripening bananas they will enjoy. In the background and unrecognizable, nonwhite workers harvest the crop for the U.S. market.

and illustration, but they show rather than tell the distinctions of race. The written narratives remark on the past and only allude to the present, while the illustrations comment explicitly on present-day racial relations in countries with a colonial heritage.

In the Haders' books, and in other texts that take an ethnographic approach to world cultures, points of identification are established and value judgments are made for child readers. Overall, modern picture books and illustrated texts participated in American mythmaking and international representation, setting certain subject matter (nonurban situations, nonwhite individuals, international groups, dolls and animals) apart from an implied child reader and in the domain of the implied cultural other. This was justified by a stated wish to create international community, but a side product was a certain degree of essentialism. Margery Williams Bianco, penning an introduction to Melicent Humason Lee's *Marcos: A Mountain Boy of Mexico* (1937), illustrated by the Haders, insists:

It is good for children of all ages to learn how other children live, how other children work, the things they see and handle in daily life. In a day of constantly widening horizons the child's story book plays a very important part. It is the first step in travel, in the knowledge of other lands and customs. More and more of late years there has grown the need for stories of just this kind. Side by side with the many friends from far-off countries, from every corner of the world, to be met in the books and pictures of today Márcos will take his place in the growing saga of childhood.[41]

Despite Bianco's earnest words about "[average] children" and "other children," the ideal reading subject for these texts may be presumed to be white and middle class by birth and by heritage. Marcos is one of many "friends from far-off countries," inaccessible to the reader, just as Lee's Guatemalan history of the banana is inaccessible to the two young white visitors, Jack and Jill. Only marginalized subjects (e.g., the small population of Chinese Americans in the early twentieth century, African Americans, migrant laborers, and international readers) likely would have the experience to notice inconsistencies between the representations and everyday life, or to comment on the implications of a shirt-less, brown-skinned laborer facing a fully clothed, plump, and pale-skinned male boss. As in Cole's *The ABC Book of People*, educators could shield a text's likely readers from troubling awareness of colonial histories and humanitarian crises, while at the same time giving accurate lessons in geography and celebrating the aesthetic appeal of national costumes and folk stories.

Yet the number of literate readers outside an implicit (indeed, often ex-plicit) norm was growing, and children's literature of this period suggests the strain of keeping up appearances. In an era of new media of sight and sound, the implied other was not so invisible or silent a witness to the implied reader's textual pleasure. No longer would it suffice for a book to include a title-page likeness of an explorer or anthropologist posing with his or her object of study; now, the object of study could be presented in sketches or photos over a series of pages, as in the ethnographic films popular in the silent era and after. In fact, given the affordable new technology, the object of study might soon represent itself. Berta and Elmer Hader's mocking caricatures of themselves as research-ers allude to the collapse of prior ethnographic conventions and testify to the difficulty of maintaining an aloof distance from the cultural other at a time when mass-reproducible images were put in circulation for readers of all ages.

Intentionally or otherwise, creators of 1930s-era picture books and illustrated work generally failed to examine stereotypical representation as a component of cultural understanding, despite so many initiatives to teach global interconnectedness. Only rarely did a text like Langston Hughes and Arna Bontemps' novel *Popo and Fifina: Children of Haiti* (1932) strive to provide an alternative to misrepresentation. *Popo and Fifina*, which offers a counternarrative to texts such as *Jamaica Johnny*, is a deceptively tranquil portrait of an island that had seen centuries of violent class and racial upheaval.[42] In this understated novel, eight-year-old Popo, his ten-year-old sister Fifina, Papa Jean, Mamma Anna, and baby Pensia leave their mountain home and move to the city of Cape Haiti so that Papa Jean can find work as a fisherman. Hughes and Bontemps scarcely mention Haiti's volatile past as a slave nation, its hard-won status as an independent black republic, and its status vis-à-vis the United States, yet the authors touch upon racial and colonial oppression as they detail the family's activities. Popo meets a boy his age carrying "chickens . . . a basket of mangoes, two bunches of bananas, and a tiny green parrot"; the boy says he is "going out to the ships to sell them," a reference to men on foreign vessels who buy cheap goods and services from the Haitian underclass (27). Popo looks forward to the day when he, too, can start "selling things to the steamers anchored near the horizon" (28). Later, the family observes a busy factory where pineapples are canned for export to the United States, and gaze at a beach where American Marines go swimming, evidence of the country's occupied status. They also pass decayed forts from the time "when Haiti was still a French possession. Old rusted guns pointed up out of the crumbled stonework" (91–92). The ruined weapons hint at the perseverance of the Haitian people over occupiers.

Hughes and Bontemps even recast the ultimate in primitivism—the moonlit tomtom scene—in a chapter titled "Drums at Night" (which predates Bontemps' 1939 novel *Drums at Dusk*, on the Haitian War of Independence).[43] Native drums operate as a prequel to violence in pseudo-ethnographic films including *King Kong* (1933) and children's stories like Armstrong Sperry's *Call It Courage* (1940). To the contrary, Hughes and Bontemps stage a child-friendly party scene where Popo resists his bedtime, confidently strolls out to see the festive lights surrounding the drummers, and enjoys the "scooting" feet of dancers accompanied by "happy booming sounds." Popo's fun ends when his older cousin escorts him safely home. Hughes and Bontemps cheerfully defuse the atavistic tension of the typical drumming scene. The wholesome affair parallels the vogue for Harlem, which J. Michael Dash, tongue in cheek, calls "a safe safari into the world of the primitive. The Harlem nightclub like the Haitian voodoo ceremony had become a plunge into the unknown, a salutary disorientation for those who were willing to indulge their wildest fantasies."[44] Anxious readers had their expectations overturned by *Popo and Fifina*'s party scene, and those opposed to American intervention in Haiti might detect what Dash, echoing W. E. B. Du Bois, refers to as a "burgeoning sense of Pan-African solidarity."[45] Hughes and Bontemps destabilize stereotypes and cultivate a feeling of alliance with the Haitian people. *Popo and Fifina*'s chapters proceed in this same calm manner, without high drama.

The novel was read with disapproval by progressive critics. Writing in *Opportunity* in January 1933, Alain Locke of *The New Negro*—who, like Du Bois and James Weldon Johnson, visited Haiti in the late 1920s—dismissed *Popo and Fifina* as "a quite flimsy sketch, a local-color story of Haitian child life."[46] Locke found the book disappointing compared to Hughes's polemical essays on Haiti, and he was not alone in thinking the authors turned off their opinions for the project. According to Violet J. Harris, Macmillan editor Louise Seaman wanted "more 'colorful' details. . . . Hughes wryly suggested they add a rum shop owned by a voodoo priestess. Bontemps and Hughes had to compromise. . . . The rum shop is included in the story, but it is a restrained portrait without the voodoo priestess."[47] The flap copy for the 1932 Macmillan edition whimsically explains that Popo's and Fifina's "funny names belong to a small black boy and girl who live on the island of Haiti. What fun they had—and how like the fun of any children anywhere in the world." Even the cover copy for the 2000 edition focuses on the tropical setting minus the politics: "We feel the majestic beauty of tropical Haiti and delight in meeting two poor but very happy children growing up in a close-knit, simple, hard-working family."[48]

Many critics also disdained writing for young readers and dismissed Hughes and Bontemps' work out of hand. Drewey W. Gunn, writing on Hughes's essays "In a Mexican City" and "Up to the Crater of an Old Volcano," comments that "Since both are in a language appropriate to children, they do not give us much indication of Hughes's great skill with American speech."[49] Edward Mullen remarks, "The influence of Haiti in [Hughes's] work was not entirely political. . . . With Arna Bontemps, he wrote an idyllic novella for children entitled *Popo and Fifina*."[50] Mullen assumes *Popo and Fifina* is apolitical even though he quotes Hughes's denunciation of the American occupation and "the officials of the National City Bank, New York," who "educate their children to read and write, to travel, to be ambitious, to be superior, to create armies, and to build banks."[51] These critics reiterate a common fairy tale of modernity, that children's texts preserve innocence, even though children themselves (like the bankers' kids) inherit and reproduce cultural ideology.

Hughes and Bontemps softened their rhetoric to appeal to a young audience keen on learning about locations and peoples outside the United States. Hughes's anger is palpable in his radical editorials on Haiti, Cuba, Mexico, and Russia for journals like the *Crisis* and *New Masses*.[52] But in children's texts—created for publishing houses that shied away from controversy—he and Bontemps focused on literary imagery to convey a comfortable sense of place and an ambience of family and racial unity. They anticipated an inexperienced but socially conscious audience that was not fully indoctrinated into adults' cultural biases. In *Popo and Fifina*, they attempted an intervention in stereotypes of race and class via the portrait of common people in a tropical locale. The book was part of the proliferation of 1930s children's literature on international subjects and predated less progressive accounts of foreign lands including Melicent Humason Lee's *Children of Banana Land* (1936) and the Haders' *Green and Gold*.[53]

Hughes and Bontemps do not preach a radical agenda, but they add instructive asides on how U.S. and Haitian customs differ, potentially raising awareness of labor and economic issues. In the market area of Cape Haiti, Popo and Fifina meet "a little smiling black girl who carried a large wooden tray on her head and a small folding stool on one arm":

> All Haitian youngsters learn to carry burdens on their heads. Popo already knew the trick. . . . He could forget the burden on his head and at the same time have his hands free to play.
> But the little girl with the wooden tray and broad smile was not out to play. She was on a business errand, and Popo could see that her tray was loaded with things to sell. (21)

Hughes and Bontemps gently commented on child labor, village life, and poverty at a time when child labor was contested in the United States.[54] They published *Popo* at an opportune moment when race, imperialism, nationalism, and proletarianism were key issues in U.S.–Haiti relations, and their challenge was to write on a heated issue while reaching a wide readership. Publishing houses restricted radical or even moderately leftist voices and skewed toward a white, middle-class subjectivity; African American author-illustrators were largely unwelcome already, due to institutional racism.[55] Hughes and Bontemps' subtleties, sometimes so subversive as to escape notice entirely, imply the conservatism they faced in the U.S. children's publishing industry.

Although Hughes and Bontemps wrote to a general audience, their foremost concern was with the young African American public. In his 1932 "Books and the Negro Child," Hughes decried textbook treatments of people of African heritage that encouraged contemporary readers to internalize inferiority:

> Geographies picturing the African natives as bushy headed savages with no culture of their own; civics describing Negro neighborhoods as the worst quarters in our cities; histories that note the backward-ness of the Negro South but none of its amazing progress in only three score years of freedom; all of the bad, depressing phases of racial life set before the black child—none of the achievements; these are what the school books usually give. . . . Only when one is no longer ashamed of one's self can one feel fully American, and capable of con-tributing proudly to the progress of America. To drive out false shame, then, with its companions, timidity and fear, is one of the duties of all grown-ups toward the Negro child.[56]

Hughes details a critical commitment to writing for children. His children's prose style often mimicked that of a middle-class white culture, and this may have been purposeful; he worked within a marginal field, closely guarded (as it is today) by conservative forces. Considered within that context, *Popo and Fifina* speaks to its cultural moment and challenges armchair-traveler visions of exotic locales.

Furthermore, the novel's stylized silhouette illustrations signal a modern context. E. Simms Campbell provided block prints of palm fronds, seaside shacks, and dark-skinned people in white hats and white T-shirts. His flat, solid-black images, which reflect the late-1920s fashion for folk art and primi-tivism, effectively absorb the reader's gaze. While all illustrations "look back" in the sense that they counterpoint a spectator's gaze, a pictured face need not confront an audience eye to eye. *Popo and Fifina*'s silhouettes allude to then-fashionable illustrations in *The New Negro* and in little magazines, yet they also obscure the characters' facial features.[57] The opaque illustrations, which complement the opacity of the mild-mannered text, could keep the audience from engaging with the characters or the island environment. In Campbell's images, Popo and Fifina express themselves only in stiff, unemotional whole-body gestures rather than in significant facial expressions. Campbell's illus-trations do resonate with the written narrative, making the Haitian popula-tion partially visible, but the silhouettes tend to objectify the Haitian other. The pictures stop short of permitting the narrative's objects and the book's

American subjects much basis for mutual understanding. Campbell, despite illustrating a text that celebrates people of African heritage, participates in the crisis of representation around nonwhite subjects of children's literature.[58]

Other attempts at counterrepresentations were not so effective, despite receiving much attention for their subject matter. Numerous picture books and story collections of the 1920s through 1940s purported to be direct translations of Native American folklore, among them Ahlee James's *Tewa Firelight Tales* (illustrated by Awa Tsireh and others) and Elizabeth Willis De Huff's *Taytay's Memories* (1924, illustrated by Fred Kabotie). In the introduction to *Taytay's Memories*, De Huff makes reference to her previous volume and the sources of her material: "Many children have found so much pleasure in *Taytay's Tales* that I have persuaded the grandchildren of Taytay to tell me other stories that he tells to them. . . . Taytay's grandchildren, as you know, are Pueblo Indians, who live in New Mexico and Arizona. They live in villages made of houses all piled one upon another. And these kind Indians have told me all of the stories herein contained. I hope you will enjoy reading them as much as I enjoyed hearing them."[59]

In protest to this flood of books, and to assert a marketable authenticity as well, William Morrow and Company published *I Am a Pueblo Indian Girl* (1939), by an author identified as E-Yeh-Shure', or Blue Corn (Figure 2.9). Four Native illustrators—Quincy Tahoma, Tony Martinez, Allan Houser, and Gerald Nailor—contributed full-page images to accompany E-Yeh-Shure's words in this unpaginated book. Nonetheless, the text offers scant information on its illustrators or author. Houser, born in Oklahoma, and Nailor, a Navajo born in New Mexico, attended various government-run schools, and both completed their studies at the Santa Fe Indian Art School. Houser appears to have had the greatest success, explaining in a note for *Illustrators of Children's Books* that he "painted murals in oils in the Indian Arts and Crafts room in the new Department of the Interior Building in Washington," in 1938, did "murals for the Indian Schools in Oklahoma and New Mexico," and "studied and worked with frescoes, secco and egg tempera, under Olaf Nordmark, the Swedish muralist."[60]

The introduction to *I Am a Pueblo Indian Girl* dismisses this long educational history and gives ethnographers credit for preserving Native art: "It is some twenty years now since the desire of an ethnologist to preserve the details of Indian ceremonies that seemed to be vanishing led to the first Pueblo Indian water-colors," writes Oliver La Farge. "The artists, fortunately, had no instruction; they simply depicted familiar matters in their own way, with the tremendous discipline of their native design behind them." La Farge, whose "we" includes himself among his readership, elevates Native ingenuity yet

### MY COUNTRY

I am an Indian girl. My name is E-Yeh-Shure', which means Blue Corn. I live in a pueblo. A pueblo is an Indian village. Some of them are four and five stories high. My people lived there many years before the white people came to this country. They tilled the soil near the pueblo much as we do now. Their hunting grounds were the plains and the hills far to the east. They brought down huge timbers from the mountains many miles away to build their homes.

There are eighteen pueblos in New Mexico. Taos Pueblo is the farthest north. Isleta Pueblo is the farthest south, while Zuñi Pueblo is the farthest west. There are eleven more pueblos called the Hopis still farther west but they are in Arizona. The distance from Taos to Zuñi is about three hundred miles, and from Taos to Hopiland it is about five hundred miles.

There are many mountains in my country. Some of the pueblos are on rocky cliffs. Acoma Pueblo is on top of a rock mesa about three hundred feet high. Isleta is my pueblo. It is in the valley. At one time it was surrounded by water and it was as hard to get to as Acoma. Some of the pueblos are in the desert. It is dry and there is very little rain.

We no longer have the hunting grounds and we do not have much land around our pueblos.

We have clear skies and we can see the beautiful blue hills far away.

FIGURE 2.9. First-person reveries by a young woman accompany illustrations from Native artists in *I Am a Pueblo Indian Girl* (1939), a book that strives for authenticity.

silences the text's ostensible creators—including the author, who is identified only as the daughter of a prominent man. La Farge makes angry reference to unethical story collectors, yet he himself reinforces patriarchal control when he calls American Indian storytelling

> a living literature, which a few white people have pirated freely, profiting by the publication of usually lame translations of poems which their makers recited free of charge. . . . Now the new and the ancient art have been brought together, and not by a white man, but by my friend, E-Yeh-Shure's father. He is a member of one of the strong families of Isleta Pueblo, an educated, enterprising man, and a complete Indian, holding fast to the good things of his own culture and his own religion. When his daughter turned her natural gift as a poet to work in English, he saw its promise, and had the inspiration to bring together Indian artists, Navajo, Apache, Pueblo, in a cooperative endeavor to make a truly Indian book. The techniques are modern, but the line, the essential union of word and picture, is very old—it is the union of the poem and the dance from which both arts take their ultimate derivation.

*I Am a Pueblo Indian Girl* consists of eight prose pieces and two poems, each printed on the left-hand page facing a color illustration on the right-hand page.

For all of La Farge's enthusiasm, E-Yeh-Shure' uses the passive voice and unexciting verbs. She uses blunt, short sentences to describe the earth, desert wildlife, the way she washes her hair, the way people of the past "tilled the soil near the pueblo much as we do now," and her enjoyment of caring for her ponies: "I am an Indian girl. My name is E-Yeh-Shure', which means Blue Corn. I live in a pueblo. A pueblo is an Indian village. Some of them are four and five stories high. My people lived there many years before the white people came to this country." The stilted selections concentrate on setting and superficial appearance, and the impersonal self-description sounds more like a museum caption than a firsthand observation, despite the first-person voice.

Similarly, the book's designers make little effort to enliven the juxtaposed words and images, although the artists' gentle, static images complement the text by picturing clay pots and a clay oven, a corn plant, deer and antelope, and regional bird species. The illustrations appear to have been composed separately and slotted to fit the prose, rather than representing a true collaboration between the young woman and the team of men. E-Yeh-Shure's account "My Clothes" describes a handmade "calico dress" and a special-occasion "black *manta* which is a dress made of black cloth woven in one of the Hopi pueblos. . . . I fasten one corner of it over my left shoulder and let the right shoulder go free. It has no sleeves. I have a wide red belt for it, woven by a woman in the pueblo here." The corresponding image pictures a woman standing stiffly in a black-cloth top layer, with an argyle-patterned scarf and cropped hair—not quite the "long knot in back of the head" that E-Yeh-Shure' claims to have. Even the mild political statements in E-Yeh-Shure's prose have a quality of stoical resignation that renders the book a curiosity rather than an empassioned testimony: "We no longer have the hunting grounds and we do not have much land around our pueblos. / We have clear skies and we can see the beautiful blue hills far away"; "There are only a few antelope left on the plains now. They run very fast. The old Indians had fast horses on which they chased the fleet antelopes. It was great fun, they say." Although E-Yeh-Shure' laments the loss of tribal land, she refers to Arizona and New Mexico as such and locates various pueblos according to U.S. borders, clearly addressing an American readership that lacks an investment in or knowledge of tribal history, Native nations, or concerns specific to the Pueblos. Despite proposing an alternative to misrepresentation of nonwhite American people, *I Am a Pueblo Indian Girl* conforms to picture-book conventions for the depiction of Others, introducing a docile speaker and predictable content.

## WILD KINGDOMS: THE ANIMAL OTHER
## IN UNFRIENDLY TERRITORY

In 1933, Viking editor May Massee (formerly of Doubleday) published Marjorie Flack and Kurt Wiese's collaborative *The Story about Ping*. This narrative of a duckling on the Yangtze River depicts Chinese culture as rural and traditional and the river as a place where fishermen live aboard unmotorized sailboats and use cormorants to catch one fish at a time. *The Story about Ping* exemplifies a common storytelling practice of its era, in which a sympathetic child or animal protagonist becomes the analogue of a non-American individual. Its title, which both supplies the duck's name and imitates the sound of Chinese words to an American ear, signals difference even before the reader opens the book. In this and similar books set in international locales, the child or nonhuman character provides a youthful point of identification while adult humans act as the cultural other. Such books identify a main character in their titles, speak on that character's behalf, and predict a biographical storytelling structure; they generally include an iconic visual representation of the character, too. The reader establishes a subjective identity in counterpoint to that of the named and pictured character even before concentrated reading commences.

*The Story about Ping* advances the animal other as a signifier of cultural difference, avoiding the need to provide insight from any but an Anglo- or European American perspective. Its author, Flack, previously had written and illustrated *Angus and the Ducks* (1930), about "a very young little dog whose name was Angus, because his mother and his father came from Scotland." This first in a five-book Angus series shows the inquisitive dog pursued by a flock of ducks and, like *Ping*, calls attention to a name as a mark of ethnic heritage.[61] Flack's books frequently focus on animals' natural lives and tribulations. Illustrator Wiese, a German émigré, had lived in China prior to his arrival in the United States and specialized in Chinese subject matter. He illustrated Elizabeth Foreman Lewis's Newbery Medal–winning *Young-Fu of the Upper Yangtze* (1932) and its follow-up, *Ho-Ming: Girl of New China* (1934); Ethel J. Eldridge's novels *Yen-Foh, a Chinese Boy* and *Ling, Grandson of Yen-Foh* (1936); Clare Hutchet Bishop's folk retelling *The Five Chinese Brothers* (1938); and his own picture books *Liang and Lo* (1930) and *You Can Write Chinese* (1945). Subsequent picture-book accounts of China, including Thomas Handforth's Caldecott Medal–winning picture book *Mei-Li* (1938), were informed by Wiese's lithocrayon line drawings, his occasional renditions of Chinese pictograms next to Western writing, his unified color schemes (often golden yellows and sky blues), and his consistent way of stylizing Asian facial features and fashion. The conical hat and cotton jacket drawn on a Chinese peasant by Wiese, later confirmed by a *Look* or *Life* photo-essay on farm life and reinforced by the costumes in the 1937 Hollywood production of Pearl S. Buck's Nobel Prize–winning novel *The Good Earth* (1931), came to signify a generic China and its inhabitants for a 1930s audience. Merely listing all these books indicates the thirties' deep fascination with a quaint rural China, denotes a sharp tendency to ignore American policies to restrict Chinese immigration, and, most strikingly, shows a willful blindness to war crimes and other atrocities in the years leading up to the Sino-Japanese War and the Nanking Massacre in 1937.[62]

Flack and Wiese's *Story about Ping* depicts an uneasy peace along a tranquil river (Figure 2.10). The unpaginated book situates its vulnerable, potentially tasty bird hero among hungry Chinese fisherfolk, allowing the nonhuman character to serve as a point of identification and diminishing the agency of the representative human beings outside narrative confines. *Ping* takes place among old-fashioned houseboats on the Yangtze River, not among Asian Americans in a modern U.S. city, and offers a limited duck's-eye view of a possibly preindustrial Chinese society. It color-codes its bright-yellow Chinese duckling, whose down is the same saturated shade as the people's skin, and three times refers to the "yellow water of the Yangtze River" (which is printed blue in the pictures, although *yangtze* translates to the English word "yellow"). Flack does not specify skin color directly in her written text, leaving this task to Wiese's unambiguous images.

Ping and "his mother and his father and two sisters and three brothers and eleven aunts and seven uncles and forty-two cousins" live on a "wise-eyed boat," and every night they come home to nest there. "Ping was always careful, very very careful not to be last, because the last duck to cross over the bridge always got a spank on the back." Wiese's lithograph shows ducks climbing onto the wooden boat via a bridge, watched over by a man in a buttoned blue shirt and short blue pants. A broad-brimmed straw hat hides the man's eyes, but he smiles slightly as he holds the reed switch with which he will sting the last duck in the row. Predictably, Ping fails to make it home one evening and chooses to stay on the river rather than be disciplined. The next morning, he paddles up to another houseboat, where a boy hops into the water and offers him some food: "'Oh-owwwwooo!' cried the little Boy, and up dashed Ping and snatched at the rice cake." Ping is captured ("Quickly the Boy grabbed Ping and held him tight./ 'OH!—Ohh-ooo!' yelled the little Boy") and taken aboard by the Boy's family ("'Ah, a duck dinner has come to us!' said the Boy's father. / 'I will

Boy on to the house boat.

"Ah, a duck dinner has come to us!" said the Boy's father.

22

"I will cook him with rice at sunset tonight," said the Boy's mother.

"NO-NO! My nice duck is too beautiful to eat," cried the Boy.

But down came

23

The basket was quickly lifted, and the little Boy's hands were holding Ping.

26

Quickly, quietly, the Boy dropped Ping over the side of the boat and Ping slipped into the water, the beautiful yellow water of the Yangtze river.

Then Ping heard this call, "La-la-la-la-lei!"

27

FIGURE 2.10. In these 1933 spreads, illustrated by Kurt Wiese, Ping the duckling strays from his houseboat on the Yangtze River. Under threat from a hungry family, Ping is released by a helpful child.

cook him with rice at sunset tonight,' said the Boy's mother"). Before Ping can be eaten, however, the Boy sets him free. Ping hears the "La-la-la-la-lei!" of the man who pilots the wise-eyed boat, and he gratefully rushes home. "SPANK / came the spank on Ping's back!" when he is the last duck on board.

Ping is the book's hero and, in all but the last two images, the only duck that has yellow down. He's a standard-issue duckling, like any duckling in the world. According to the third-person narrator, Ping cries, "Quack-quack-quack-quack!" when he is captured and feels "very sad" until the Boy sets him free. On the one hand, in the sense that he looks ordinary, says "quack," and apparently experiences a common emotion, he is a unified character that suggests similarities between the United States and overseas locations. A duck is a duck is a duck, as the Marx brothers might have said in the same era. On the other hand, the Chinese people wear culturally specific clothing and do not stare out at the reader, as Ping does on the book cover and title page. They do not engage with the audience except as objects for inspection. Unlike the duck, the human beings remain enigmatic; their "OH!—Ohh-ooo!" and "La-la-la-la-lei!" exclamations are indecipherable. The adults, from the houseboat owner with the switch to the smiling, hungry family that plans to eat Ping, pose a threat. Only the boy protests Ping's fate (yelling "NO-NO! My nice duck is too beautiful to eat") and sets Ping free, but even the child's compassionate act might be attributed to selfishness. The unpredictable human presence casts Ping's houseboat existence into question; a non-egg-laying male is likely to end up in the stew pot soon enough.

But Ping's future is not the issue. Instead, imaginative American readers of the thirties could use *Ping* as a one-way window onto people and practices in the distant country of China, in an era when the Chinese American population actually was declining because of immigration restrictions. The Page Law of 1875 and the Chinese Exclusion Act of 1882, both of which restricted Asian immigration, were extended indefinitely in 1902 and reinforced by additional immigration restrictions in 1924; new quotas were not established until the forties.[63] Although Chinese American citizens and Chinese nationals were staples of photo-magazines, actual Chinese Americans were seldom seen by most young Americans in the 1930s and would have been objects of curiosity. *The Story about Ping* does not necessarily protest anti-immigrant restrictions, given that the book's adult characters are not to be trusted (and neither is the boy's young sister). As a picture book, it conveniently overlooks U.S. policies of its day. Yet it is worth noting that the boy child and the careless duck form an alliance that saves Ping's life. As does *Little Annie Rooney, The Story about Ping* implies that hope resides in coming generations.

Another popular text, Munro Leaf and Robert Lawson's *The Story of Ferdinand* (1936), similarly posits an ingenuous animal other in grave danger from ethnic adult types (Figure 2.11). Where *The Story about Ping* features a Chinese duckling, *The Story of Ferdinand* famously concerns an unaggressive bull calf in a bullfighting-obsessed Spain. *Ferdinand's* male hero has a Spanish name but no defining national characteristics other than a stalwart, unexamined pacifism. The initial spreads, featuring Lawson's distinctive, sharp pen-and-ink and tempera images, focus on Ferdinand's gentleness: "All the other little bulls he lived with would run and jump and butt their heads together, / but not Ferdinand. / He liked to sit just quietly and smell the flowers." Ferdinand's story progresses from spread to spread in placid phrases and sentences without undue punctuation. The consonance of the *S*'s and assonance of the *U*'s in "just quietly" suggests a lulling whisper or blissful complacency.[64] Lawson's tightly composed, high-contrast illustrations instill drama. The images depict Ferdinand's Zenlike demeanor but also foreground his growth from a gangly calf to a muscular, meaty bull. A chart carved in a dead tree indicates the passage of two pleasant years in Ferdinand's life, yet a feathery vulture sitting patiently on the stump forebodes big trouble.

Eventually, "five men came in very funny hats to pick the biggest, fastest, roughest bull to fight in the bull fights in Madrid." Again, the author and illustrator mingle the comic and sinister in the mention of "funny hats" and the illustration of five unsmiling talent scouts, who glare menacingly at the audience and, presumably, at the sweet-natured title character with whom the reader is encouraged to sympathize. Young bulls show off for the five men while Ferdinand wanders off to smell the flowers. But Ferdinand accidentally sits on a bee, occasioning the narrator's question:

> Well, if you were a bumble bee and a bull sat on you, what would you do? You would sting him. And that is just what this bee did to Ferdinand.
>
> Wow! Did it hurt! Ferdinand jumped up with a snort . . . pawing the ground as if he were crazy.

This violent behavior delights the shifty bull appraisers, who cart the unsuspecting Ferdinand off to Madrid. Rhetorical questions, information-heavy sentences, and alarmed interjections signal an end to Ferdinand's tranquil lifestyle, and Lawson's illustrations continue to carry dire warnings. Vultures perch on roadside signs, city rooftops, and the lip of the bullfighting arena. Caricatures

FIGURE 2.11. In Robert Lawson's energetic illustration for *The Story of Ferdinand*, five sinister Spaniards cheer and plot for a bullfight after gentle Ferdinand is stung by a bee and goes on a snorting, kicking rampage.

establish the cowardice and vanity of the bullfighters; the slouching Bandilleros ("with long sharp pins . . . to stick in the bull and make him mad"), scrawny Picadores, and primping Matador swagger into the bullring, and Ferdinand himself goes unpictured for five spreads. At last, the text draws attention back to the animal, who is pictured in a very long shot, peeking from a dark tunnel and into the sunlit bullring: "Then came the bull, and you know who that was don't you?—FERDINAND." With the whispered subscript capital letters advertising Ferdinand's meek entrance, the suspense reaches its peak. The bullfighters sweat and grimace with fear of the coming fight. But Ferdinand, entranced by the scent of flowers worn by the Spanish women, "just sat and smelled" rather than rising to the fight: "The Matador was so mad he cried. . . . / So they had to take Ferdinand home. / And for all I know he is sitting there still, under his favorite cork tree, smelling the flowers just quietly. / He is very happy." A four-spread sequence promptly removes Ferdinand from the fateful ring, returns him to his pasture, and situates him in a timeless fairy tale realm that bookends a "Once upon a time in Spain" introduction. Lawson's closing, wordless image of a daisy shedding its petals might imply Ferdinand's mortality, but otherwise the mellow bull maintains his nonconformist stance.

Leaf and Lawson's persuasive balance of first-person written text and satirical imagery establishes admiration for the bull and mistrust of the Spaniards. *The Story of Ferdinand* centers on the alien custom of the bullfight as conducted by deadly cultural others and experienced by an endangered animal character. It does not provide its title character with a voice (although Walt Disney's widely circulated 1938 animation gives him, as a calf, a twee accent), but it excites sympathy in its rhetorical questions to an unseen "you" and assures the reader that, "for all I know," the bull is safe and sound.

According to Gary D. Schmidt, Leaf "chose a bull because he wanted to write about an uncommon animal; he chose the name Ferdinand because King Ferdinand was the only Spanish figure he knew."[65] Yet Leaf and Lawson's publisher was far from uninformed about the world situation, and the unstable political climate contributed to the book's eventual best-seller status:

> They offered the book first to Little, Brown, got turned down and
> went to May Massee at Viking. Although Massee worked to get a
> small 5,200 print run accepted, "The publisher was only mildly enthu-
> siastic about the book. Civil War erupted in Spain, and Harold Gins-
> berg, president of Viking, suggested holding back publication until 'the
> world settles down.'" But Massee persisted, despite the fact that all of

the advertising money for that session had been allocated to William Pène du Bois's *Giant Otto*, the book that Viking was most enthusiastic about. "*Ferdinand* is a nice little book," suggested Ginsberg, "but *Giant Otto* will live forever."[66]

Unsurprisingly, *The Story of Ferdinand* provoked controversy, along with a marketing juggernaut of toys and some sixty translated editions. Needless to say, it was read much differently in its originating decade than it can be read today. Not only did *Ferdinand* feature a male hero who bucks gender norms, but also the book appeared as the Spanish Civil War was pitting Loyalists against General Francisco Franco's Nationalists, and communists (including Mexican and Soviet supporters) against fascists (backed by Hitler's military), and otherwise previewing the Allied–Axis showdown of World War II.[67] *Ferdinand* was banned in Spain and Germany in the late 1930s, but several long years later, "after the fall of Berlin, 30,000 copies were distributed to the children of that city as a mission of peace."[68] In the United States, where Eleanor Roosevelt had proclaimed herself and her husband fans of the book in the thirties, *Ferdinand*'s reception was popular, but its message had potential to cause consternation, given post-1941 public sentiment about the honor in putting up a fight. "Is Leaf and Lawson's *The Story of Ferdinand* the first American antiwar picture book?" ask Joseph and Chava Schwarcz. "[There is] a mild early whiff of the antihero, of flower children and nonviolent resistance movements."[69] Leaf maintained neutrality, saying the book "was propaganda all right, but propaganda for laughter only.... If the book fails to make you chuckle, there is no excuse for its existence, as far as I'm concerned."[70] The book did appeal, and still does, to people of various political beliefs. *Ferdinand* seems to provide a worthy lesson for children, although its grown but childlike hero demonstrates a moral code that proves hard to live by for mature human adults. *Ferdinand* is a comic story, and arguably an infantilizing and possibly feminizing story as well, for it pictures its hero as a shy loner whose only friend is his mother; there is humor in the irony of the bull's tough looks and gentle disposition, and a clear challenge to masculinity, albeit via anthropomorphism. *Ferdinand* also builds its humor at the expense of Spanish people, whom Lawson visually stereotyped.

*The Story of Ferdinand* and *The Story about Ping* belong to a specific context and a thirties account of otherness. At one level, they respectively associate Spain with a pacifist bull or conscientious objector cruelly abused by Spanish people, and China with a risk-prone yellow duck, almost eaten and barely rescued after misbehaving. Yet, almost a century later, few children's texts match these popular books for name recognition and wide distribution. Today, *Ferdinand*'s and *Ping*'s ideal readers know little about U.S. foreign policy and international conflict, and much less about the events of the thirties that drew the authors' and illustrators' attention to particular nations. Yet these texts still help American readers develop connotations of Spain, China, and the individuals (coded as animals) who live there. In presenting limited possibilities with regard to ethnicity, these texts discipline young readers' imaginations. Everyday life might contradict the written or visual information sufficiently to disrupt established conventions; readers might enjoy these texts for their accounts of peacefulness, compassion, and responsibility. A concern, however, lies in the scarcity of texts providing alternatives to established stereotypes, making alternatives difficult to imagine.

## IMPLIED READERS, IMPLIED OTHERS: FOREIGN AND DOMESTIC CHILDHOOD ON THE PAGE

Children's texts construct and imply an ideal readership. In the process, they also construct and imply their Other, an alternative and unwelcome subject position. Often, reader-response critics designate only the implied reader, a generic child, and fail to acknowledge that the text excludes certain young populations. Even if the formal structures and explicit content are nondiscriminatory to everyone, fitting an all-inclusive "child" category, not every reader is deemed worthy of membership in this (often middle-class, white) demographic. Perry Nodelman writes, "All texts imply in their subject and their style the sort of reader most likely to respond positively to them. . . . In requiring us to possess the interpretive skills they demand and to know how to enjoy the pleasures they offer in order to get the most out of them, literary texts invite us to become something like the reader they imply as we read them."[71] Nodelman's affirmative critique nonetheless suggests that the welcome reader has an alter ego, the potential outsider, because not every individual can answer (or is willing to answer) a text's invitation.

The implied reader of an animal story might answer the text's invitation solely on the basis of the animal character's nonhuman status. This allows for a foreign setting and context often populated by people judged as different from the text's likeliest audience. International stories frequently introduce a sympathetic animal protagonist in mortal danger from racialized or nationalized humans, and the reader's affiliation lies with the hero rather than with the antagonists. A gentle version of this narrative, *Curious George* (1941), shows the childlike, joyful creature on a journey from his native habitat to a controlled zone. At the zoo, Curious George's mischief is curbed, and he can reside as a kind of naturalized, nonoriginal citizen; in this case, too, bemused readers identify Curious George's charming naïveté and klutzy accidents (falling overboard a ship, mistakenly phoning the fire department, being hoisted aloft by a balloon bouquet) as justifying good-intentioned discipline.[72] Such picture books either affiliate human, especially child, physiognomy with an animal other or associate an animal with the human ethnic group in its habitat.

Conversely, Brunhoff's *The Story of Babar, the Little Elephant* opens with idyllic scenes of elephants enjoying jungle life, vilifies the white safari hunter who kills Babar's mother in her own homeland, and then venerates an elderly white urbanite who provides for the African elephant's socioeconomic salvation. The original *Babar* "represented something avant-garde and was an early protest against the slaughter of elephants," according to Jean Perrot, who rejects colonial interpretations of the book and connects the shattering of rural peacefulness and the urban commotion to a 1928 ideal of "the 'garden city,' the utopian incarnation of a certain form of communal living."[73] Perrot argues that Brunhoff memorably translated the mass poaching of elephants for their tusks, carried out by heartless humans in the African bush, to picture-book pages, along with depicting the young elephants in a parkland that had become uncommon for the cosmopolitan modern child. He disagrees vehemently with the position of Herbert Kohl, whose point of view is that Babar casts naked elephants, representative of black African people, as the colonized subjects of wealthy, "civilized," white French city dwellers, who gladly initiate Babar into their materialist customs. After his city sojourn, Babar—mutually representing his elephant heritage and the city folks' school—returns home, where he is crowned king and presumably rules on behalf of his imperial masters. Other critics take the middle ground. Adam Gopnik, reviewing an exhibit of Jean and Laurent de Brunhoff's work, comments, "The de Brunhoffs' saga is not an unconscious expression of the French colonial imagination; it is a self-conscious comedy *about* the French colonial imagination and its close relation to the French domestic imagination."[74]

A character like Babar or Curious George can range into a nation not his own, either to learn new customs there or to become part of an amusing spectacle. In contrast, if the international tale's protagonist is a child rather than an animal—such as the heroes of *Lucio and His Nuong* or *Jamaica Johnny*—he or she resides in a national homeland, impresses skeptical adults, and meets with wonderful success on native grounds. Unlike an ethnoracially coded animal, the international child protagonist may not venture outside national boundaries, although he or she is welcome to be clever and productive on native ground. Therefore, although stories with international topics reach American readers, their characters do not cross U.S. borders, contributing to the perception that nonnative English speakers, many nonwhite people, and people with non-U.S. customs must be foreigners rather than potential citizens and neighbors. And although such texts do represent diversity in words and pictures, they require their implied reader to assume a spectatorial or ethnographic perspective upon the struggling Other.

In their illustrated, unpaginated novel *Boomba Lives in Africa* (1935), Caroline Singer and Cyrus LeRoy Baldridge base their fictive, ten-year-old West African protagonist on "a friendship with a certain brown Boomba of the Sierra Leone hinterland." In their introduction, they attest to having spent "more than a year in tropical Africa" and explain, "The narrative is frankly fiction. But its minor incidents and its setting are drawn from first-hand observations in a hinterland village, the counterpart of Mabai, among a people whom we have chosen to term the 'Dimbas' lest, giving them their correct name, we be suspected of posing as anthropologists." Singer and Baldridge defend themselves against an anthropologist label, or perhaps against accusations of failing in scientific objectivity. Unlike the Haders, who make a visual joke of anthropological data collection, Singer and Baldridge go out of their way to reject it. Yet, to support their book's authentic foundations, they allude to research assistance from "Achimota College, the Gold Coast, West Africa. The emblem of this college—uniquely chartered under the British Crown—is the piano's key-board. For, deprived of either its black or its white keys, a piano is rendered useless as a musical instrument."

Singer and Baldridge call for racial harmony yet celebrate a colonial institution in the process. They then open their narrative with heavy-handed didacticism around skin color: "Some people call Africans 'black.' But no 'white' person is ever a really white white. And no 'black' person is ever a really black black. This boy [Boomba] is a beautiful dark brown. Do not ask anybody why. For nobody knows why some people are brown and why others are not." The authors continue with instruction on village life and customs, including the trading of handwoven cloth and weapons, described in ethnically and racially politicized terms:

> Wanting the Africans' land and good African things, white nations
> have taken nearly all of Africa away from the brown African tribes.

This was easy to do. For nations are bigger and stronger than tribes. The Dimbas no longer own the country where the Dimbas have lived for hundreds of years. All over Africa are white Traders with stores. These white Traders go to Africa to get African things which they can send away and sell. . . . Selling machine-made things, the white Traders have put the Africans, who made things, out of business. . . . Today a fine hand-woven African cloth is so rare that only a Chief can buy one. That is why such a cloth is called a "Chief's Cloth."

As in their acknowledgment of their colonial hosts, Singer and Baldridge sit on the fence. They criticize imperial conquest, on the one hand, while implying a survival-of-the-fittest outcome in the unbalanced struggle between large but anonymous "white nations" and generic, weak "brown African tribes," on the other. The authors do not identify the white traders by country of origin.

The mock-instructive setup of *Boomba Lives in Africa* supports the story of a compassionate boy who protects his pet gazelle against a marauding leopard. The narrative is undoubtedly sympathetic to its ten-year-old child hero, however lacking in accuracy, and culminates with Boomba's use of a flintlock gun, euphemistically described as "an odd thing [bought] from white-skinned strangers." This occasions a closing lecture on colonial control of African subjects' education and defense. For killing the dangerous leopard (albeit wasting gunpowder his father had forbidden him to use), Boomba is rewarded by his village's "Paramount Chief" with the promise of attending a boys' school and learning to hunt with his father. This comes with certain conditions, though: "[At 'Bush School,' Boomba and his fellow students] learn warriors' songs and dances. But they do not become warriors. White nations have taken the guns from the tribes. Today no Dimba village may have more than one gun. And this gun may not be new. That is why Boomba's father has the only gun in Mabai and why his gun is a muzzle-loader flint-lock." Singer and Baldridge visualize an international location—albeit a generic African continent—and create a sympathetic main character with great regard for his pet animal. Yet they also render ethnoracial outsiders distant and nonthreatening, cordoning them off in their place of origin and literally disarming them, lest they use weapons unwisely and outside the limitations the white traders appear to have set.

Picture-book creator and novelist Armstrong Sperry, who won the 1941 Newbery Award for his Polynesian-themed *Call It Courage*, specialized in international books of this nature. Sperry had attended Yale Art School prior to the First World War, but dropped out when he joined the Navy. After his service, he went to New York, took courses at the Art Students League, and worked as a graphic illustrator and advertiser. In 1925, already weary of his advertising career, he signed on as an "assistant ethnologist" with the Bishop Museum of Honolulu and traveled throughout the Pacific as part of the "Kaimiloa expedition," visiting islands and meeting populations about which his seafaring great-grandfather had told him stories as a child.[75] Sperry recalled the warm welcome he received from island inhabitants, whom he later depicted in his pictorial books. In his Newbery Medal acceptance speech, he explained how Opu Nui, "the Tavana Rahi, the Great Chief of Bora Bora," welcomed him into the family home and gave him a comfortable place to sleep. During Sperry's visit, a blight on vanilla beans on all the neighboring islands caused the market price of vanilla to skyrocket, resulting in a shift in the island economy and a rise in local crime between those who were losing their livelihoods and those who still had vanilla to sell. "It was a terrible experience to see this change come over the island; above all to realize that the civilization for which I stood should have brought it about," Sperry said.[76] Yet when he made plans to leave, Opu Nui convinced him to stay longer and avoid the hazardous February weather at sea. When a storm hit the island, Sperry felt grateful to have been forewarned by his generous host.

Yet, for all Sperry's experiences, which acquainted him with the potential hardship of life in the South Seas and with knowledge of Western dangers to traditional cultures, he promoted a largely Romantic view of life in Bora Bora. Despite the islanders' keeping him safe from bad weather and from the economically induced crime wave, he irresponsibly characterized them as "the race of friendly savages who peopled [Bora Bora's] shores." As he told the Newbery Medal audience, he enjoyed his tropical adventure à la Gauguin ("long before Hollywood had discovered Tahiti") and found "that in the South Seas, Time stands still. It becomes only one more illusion of civilization. When every day as it comes is just like the day that has gone before, the sense of the division of time by minutes and hours quickly vanishes."[77] This reductive, primitivist attitude made its way into Sperry's later picture books: *One Day with Manu* (1933), a story of a boy in Bora Bora who roasts a delicious pig for a gluttonous, lazy ruler named King Opu Nui, after Sperry's host; *One Day with Jambi in Sumatra* (1934), in which a boy, with help from his companion elephant and monkey, participates in killing a tiger; and *One Day with Tuktu, an Eskimo Boy* (1935), a story of an Inuit who takes part in a polar-bear-hunting expedition. Sperry's *Little Eagle, a Navajo Boy* (1938) follows the same coming-of-age trajectory as the "One Day with" trio. (Only *Little Eagle* is paginated.) All four texts feature wide-angle landscapes and brilliantly multicolored illustrations that alternate with black-and-white imagery. *Manu's* illustrations, usually framed in rectangular or implied borders, show Manu and his friends surfing with porpoises, wading in the sea, and climbing palm trees; some spreads include descriptive captions, including one that compares Manu's elevated bamboo home to a birdhouse. The boys slide down a waterfall and swim in a lagoon, smiling and having fun. In Sperry's pictures, Manu's Bora Bora and Jambi's Sumatra look like theme parks with bountiful resources and endless opportunities for play (Plate 12).

In each consecutive book—*Manu, Jambi, Tuktu,* and *Little Eagle*—Sperry signals superstitions and indicates that the people under discussion have spiritual beliefs distinct from the reader's. The text of each usually takes the past tense and includes italicized words or chants in the hero's "native language," or at least semblances of these words according to Sperry, adding to the curiosity factor. Very often this feels gratuitous: In *Manu,* the people of Bora Bora cry, "*Aue!*" instead of "Oh!" with italics to indicate a Pacific Islander is speaking. When Manu dives off a waterfall, the text reads, "*Aue!* What fun! He'd like to do it all day!" *Little Eagle* includes a dubious glossary of "unfamiliar words," many unnecessarily defined or suggestive of Native American political issues elided in the text; these include "ei yei!" defined as "an exclamation"; "hard goods," said to be a "Navajo expression for jewelry"; "o'o," which means "yes"; "Pendleton blanket," otherwise known as a "trade blanket"; "pinto," which is "a spotted pony"; and "Washindon," "the Navajo word for the government at Washington" (n.p.). Sperry's attention to trade goods implies the exchange economy that helps support Little Eagle's Navajo family, although the book focuses on the family's abundance of silver necklaces. The misspelled "Washindon" is not a real word but a demeaning implication of Navajo mispronunciation and ignorance.

All of Sperry's books, although written in affirmative terms, emphasize us-and-them differences between the implied young reader and the implied other or object. The books visually and verbally note the characters' skin: Jambi's "skin was the color of wild honey," as sweet as the delicious produce he enjoys in Sumatra; Tuktu's skin is "copper-colored"; and Little Eagle's skin makes him a natural part of the landscape, for it is "as coppery-red as the cliffs of Arizona's Canyon de Chelly, where he lived." The texts focus on unusual foods and the subjects' crude, impolite eating habits (Tuktu eats raw seal meat from a knife, Manu drinks messily from a coconut), while describing the youths' mature willingness to labor for their families and communities. The books focus on fun—there are not many pictures of adults, and particularly few of girls or women outside *Tuktu's* and *Little Eagle's* family portraits—but the importance of gendered labor is studied as well. Women and girls do domestic tasks such as sewing and washing; Jambi's mother cooks and weaves while his sister spins thread and dyes cloth. Men do the more dangerous tasks, the most glamorous of which is building a tiger trap in the jungle. Ordinarily, Jambi's father plants and harvests rice, and when Jambi is not fishing he helps in the fields by guiding a plow behind a water buffalo: "In Sumatra everyone has to do something to help the family. The women make *sarongs* and baskets and beat jewelry out of silver to sell in the Market Place; the little girls spin thread, and dye it, and learn to weave and cook; the men hunt and build and cultivate the land. Silently Jambi clung to the plow. This was his part. . . . When crops failed, people starved." Although Jambi enjoys a bounty of rice at home—at a typical breakfast, "The little boy helped himself to a bowlful of steaming rice and a rosy, juicy mango"—the details of plowing and planting qualify Sperry's overall depiction of bountiful living. Remarks such as "When crops failed, people starved" underscore the fact that Sperry wrote in the middle of the Depression, producing coming-of-age tales that praise family self-sufficiency and detail effortless, mouth-watering meals.

Sperry places the child in close communion with animals as well, whether as food, as friends (*Call It Courage* features an albatross), as predators (Jambi dares to face a tiger, Tuktu dominates rebellious huskies and—needlessly, out of superstition—kills a polar bear), or as domestic animals (Little Eagle is an expert horseman; Jambi pals around with an elephant and monkey) (Figures 2.12 and 2.13, Plate 13). Further, Sperry includes medicine men, elders, and tribal chiefs, who inspire respect or fear in the story but seem backward or ridiculous to the reader. His patronizing depiction of King Opu Nui in *Manu* seems the worst depiction, based on his relationship with the actual dignitary. In *Manu*, Opu Nui is a greedy authoritarian who "was always declaring Feast Days": "King Opu Nui, whose name meant Big Stomach, had said that there should be a feast that night, and that each man must bring twenty coconuts. . . . These people in Bora Bora have enormous appetites. By the time they are sixty or seventy years old, they all have huge stomachs, just like King Opu Nui. The King, on top of a full meal, very often ate a whole bunch of bananas. . . . Everybody would eat and eat until he couldn't hold another mouthful, and then he would lie right down to sleep wherever he might be." Opu Nui's people act like gluttons at the feasts, although otherwise they eat poi almost exclusively. With firsthand authority, Sperry states that poi, made from breadfruit, is a "thick, sticky mess" that "tastes like sour billposter's paste," and implies that "you," the audience, are lucky to avoid it. If the common folk indulge themselves child-ishly, Opu Nui's appetite is the most childish of all. Thanks to the bountiful natural resources on the island (apparently vanilla beans are plentiful), the king whimsically declares festivals when he wants his tribal subjects to feed him. In addition, a feast requires the villagers to slaughter numerous pigs so that the king may give credit to the best one; there is no concern for waste. Contrary to what Sperry knew about the island, his fictive Bora Borans lead a life of luxury and sloth, eating too much and securely falling asleep anywhere they wish, like infants. One color spread shows them loaded with food for a feast, parading past palm trees, playing leisurely music as they go.

The texts also differentiate the hero and his family or tribe from "the White Man." *Manu* includes references to the White Man's names for constellations, as opposed to the cosmology of his own people. *Jambi* references an almost tele-pathic communication among islanders, used in the book when Jambi and his elephant kill the tiger and impress "His Highness the Sultan Pera-Pat Nopan," who gives Jambi one of the coveted tiger's teeth as a reward: "In Sumatra, as in all the other islands of the Pacific Ocean, the natives have a mysterious way

JAMBI AND KOKO AND WANG FOLLOWTRAIL OF THE TIGER INTO THE JUNGLE

FIGURE 2.12. The stylized spreads of *One Day with Jambi in Sumatra* (1934) picture a hardworking, daring boy and cast Sumatra as a leisurely place threatened by a tiger.

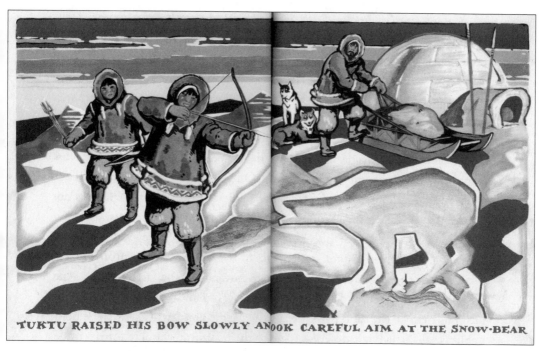

TUKTU RAISED HIS BOW SLOWLY ANᴅ TOOK CAREFUL AIM AT THE SNOW-BEAR

FIGURE 2.13. *One Day with Tuktu, an Eskimo Boy* (1935) pits a brave child against a vicious polar bear and recalcitrant sled dogs. Sunset-hued spreads valorize hunting and Arctic survival in this departure from Armstrong Sperry's usual tropical locales.

of sending news. White men call it the 'grapevine telegraph.' When an event of importance takes place, news of it reaches the most distant villages in no time at all. How it is done I cannot tell, for no white man has ever been able to discover. . . . So it was that news of the tiger's death reached the village long before Jambi did himself." Sperry's first-person "I" places *Jambi*'s narrator in the ethnographic role of astonished observer. In another example, the Inuit boy Tuktu, whose father exchanges fox pelts for ammunition, matches, and other basic supplies at a trading post, observes, "The White Man was mysterious in his ways. If a fox skin were perfect, he would pay a big price, but if it had so much as a speck of summer brown, the Trader would throw it out." Tuktu uses this knowledge when doing his own trapping, because he hopes the whites will be generous enough to provide his family with "tea and sugar, and scraps of iron to fashion into harpoons," as well as "a knife, a box of striped candy, and some ship biscuits that went *crunch-crunch* between his teeth." Although he seems self-sufficient, Tuktu nonetheless worries how to appease the White Man, whose steel sewing needles are "so much better than the Eskimo needles made of bird bone."

Among Sperry's books, *Little Eagle* dwells at length on ethnoracial differentiation, given its U.S. setting (Figure 2.14). In this sense, it proceeds in opposition to most picture-book tales of the Other, which restrict fictional ethnic types or nonwhite child characters either to the past (in the case of Native Americans) or to non-U.S. settings. *Little Eagle* features an assimilationist protagonist eager to go to the white Americans' "Government school," where his sister has spent three years and where her fiancé has trained to be an auto mechanic. Little Eagle's desire to attend the school occasions his immense disrespect for his great-uncle, "the Ancient One," whose "memory reached back to those days in 1863 when Kit Carson's soldiers had driven the Navajos out of land that had been theirs for centuries" (16). Little Eagle protests, "But that was long ago, Great-Uncle" (17). He indulges in a reverie, "his eyes shining with the vision. To see the distant settlements of the white man; the 'Iron Trail' of the railroad; the automobile that traveled faster than the fastest horse! And those pictures that moved and talked—'movies' men called them—more miraculous than all the sand paintings of the Medicine Men." (17–18). The book implies that Little Eagle deserves to go to the boarding school to learn a trade, regardless of what elders say to the contrary, regardless that his father is a silversmith who can teach him, and regardless of the brutal white takeover of Native tribal land in his recent history. What's more, Sperry's positive account of the government school stands in contrast to the lived realities of such institutions, which forcibly removed children from families, observed English-language-only policies, and specifically operated to dilute tribal cohesion.[78]

Notably, Little Eagle's yearning to attend the school is not the only source of conflict; another is between Little Eagle and an unnamed Ute who tries to steal his prized pony. Little Eagle is shot in the shoulder by the Ute, but he recovers his horse and recuperates. This near-fatal clash places the narrative focus on hostilities among Native peoples, eliding evidence that white and Native cultures are at odds. Little Eagle competes with other Native men, and he craves the wisdom available at the government school. Thanks to another tribal elder, who intimidates the Ancient One and rudely tells him, "The sparrow does not challenge the vision of the eagle," Little Eagle's wish is granted. An informed reader might wonder whether, despite Sperry's travels, he could not overcome imperialist clichés instilled in his own youth or whether he dismissed his concerns in order to provide American children with the same affectionate, exotic portraits of island paradise and Indians that had led him to his successful writing and illustrating career. In any case, Sperry does all his international subjects a great disservice.

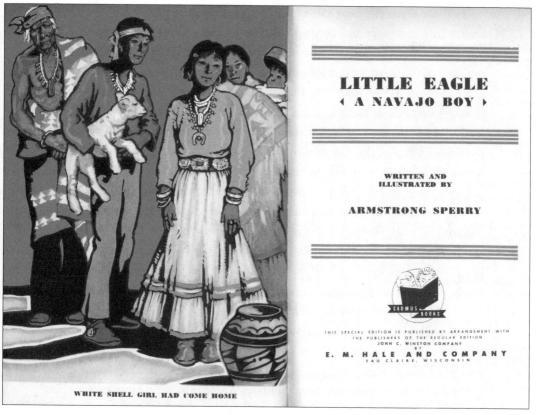

FIGURE 2.14. In Armstrong Sperry's idealistic *Little Eagle: A Navajo Boy* (1938), White Shell Girl returns from three years at a U.S. government school, and her brother Little Eagle dreams of going to the school himself.

Like *Boomba Lives in Africa*, Sperry's books acknowledge the vastness of the world and diversity of populations, potentially expanding modern readers' range of interests. Book reviewers verify that author-illustrators such as Sperry did considerable research or gained invaluable firsthand knowledge overseas, whether growing up abroad or sightseeing. Yet these texts define the reader as a middle-class armchair tourist observing faraway children from the safe cocoon of a Western home, rather than one with firsthand daily contact with multicultural American citizens or with a traveler's mobility. These texts model cultural standards of invisibility and visibility, absence and presence. They suggest how and under what conditions certain people and things might be made visible to a young audience in a given era, and all too frequently normalize hierarchies among white American children and children of color, represented as living elsewhere.

In these texts, the fairy tale of modernity created expectations of middle-class, white centrality at a time when that dominant culture was under diffusion nationally and globally. Modern actualities sometimes contradicted textual content. Where some works outwardly upheld narrow standards of racial and ethnic purity—whether by focusing exclusively on white characters or by insisting that ethnic and racial "nationality groups" existed only in their native lands—other written, pictorial, and cinematic evidence of cultural diversity prefigured a drastically different reality. Mass-produced information thus had the capacity either to reinforce or to destabilize the fairy tale of modernity as provided in so many picture books and illustrated texts for young readers.

Every children's text—then and now—implies something about its reader's nationality, race, intellectual ability, and socioeconomic potential. This implication takes place not only through narrative, pictures, design, and packaging but also through the visual information provided in words and punctuation. Colloquial or formal words are visible on the page, closely studied and pronounced by the person who practices them aloud. Within an English-language text, non-English terms often appear in italics and in a glossary. Animals make distinctive sounds for a reader to imitate, whereas human voices and dialects are complicated by variable spelling and idiosyncratic punctuation. Some characters speak in authoritative commands or onomatopoeic grunts that end in exclamation points; others speak a regional vernacular, dropping g's from their gerunds; still others speak the Queen's English. Novelty words and alternative spellings cue readers to the multiple ways of using language and the multiplicity of speakers; characters spice their conversations with idioms or non-English vocabulary, which may be offset by italics, footnoted, or translated in a helpful glossary. Experienced readers can determine whether a speaker is urban or rural, European or British, Anglo- or African American or otherwise, based on the look of printed words and the sound of language, whether it is imagined while reading silently, overheard in a read-aloud session, or imitated.

In modern picture books and illustrated texts for young readers, international characters teach implied Anglo- or Euro-American readers how to identify a non-American, non-Western, and perhaps nonhuman perspective. Books featuring foreign characters introduce U.S. children to their "friends" in other countries without suggesting that those friends are their peers or concentrating on the children's coeval existences. Further, authors remind readers that the characters are not speaking English, or provide dialects and thick non-American accents to establish the cultural other. Fashions for dialect writing, and for representing non-American voices in print, imply a modern public attuned to linguistic diversity. The printed language is English, but far from the formal English to which an implied reader presumably is accustomed in school. For example, English writer-illustrator Cecil Aldin, who crafted a name and a voice for a dog in his *Mac: The Adventures of a Scotch Terrier* (1927), received an enthusiastic review from the Boston Bookshop for Boys and Girls:

> The Bookshop is always a jollier place when "Mac" is in it. "I tell't him ma name, every sylup of it, Macgillysloganardnamurchanmore; and says he, 'Is it the long or the short of it ye're after giving me?' The short of it,' says I, 'Is Mac.' " We beg the publishers in England to reprint this book.[79]

The Bookshop staffers select a piece of precious dialogue for their review and anticipate that children's educators and librarians will be amused by Mac's long name and odd speaking style. Certainly, there is pleasure in decoding the unusual spellings and play in pronouncing the multisyllabic name, and the editors' unreserved praise of this comical first-person narrative suggests that adults of the period judged such material worthy entertainment for young audiences. Yet the book's representation of cultural difference raises no eyebrows. The reviewers seem untroubled by the lack of proper spelling and textbook English, perhaps because the terms are given as dialogue and not in exposition, and they happily invite a comic representation of the cultural other. Scotland is represented as a dog with an unusual name, as in Marjorie Flack's *Angus and the Ducks* three years later, or as a quirky bagpipe player in Munro Leaf and Robert Lawson's *Wee Gillis* (1938), a picture book about a meek boy torn between brutish relatives in his parents' rival clans of Scottish Highlanders. Certainly a reader can take pride in his or her own or another's unusual name, and can show equal respect for people of dissimilar ethnic or racial backgrounds. But the clownish figures of Mac and Wee Gillis, visualized and voiced on the printed page, maintain the separation between the normative English speaker and the peculiar stranger who mutilates the mother tongue, albeit in a silly or charming way.

Much depends on the source of the text that dissociates a manner of speaking from formal English usage. Inscribed imitations of African American voices, alternately by Harlem Renaissance writers, folk historians, and middle-class Anglocentric writers for children, complicate the issue of valorization or condemnation of difference. With rare exceptions, such as Langston Hughes's poetry anthology *The Dream Keeper* (1932, illustrated by Helen Sewell)—which alternates between a racially undifferentiated voice, a voice identified as African American speaking to a black readership, and a black idiom that Hughes designates "the blues"—children's texts tend to present dialect that constitutes an Anglo- or Eurocentric subject's social dominance.[80] For example, author-illustrator Ellis Credle found welcome audiences for her depictions of class and race, which today are troubling. Credle's *Across the Cotton Patch* (1935) describes two well-off, mischievous white children and their three African American friends on a former plantation (Figure 2.15). A white girl named Nancy Elizabeth is nicknamed Pig-Tail by the black tenant farmers whose log cabins are "across the cotton patch" from her parents' stately manor house. Pig-Tail and her brother, Billy, do not like playing in their own yard and prefer the environs of twins Atlantic and Pacific and their little sister, Magnolia Blossom. The children get in trouble for hitching a pig to a cart and for attempting to build a tobacco smokehouse, although they effectively punish themselves by chewing the tobacco and getting sick. Credle refers to "darkies" with careless glee, renders the white children's statements in noncolloquial English, and writes the African American characters' voices in a distinctive vernacular. She repeatedly differentiates the children despite their close friendship and takes care to mention that the black children receive harsher punishment for their antics than do the merely mischievous Pig-Tail (the ringleader) and Billy. Credle's rough lithographs, printed in black ink, contrast the blond children with the African American ones, although arguably all the characters receive a similarly exaggerated visual treatment.

Credle, a schoolteacher-turned-artist who created a mural for the Brooklyn Children's Museum, mimes an American regionalist style and alludes to Gág's *Millions of Cats* in the landscape layouts of her text and imagery. Like Gág, Credle intimately recalled small-town life but welcomed modern urban living, too. In a biographical note, she recalls growing up in rural North Carolina, alludes to slavery, and implies that the Old South is outmoded: "Decaying plantation houses and weed-choked gardens made me always conscious of a dead past." She asserts that art school in New York, including a stint at the Art Students League, taught her "that North Carolina was not the center of the universe and that people of Anglo-Saxon blood were not always as superior as I had somehow come to believe. The gradual education of my conscience may be easily traced in my books."[81] Yet Credle does not specify which books represent the education of her conscience. If *Across the Cotton Patch* is among them, then her racial understanding had a long way to go even by midcentury standards, for the book keeps stereotypes firmly in place. *Cotton Patch* received

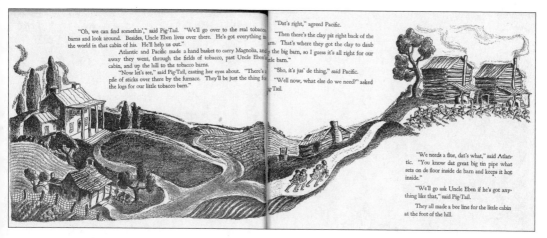

The text within the illustration reads:

"Oh, we can find somethin'," said Pig-Tail. "We'll go over to the real tobacco barns and look around. Besides, Uncle Eben lives over there. He's got everything in the world in that cabin of his. He'll help us out."

Atlantic and Pacific made a hand basket to carry Magnolia, and away they went, through the fields of tobacco, past Uncle Eben's cabin, and up the hill to the tobacco barns.

"Now let's see," said Pig-Tail, casting her eyes about. "There's a pile of sticks over there by the furnace. They'll be just the thing for the logs for our little tobacco barn."

"Dat's right," agreed Pacific.

"Then there's the clay pit right back of the big barn. That's where they get the clay to daub the big barn, so I guess it's all right for our little barn."

"Sho, it's jus' de thing," said Pacific.

"Well now, what else do we need?" asked Pig-Tail.

"We needs a flue, dat's what," said Atlantic. "You know dat great big tin pipe what sets on de floor inside de barn and keeps it hot inside."

"We'll go ask Uncle Eben if he's got anything like that," said Pig-Tail.

They all made a bee line for the little cabin at the foot of the hill.

FIGURE 2.15. In this 1935 spread, Ellis Credle pictures a plantation house "across the cotton patch" from tenant farmers' log cabins. Her illustration echoes the rolling landscapes of *Millions of Cats*.

a second printing in 1935 and subsequent reprintings in 1936, 1938, 1942, and 1945, attesting to a decade's popularity.

Credle did explore white rural life elsewhere without harping on the jarring social disparities of *Across the Cotton Patch*. *Down, Down the Mountain* (1934) introduces two earnest siblings who live in poverty in the Blue Ridge Mountains and raise turnips to trade for their first pairs of real shoes (Figure 2.16). Visually, the book is memorable for its blue-and-brown-ink lithographs, which eschew even black-ink type. Later, Credle departed from human protagonists and U.S. subjects altogether in *Pepe and the Parrot* (1937). In this international-animal-in-trouble story, Mexican dog Pepe is frustrated when his human guardians, Mama-cita and Papa-cito, bring home a parrot that teases him. Credle uses an American regionalist style, possibly influenced by Mexican painters such as Frida Kahlo, Diego Rivera, and José Clemente Orozco, who were active on the New York scene in her day. For *Pepe*'s printing, reminiscent of *Down, Down the Mountain*, she chose an unusual, fuchsia-and-teal palette on pale blue-green speckled paper to achieve a sun-blasted brightness. Even the printed text appears in a deep turquoise, so no black or primary hues intrude on the tart tertiary hues. The color scheme of *Pepe and the Parrot* catches the attention, and its hardworking people give a vague account of class, yet its dog story primarily shows off a quaint Mexican locale (Figure 2.17).

As these examples from Credle illustrate, the pictorial texts of modernity register and reinforce an ongoing crisis of representation that can be attributed

FIGURE 2.16. The subsistence and financial concerns of the 1930s are implicit in Ellis Credle's upbeat Appalachian story *Down, Down the Mountain* (1934).

to factors including industrialization, modernization, decolonization, and anxiety around miscegenation and ethnoracial mixing. Like the machine-conscious art and class-sensitive literature of their era, texts on diversity attest to an alternately distressing and exhilarating state of flux in cultural production and society. They reflect a nation's anxiety as tradition gives way to modernity. In many ways, popular picture books organize a cultural imperialist point of view, naturalize middle-class whiteness, and compartmentalize populations by picturing Indians in India, Africans in Africa, nonwhites as the underclass, and so on. Some blatantly ignore the existence of working-class and nonwhite children, caricature spoken vernaculars and appearances, or idealize rustic life. In this way, children's texts erase matters of difficulty or make issues conditionally visible.

Whether celebratory, ambivalent, or condemnatory of diverse populations, modern picture books and illustrated texts make cultural discrimination a matter to which children must attend. These texts take for granted a young child's ability to categorize people by external traits. Miscegenation and desegregation may be avoided as overt topics for children's texts, but they remain detectable

PEPE AND THE PARROT

Once upon a time, in the great warm mountain land of Mexico, there was a little dog named Pepe. He had a round nose and a long stringy tail and two great big ears that stood straight out from his head.

FIGURE 2.17. Printed in an eye-straining, humid pink and teal palette, Ellis Credle's *Pepe and the Parrot* (1937) depicts Mexico in terms of a rivalry between pets.

in texts' very resistance to diversity. Otherwise exceptional texts such as Lorraine and Jerrold Beim's picture book *Two Is a Team* (1945, illustrated by Ernest Crichlow)—unusual for its portrayal of an African American boy and a white boy as partners who want to start a grocery-delivering business—do not verbally acknowledge their racial dimension. *Two Is a Team* shows the boys trading ideas and occasionally disagreeing before coming to a fair resolution, yet, for all the affirmative work, the cover subtly foregrounds its white boy, who appears to stand in front of his friend.

Thus, picture books, illustrated texts, and other highly mediated modern media give qualified visibility to racial and ethnic types. Although nonwhite or culturally differentiated individuals are visible in the children's texts of the early twentieth century, they always are under discursive and visual restrictions. Narrative styles and visual cues divide "us," in the dominant category, from "them," in a subordinate group; there is a powerful observational quality and detachment in the illustrated books published from the 1920s through the early 1940s. Representational constraints operate in all texts, from fairy tale retellings to modern texts about places outside the United States. Of course,

there can be no guarantee that a children's text produces a particular sensibility or set of beliefs, whether moral or amoral, optimistic or pessimistic, open-
minded or bigoted, radical or conservative, or that the children of the twenties
through the forties were made any more or less open to diversity by the picture
books they encountered. A disciplinary text and its visual accompaniments do
not poison the minds of children any more than a prayer and a religious icon
guarantee that their holder will lead a moral life. Young readers need not take
an image's imperialist connotations to heart or believe that all children prefer
a Western lifestyle. Neither is it relevant whether writer-illustrators feel any
imperative toward political correctness or produce what they consider an all-
inclusive (or exclusive) work of art, because "every text is eternally written *here
and now*. . . . The birth of the reader must be at the cost of the death of the Author."[82] Yet even if the interpretation and psychological impact of a given book
are relative to the individual reader, dominant ideas circulating in the field of
cultural production are reinforced by texts, experiences, and corporate interests. The children's text stands as a powerful system of representation, one that
demarcates cultural difference and naturalizes ways of reading. The children's
text, like the child, is not an innocent but a dialogic mode that hails the avid
reader and makes that reader complicit in its representation of the world.

# Sentient Machines: Lonesome Locomotives and the Mechanized Modern Body

## "VICTIMS OF INDUSTRY":
### LOITERERS, LABORERS, AND CHILDREN

Children's texts of the twenties and thirties pursued a national myth of progress in a proletarian vein, fetishizing powerful machinery and human labor alike. During the twentieth century's early decades, people began witnessing huge machines with comparatively small drivers—not just locomotives and trolley cars but gigantic building equipment and wrecking balls that tore into wood and brick structures that had outlasted their usefulness. Human drivers' intentional movements were in turn translated into machinery's animal-like motion as cities went up and old buildings were torn down.[1] New modes of attention and perception were necessary in this altered environment, in which fairy tales of modernity expressed older generations' ambivalence toward speed and progress.

In a 1926 book review for Anne Carroll Moore's *New York Herald Tribune* column, "The Three Owls," Leonore St. John Power called New York City residents the "victims of industry" who "indulge all their senses in scenes that put commerce and industry into the high realms of imagination. They loiter, these newspaper readers, on hazardous boardwalks to watch a huge clamshell dredge swinging tons of earth and rock onto trucks with a precision that is fascinating."[2] Power described passersby who were engrossed by the sight of a skyscraper under construction, emphasizing the rickety boardwalks and the skill of the laborers. Certainly twenty-first-century spectators at construction sites can still relate to the fascination these 1920s gawkers experienced: white-collar workers set aside their daily newspapers and delay their lunch hours—symptoms of a society and labor organized by time—in order to watch a clamshell dredge in action. Today, construction equipment and tall buildings are a familiar sight, and 1920s urbanites were captivated by the lively scenes of industry around them. "New York gives its loitering citizens a magnificent opportunity to find rare characters among machines," Power observed. She described her firsthand experience of this phenomenon:

when a subway excavation started under the windows of the Children's Room of the Public Library [on 53d Street in Manhattan]. Blasts shook the building, dirt and smoke were a menace to pictures and furniture. Engineers came in, looked at the broken window panes, observed the shape of cracks in the walls, wrote in little books and went out. Being in charge of the room I felt aggrieved at the destruction and resented the progress that made subways essential. Then one day outside appeared a steam-shovel. It belched black smoke, its whistle shrieked, and its great iron arm swung almost into the window. After a few days the steam-shovel asserted its individuality. The children looked at it, named it "Jonathan," and knew its tempers and pleasantries. The man who sat in the little house attached to "Jonathan" looked in our windows and bade us "good morning." . . . "Mercy, there is 'Jonathan' heating up his works" was a less tempestuous view of clouds of black smoke than the less personal one of the nuisance of steam-shovels.[3]

Power indicated how machines—and, less so, the workers who operate them—fascinated not only children but adults. She implied that people of all ages not only watched the machines but identified with them. Library-going children gained an understanding of how machines empowered human beings, and they allied themselves with Jonathan, the steam shovel, which "asserted its individuality" over that of "the man who sat in the little house attached to" it. Jonathan's master, sitting in this little house, seemed to be doing nothing of importance, whereas the machine resembled a beast. Power resisted the children's enthusiasm and considered machines a "nuisance," but she finally indulged her audience (who could not concentrate on their library books) and went along with the symbols of progress. Although nervous about the cracks in the walls and the shaking building, the librarian felt relieved that the children found an alternative to an adult's "less personal" relationship with the noisy, dirty machine.

Power experienced firsthand the responses of adults and children to technological upheaval and the transformation of landscape. Through illustrated books, other mass media, the aggravation or excitement of adults around them, and their own spontaneous reactions, the children of 1926 were finding ways to interact with their everyday environments, in some cases establishing imaginary relationships with nonliving things, effectively treating machines as toys. Giving a steam shovel a person's name and dismissing its operator need not be condemned as damaging to the young psyche, yet the children's impulse to anthropomorphize the steam shovel suggests how modern identity and affect were shaped. As Marshall Berman contends, "[In futurist thinking, it] appears that some very important kinds of human feeling are dying, even as machines are coming to life."[4] Similarly, Donna Haraway describes a possible outcome of mechanical anthropomorphism when she writes, "Our machines are disturbingly lively, and we ourselves frighteningly inert."[5] Power does not say whether the steam shovel strikes her as uncanny, yet her mingled frustration and bemusement betray an anxiety around technological progress and children's futures.

With the arrival of an exciting distraction like Jonathan the steam shovel, the quaint, pre-automobile-era mind-set disappeared. The adult's past and knowledge lost their meaning in the noise and smoke of new construction, and elementary-school-age children acquired a new sensibility as they encountered technological and other creative innovations. Power's remarks raise the question of how young children, soon to be Depression-era teenagers and adults, made sense of the lumbering machines in their midst. Although Power and others affiliated with Anne Carroll Moore's "Three Owls" columns for the *New York Herald Tribune* touted old-fashioned fairy tales and folktales as a potential cure for what ailed modern America, the here-and-now was upon them; distractions meant they had to reinvent the preindustrial oral tradition they were working hard to sustain. Like Moore, who avidly detested comics and other modes of mass entertainment appropriated by the young, many aficionados of children's literature outwardly protested modernization while being unable to resist it.

Children's literature began to engage with the society of the spectacle. "The spectacle is not a collection of images; rather, it is a social relationship between people that is mediated by images,"[6] and modern picture books and illustrated texts provide imaginative, ideologically charged explanations of the spectacles of modern life. Jonathan Crary characterizes the spectacle as "the development of a technology of separation" among heretofore social individuals, and places it in parallel with "the production of docile subjects, or more specifically the reduction of the body as a political force. . . . Spectacle is not primarily concerned with a *looking at* images but rather with the construction of conditions that individuate, immobilize, and separate subjects, even within a world in which mobility and circulation are ubiquitous."[7] Crary says the spectacle is characterized by "the management of attention"; this can be seen in the way children's texts strive to manage readers' perceptions of construction, labor, and social hierarchies. Many picture books and illustrated texts of this time implicitly deny the technologies of separation, focusing closely on resources, tools, and industrial processes, and echoing Power's account of communal loitering to observe noisy work sites. Texts direct attention to how buildings are constructed and roads are paved, how steel mills and cotton mills work, how a transatlantic steamer operates while passengers lounge in their cabins, and how trains transport commuters or deliver goods from the factory to the store. They investigate common machines, mass production, and distribution of goods, yet, despite a superficial focus on civic-mindedness, separation goes into effect, regulating human conduct in the process of construction and in the built environment.[8]

Popular children's books of the time present workers as an integral component of a visceral here-and-now world that is driven by a combination of animal muscle, fossil fuel, cold metal, and money.[9] In this realm, skilled humans and practical machines work as intimate partners; the middle-class child's identity is constructed around automatons, urban scenarios, and industrial machines that transform the rural landscape and produce consumer goods. Many texts call for sympathy and a concern for social justice but seldom, if ever, propose alternatives to class hierarchies, mind-numbing assembly-line jobs, and industrial production and consumerism. Publishers of juvenile literature, responsive to what amazed children and their parents, fetishized machines in picture books such as C. B. Falls's *Modern ABC* (1923) and Elizabeth King's *Today's ABC Book* (1929).[10]

In *Today's ABC Book*, as in Falls's work, King provides an Aeroplane-to-Zeppelin listing of machines that children saw in their everyday environments (Figure 3.1). Her illustrations, framed in black-and-blue rectangles with rounded edges, include a Dredge in a river, a locomotive Engine, and a Steam Shovel—all in operation around the modern city and country. Also like Falls, King alludes to military defense with an iconic B (Battleship), N (Navy), and U (U-boat), but, unlike Falls, she provides short definitions for each pictured item, printed alternately in blue or red ink. In particular, she points out distribution methods between urban and rural spaces. F stands for Freight, and readers learn that "FREIGHT cars bring to the city spinach and string beans and potatoes and all the other good things that the farmer grows. They take to him things that he needs from the city." Farming methods reemerge around the letter *T*, for Tractor: "Farmers used to use horses to pull their ploughs across the fields but now many of them have tractors to do the work. TRACTORS have no wheels but move along like caterpillars. That is why they can go over the soft earth without sinking into it." King's analogy between the caterpillar and tractor, comparing the natural creature to the less familiar machine, suggests the relative newness

FIGURE 3.1. Like C. B. Falls, Elizabeth King pictured familiar machines of war and industry in her modern alphabet, *Today's ABC Book* (1929).

of the tractor (especially to the librarians, teachers, and parents of 1929). An attachment to nature, despite or because of these huge new machines, resonates in King's work. For instance, when people ride in the letter-R Roadster, "the top of the roadster can fold up . . . and on bright sunny days it can be tucked away so that you can see the sky and the tree tops." King alludes to the relatively recent pleasure of the Sunday drive for the modern family.

Publishers responded as much to adults' anxieties as to children's desires, and their texts implicitly recommended adapting to the latest technologies without forgetting old-fashioned ways. George E. Bock's *What Makes the Wheels Go Round* (1931) provides stylized diagrams of a dam and hydroelectric power plant, and a locomotive engine, in high-contrast black and white with hints of primary colors (Figure 3.2, Plate 14). Bock's loquacious and technical text describes the inner workings of machines, but the pièces de résistance are the oversize illustrations, fit for memorization by future engineers of America.

Other writers and publishers notably responded to industry through their marketing of informational textbooks like Harper and Brothers' City and Country series, launched in 1927, which included evocative frontispieces but few illustrations.[11] These tiny, informational textbooks promoted inquiry over complacency, as an advertisement indicates:

> Here at last are some books designed to answer the endless queries of children about the everyday things of everyday life. Where does our milk come from? How does the bread get wrapped up? What happens when we telephone to our next-door neighbor? How did people get around before they had railroad trains and subways? . . . The modern schools make trips to the dairies, the milk laboratories, the telephone exchange, the wharves, the printing plants and so on a part of the curriculum. . . . And these books fill in the background for these visits, and give the little readers a sense of the romance in subjects they are apt to take for granted.[12]

Addressing parents, teachers, and other book buyers, this ad indicates the "romance" in things potentially "taken for granted" by modern children and implies a modern fear of old ways being forgotten. Urban children were introduced to industry through such books and their civics curricula, which both demystified labor and indicated trade occupations to which children might aspire.

Jeanette Eaton styles *The Story of Transportation* as a didactic conversation between siblings Tom and Mary and their parents. After giving a prehistory of

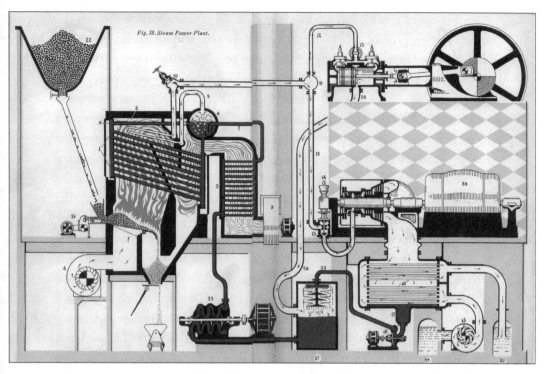

FIGURE 3.2. George E. Bock's *What Makes the Wheels Go Round* (1931) diagrams a steam power plant for future engineers.

American technology in accounts of Native American travel in canoes and on foot, Father laughingly reminds Tom and Mary "that the white men knew ever so many things the Indians didn't know. White men had known how to make wheels for ever so long before they got here to this country and they began to make wagons here right away" (8–9). He describes "a big giant which became such a wonderful friend to men," the "giant Steam" (14), which drove the original steam locomotives, here known as "The Brave Little Engines" (17). "Yes, everyone ought to remember with affection all these first brave little engines," says Father. "They were like pioneers. They pushed their way through new country where very few people lived and brought them in touch with big cities" (21).

Steam derives from the natural resources of water, wood or coal, and fire, and needs to be "tamed" like a wild animal. The engines themselves, man-made from metal and glass, have the human quality of "bravery" and are equated with "pioneers." Later, the children's parents introduce Steam's cousins, the "giant Electricity" (26–27) as well as "a new force in the world to help people get their wish to go faster. Those fairy godmothers [engineers] have been as busy as bees and they have discovered a new giant . . . [to] drive light conveyances swiftly through the water, over the ground, and in the air. You know what it is—Gasoline" (42–43). *The Story of Transportation*, then, focuses on people's "wish to go faster" while nostalgically reflecting on developments that make this wish come true. Its generic family lives in an urban apartment with easy access to buses and subways, familiarizing suburbanites with the wonders of public transit. Eaton concludes by suggesting that, through their parents' know-how, Tom and Mary have gained hindsight, an attention to progress, and a modern subjectivity: "When they rode on the street car they watched the motorman turning the electric current on and off and they thought of the old days when the horse cars rattled along the streets. When they took the subway under the river they remembered the story of how that tunnel was built. And every time they went with Mother on the railroad to another town they thought of the giant Steam and tried to imagine what it was like before he came—what it was like when the Indians had to walk along the trails all day long or paddle canoes up the winding river" (50–51). *The Story of Transportation* encourages historical consciousness while celebrating ingenuity and then-cutting-edge technologies. Not incidentally, it also lends animal qualities to fuel and human traits to inanimate devices.

The Harper series, presented in small hardcover volumes, was published at the same time as flashier pictorial books like Berta and Elmer Hader's oversize, jewel-toned *The Picture Book of Travel: The Story of Transportation* (1928) (Figure 3.3). In their narrative, the Haders represent exotic modes of transportation outside the United States; the book cover is adorned with a silhouette of a man pushing a rickshaw. In an image printed in blue and black on white, showing white-robed people with shadowed faces and a camel caravan "in an Oriental city," the Haders allude to the present but suffuse it with mystery and legends of the past. They foreground the animals and downplay the human residents of the nameless city as they speculate on the caravan's members: "Perhaps some of them are old camels who in the World War carried a brave master to battle. As the long line streams by and swings out on a desert trail, all the magic of the Arabian Nights is in the picture. Time has not brought enough railroads to this far, strange part of the world to displace the caravan. So we look at 'carrying' being done just as it was several thousand years ago."[13]

Festive four-color prints picture "two rajahs" aboard an elephant and "princes of Siam" riding in a howdah ("In Siam, the white elephant is sacred") (30–31). Most of the people in the image are seen in silhouette or, like the Indian women carrying jars of water on their heads, are turned away from the audience. One child in the Indian image faces front, establishing a young person as reference point for the reader. The Haders demonstrate a preference for preindustrial modes of transportation in exotic locales, amplified by an imagined scene, late in the book, of muscular men dragging a log using wheels made of wood. The Haders' text asks the reader to compare the sounds of a contemporary city to this time, long ago: "How many sounds can you remember hearing on a city street? Horns barking, bells clanking, engines purring, brakes grinding, the policeman's whistle, the roar of the elevated train, the rattle of a trolley car—how many more? Did you ever hear the wheels?" (38). An American audience, familiar with trolleys, elevated rail lines, and other street traffic, is asked to imagine prehistory, associated with imagery depicting foreign lands (Plate 15).

Contemporaries of the Haders described American transport and industry. William Clayton Pryor (later with his wife, Helen Sloman Pryor), created the Pryor Photographic Picture-Books for Harcourt, Brace and Company. Each of these squarish books featured explanatory text on the left-hand side, paired with full-bleed black-and-white photographs on the facing page, telling stories in a kind of visual sequence that very much depends upon the written narrative. In *The Train Book* (1933), *The Fire Engine Book* (1934), *The Steel Book* (1935), and *The Cotton Book* (1936), a family goes on field trips to learn about technology and production. Like Eaton's *Story of Transportation*, the Pryor Photographic Picture-Books feature a sister and brother learning about technology from their parents (mostly their father).

The most successful endeavor, one that paralleled the Pryor books, was Maud and Miska Petersham's 1933–39 Story Book series for the John C. Winston Company. In each book, the Petershams chart the evolution of machines and the transformation of raw materials such as gold and oil while asserting that humans control engines and resources, not the other way around: "Machines, like huge giants, do the work. But men make the machines, and men do the thinking. Men have been thinking and experimenting with iron and steel ever since early man discovered iron."[14] The Petershams' color-printed histories of technology magnify the human, as opposed to machine, role in invention, indicating that good things can come of the cooperative work between laborer and heavy equipment. In *The Story Book of Transportation* (1933), the Petershams give a chronological account of the development of conveyances like the steam engine, the railway train, and the passenger automobile. Lithographs compare a "1908 Wright Flying Machine," backlit by a triumphant sunrise and flying over a rather unsafe expanse of water, to "Today," represented by a more expansive picture of a dirigible drifting above a city of skyscrapers and accompanied by a fleet of fighter planes. Individual picture books such as *The Story*

FIGURE 3.3. Berta and Elmer Hader examine mobility and acceleration in *The Picture Book of Travel* (1928).

*Book of Wheat* and *The Story Book of Corn* were bound in multichapter volumes to become *The Story Book of Foods from the Field: Wheat, Corn, Rice, Sugar* (1936) or *The Story Book of Wheels, Trains, Ships, Aircraft* (1935). Alice Payne Hackett notes that "twenty titles in the *Petersham Story Books* series have sold 1,728,000," signaling these texts' popularity as sources of information about the lived and industrializing world from the Depression era through the mid-1940s, when these books were still available in reprint editions.[15]

From the Haders' bold prints of an exotic East, to the Petershams' more delicate, meticulously shaded color lithographs of changes in North American transport, to Pryor's photographs of steelworking and the transformation of cotton, nonfiction writers worked to describe modern industry in the young reader's modern context. Exciting machines used in mass transit and construction, especially ships and trains, received ample coverage for a child audience, and natural and man-made resources in clothing and familiar appliances—cotton, silk, wool, corn, wheat, steel, rubber—received detailed notice as well. The focus on taken-for-granted tools, raw materials, and assembly-line necessities indicates an expectation that children would be entertained and informed by edifying stories of production. In this sense, the nonfiction picture books and illustrated text series recall the here-and-now stories of Lucy Sprague Mitchell and the Bank Street School. Through these books, children living near steel mills, for instance, could receive an account of what went on in these mysterious factories; children putting on their sweaters could get a sense of where wool came from. The repetitive attention to the history of transportation and to food ingredients, however, also implies an anxiety among adult cultural producers that modern children would not feel curious about the alienated origins of their groceries and clothes. Children were to be armed with practical understandings of the modern world so that they might become active engineers of the future, as opposed to passive victims of industry.

## MOTOR SKILLS: REEVALUATING TECHNOLOGY
## AND THE WORKER

In 1929, writer Hildegarde Hoyt Swift and illustrator Lynd Ward published *Little Blacknose: The Story of a Pioneer*, a chapter book that takes seriously the analogy between "the brave little engines" and nineteenth-century homesteaders. Little Blacknose is the first locomotive, otherwise known as the DeWitt Clinton engine, sand-cast from molten iron:

He was new, brand spick and span new, just freshly dressed in a shining coat of black, and he had a long black nose that stuck straight up
in front of him, like an upside-down elephant's trunk. He didn't mind
the heat, for he had been born from it—born from the furnaces, shaped
on the anvils, put together by the labor of men. To be sure, when they
had hammered the rivets into his side, he had shrieked with pain, but
he was finished now—that was all over. He was finished and ready.
Ready for what? Who was he? What was he? Where was he going?
Oh, did he wish he could find out![16]

Little Blacknose feels pain, like a living creature ("he weighed as much as forty
fat men or one big elephant," [12–13]), and he is something of a Frankenstein
creation; Swift emphasizes designer David Mathew, who first envisions the
engine, as well as a foundry worker named Joe who forges the engine in his
workshop. Using a third-person omniscient voice that implies the DeWitt
Clinton engine's own internal viewpoint, Swift describes Blacknose's "foundry
birthplace" (10) in 1831 New York City, where children play ball in the streets:
"No monster cars came rushing by to make it dangerous. No skyscrapers shut
out the light. No roar of traffic hurt the ears" (11). Her descriptions of looming
skyscrapers and noisy traffic betray ambivalence toward modernity, yet readers
are meant to adore Blacknose, a harbinger of modernity who will be pushed
aside as new machines take his place. Curiously, Ward's accompanying images
do not lend much personality to Blacknose, although one image appears to
show Blacknose squeezing his "eyes" shut (102). Prior to Watty Piper's *The
Little Engine That Could* (1930)—initially illustrated by Lois Lenski but more
famously illustrated by George and Doris Haumann, whose images survive in
most reprints today—machines seldom had faces; one close-up seems to show
Blacknose's closed eyes, but these are as much part of the symmetrical design
as they are anthropomorphic details. Most of the time, Ward creates grainy
images of a sooty-black engine with background tints of green, blue, or rust-
orange. His symmetrical framings acknowledge Art Deco composition and
recall Georgia O'Keeffe's stark vertical compositions of New York skyscrapers
by night, painted in the late 1920s.

Little Blacknose, destined for a debut in Albany, is first loaded onto a Hudson River steamboat. He resents having to ride ("It's an insult. . . . Shall I never
go by myself, shall I never be really free?" [12]) but feels better when the boat
greets him as its fellow "Brother of the Steam! I am proud to be carrying you

up the Hudson. I hear my firemen talking about you. . . . They say you will change the land as I have changed the water" (14–15). Human gossip precedes Blacknose's arrival, but Blacknose cannot reply to his brother boat, because "he [Blacknose] had been built without any bell or whistle, and as his steam wasn't up, he couldn't speak at all" (15). This involuntary silencing troubles him still more when he is insulted by a roan horse, which is losing part of its job to him ("'For years, rain or shine, we've pulled the coaches over this rail-road,' the old horse raved" [25]). Blacknose hears the horse's venomous rant and thinks, "WHEN MY STEAM IS UP I'll put the fear of death into you back-woods horses!" (24–26). Here the horse mouths the angry sentiments of coach drivers as opposed to four-legged animals, removing the human element and shifting the focus to Blacknose's reply. The horse represents the hopeless "back-woods" point of view, and the more modern Blacknose reacts with irritation; Ward pictures their confrontation in the frontispiece, in which the bony horse lifts its front hoof and cries, "You horrid brute!" Ward's image, which cultivates a measure of the reader's sympathy for the horse, somewhat contradicts Swift's narrative, which takes the engine's point of view. The reader of 1929 could view Blacknose simultaneously as an agent for change, whose opinion counts for more than the horse's, and as an outmoded nineteenth-century artifact, thus worthy of nostalgia.

When Blacknose speaks, it is in onomatopoeic words or with hissing *s*'s, and he takes pleasure in frightening the domestic animals of Albany; a sign of his familiarity comes when cows no longer recoil at his puffing. Notably, horses continue to pull the coaches in bad weather while Blacknose stays in a dry shed, but the roan horse levels an ominous warning: "Some day you'll know how it feels to work like a horse. There's another creature coming to take your place. . . . We'll get even with you yet!" (62) Elsewhere, the horse is depicted drenched with rain or shaking with exhaustion from heavy labor on the rail line, evidence of the hardship endured by flesh-and-blood beasts of burden (90), but its unpleasant temper does not endear it to readers. Blacknose is a more sympathetic and more durable figure. Swift's focus on the engine directs attention away from the plight of abused animals, which had been the sentimental trump card of Anna Sewell's *Black Beauty* (1877), Hugh Lofting's Doctor Dolittle series (started in 1920), and other novels protesting animals' mistreatment.

In Swift's narrative, Blacknose admires human beings, and his affection manifests itself in problematic statements. He likes the foundry worker, Joe, who gets "all black and grimy" (5), and he senses an affinity with a conductor:

A tall black man strode through the crowd, holding what looked like long strips of newspaper.

"This man is the right color," thought Blacknose. "I wonder if he was born in a foundry. I wonder why all men can't be that nicer shade, like mine." (45)

Like the foundry worker, the conductor is naturalized to the railroad and well-oiled machinery by the color of his skin. In these instances, Blacknose's affection for the men carries a troubling subtext, merging the dirt-covered worker with the machines he forges and implying that the African American conductor (ancestor to the Pullman porters) is a mechanical man. Blacknose speaks of them as coworkers, dehumanizing them in the process.

Blacknose compares passengers' appearances and feelings to his own, too, noting a woman's "black eyes . . . like two nice, delicious, gleaming pieces of coal" and wondering, when a queasy girl grips her midsection after a bumpy locomotive ride, "Why does she hold her boiler? . . . She looks as if she felt as I do when I swallow too many chunks of coal at once! . . . Oh, dear, I must have shaken them up too hard!" (75) Ward's image shows the girl and her mother hanging their heads, emotional stand-ins for the regretful engine. Blacknose, meanwhile, wishes he could provide people with smoother transportation, naively failing to predict that new inventions will do just that.

Blacknose resists the notion that he can be displaced, but he sees men pointing to him and overhears them discussing "a great monster, twice the size of this one!" (66), which has just arrived from Liverpool. "It was so big, so black, so terrible, that poor little Blacknose was horribly frightened. His smoke stuck in his smoke-stack, and he choked in misery and fear. . . . The people had eyes only for the new engine, but the old red horse was watching him—watching him—and laughing!" (68–69) Eventually, Blacknose and the English locomotive, John Bull, become friends ("How he had hated and feared him at first! How he loved him now!" [105]). Soon both are at risk of ending up on the scrap pile. Blacknose sputters and hisses, "'I fffffear I shshshall be ssssscrapped sssssoon.' / He had heard that was what happened to worn-out engines. They were just broken up, thrown away, sold for old iron. Would it happen to him?" (109).

With the passing of decades, Blacknose is packed away, but in the closing chapters Swift redeems the engine. She describes the uncannily dreaming machine, awaiting its release into the modern world: "For fifty years little Black-nose dreamed and rested, dreamed and rested in his station-corner. A thick gray coat of dust settled on his proud black boiler, and telltale streaks of rust grew in his side." (115) Although marked with signs of mechanical aging and entropy, he is not scrapped or forgotten. Instead, he is returned to the foundry, "re-built and re-shined" (121) for the 1893 World's Fair in Chicago, where the "poor car-sick little girl," now a grandmother, brings her granddaughter to see him (125): "So he was forgiven, after all these years! The poor car-sick little girl with the black eyes, she had forgiven him and said he was 'a darling' too! Little Blacknose felt very warm and happy" (127).

After another long and dusty interlude, Blacknose is featured at "the hundred-year birthday party of the New York Central Railroad" in Albany, then transported to the Grand Central Terminal for display in the ultimate modern hub of railway travel. When a young whippersnapper mocks Blacknose as a specimen of outmoded technology, an older man snaps, "A pioneer, that's what he is—a pioneer! And incidentally, he made your father's money, boy, and don't forget it!" (148). The older man points out Blacknose's onetime economic position and, more important, implies that the capitalist marketplace indeed has an appreciation for old products that have lost their use-value. Moreover, the grown humans—the grandmother, the old man at Grand Central Station—might be viewed as animate antiques in their own right, transmitting their collective memory of transportation history to a younger, faster-moving generation.[17]

Similarly, Dorothy Walter Baruch's *Big Fellow: The Story of a Road-Making Shovel* (1929, with realistic black-and-white pictures of the shovel by Jay Van Everen) and its sequel, *Big Fellow at Work* (1930, illustrated by the Haders), lend human qualities to a gas-powered shovel and even to the dirt and rocks it pulverizes. The first novel, *Big Fellow*, opens with a wish to inform children and mothers about the astonishing animated objects in the everyday environment. Baruch dedicates the book: "to those children who stand entranced in front of the huge monsters of construction which inhabit this modern world on all sides—to those children who stop to gaze in wonder at the whirling of a concrete mixer or the digging of an excavating shovel—to those children who, seeing such things, propound countless questions—and more especially to their mothers—this book is sympathetically dedicated."[18] If nonliving machines are "monsters" that "inhabit" a construction site, Baruch's narrative bears out this metaphor. She makes fathers conspicuous by their absence and implies that mothers do the work of child rearing but may be unable to answer their daughters' and sons' questions about the active machines that do the work in the public sphere. Her account, in which a child gets a behind-the-scenes glimpse of working life, recalls Power's observation of urban loiterers who stop to watch construction.[19]

*Big Fellow* introduces a boy named Ned, who customarily plays and rides his bicycle along a dirt road: "No—no streets at all. Imagine! No smooth, paved streets!" (1–2) The book focuses on the strangeness of a child's riding a bicycle on anything other than a concrete path, although a dirt road would not be that unusual for adult readers of 1929. As Ned rides his bicycle across the uneven ground, the words "bumpety bump stop / bumpety bump stop" trace sharp-pointed, up-and-over triangles on the page. Baruch's onomatopoeia and concrete (or dirt-road, as it were) prose-poetry convey the dreariness of Ned's situation while alluding to the principles of Lucy Sprague Mitchell's 1921 *Here and Now Story Book*; when readers speak the "bumpety bump stop" aloud, they simulate the lurching bicycle's sound and movement. There must be a better way to ride, and poor Ned develops a great interest in the cement mixers, road-grading machines, and steamrollers making ready to pave his oppressive dirt roadway.[20] He adores seeing the road-building equipment in action, and one day he pedals to a factory where all the machines are stored: "And here something strange happened: All of a sudden, Ned's bike turned into the gate—quite of its own accord, it seemed" (28). Ned's bicycle has a mind of its own in this enchanting modern setting, and Ned happily follows it.

At the factory parking lot, Ned talks to the machines as though they were sentient beings:

> "You surely are fine fellows," he said. "You surely have strong tractor bases, haven't you, to move you steadily over even the roughest, bumpiest kind of ground? . . . And powerful dippers with shiny, sharp new teeth to bite, bite, bite into the earth.
>
> "My, but you all look strong. . . ."
>
> Suddenly he stood quite still. Absolutely still! His eyes grew bigger and the joyous smile left his face. He stared sadly at a great, new gasoline engine shovel that stood in the corner of the yard, a small distance apart from the others. His voice was full of pity as he exclaimed: "Why you poor, poor thing you! . . . I wonder why they neglected you, Big Fellow. I wonder why they left you ***without*** your BOOM and DIPPER." (32–33; emphasis in original)

Ned's admiring words and simpering inquiries mimic a farmer's affectionate words to domestic animals or a teacher's praise for a group of very young, well-behaved children. But when Ned sees the gasoline-powered shovel without its most potent working parts, he abruptly stops smiling and is overcome by "pity."

In distress over the emasculated machine, Ned calls out to the laborers on the work site, who reassure him that they are casting a new iron dipper for Big Fellow. He watches in elation as they pour the molten iron.

On his next visit to the factory, Ned finds that Big Fellow has been rebuilt by the workingmen. He is further delighted when a foreman, Bill, invites him to "just lean back in your chair, young man, and make yourself as comfortable as can be" (64). Bill tells a story about mining iron-rich rock, which can be used to make machine parts. The foreman, whose name and rank distinguish him from the undifferentiated machine operators working for him, anthropomorphizes not only the gasoline shovel but the red rock that it digs. He describes how an autonomous machine conquers the natural world:

> Red Rock was frightened, terribly frightened. It had been used to nestling peacefully down in the slopes of Red Mountain, and now, all of a sudden, it was scattered in great heaps. . . . Red Rock trembled when the shovel's iron teeth sank in, biting burra, burra, burrrrr!
>
> . . . Into a dump truck tumbled Red Rock, still trembling. . . . It wasn't used to being torn from Red Mountain.
>
> "Oh!" it moaned. "Oh," it groaned. "What is happening? . . ."
>
> "Lie still and stop your nonsense," cautioned the engine of the dump truck, while its starter went "ggerrr." (66–71)

In this imagined conversation between nature and machinery, the rock expresses horror as the engine chews it mercilessly. Ultimately this rape of the land is justified by the disturbing text, however: the quivering rock, although it is terrified by "the hugest, highest, most enormous furnaces" (83), is depicted as enjoying its violent transformation. When it is poured out again for use in making new tools, the rock exclaims, "Look at me! How I shine and shimmer! How I glisten and gleam! I am no longer shabby Red Rock, I am gleaming, molten Iron Ore" (85–86).

Baruch's *Big Fellow* presents incursions on the natural environment as both brutal and necessary. The primary actors in the drama include dynamic, even sadistic machines (not men) that know what is best for the world around them and do not hesitate to "bite" deeply into it, ignoring its fear and pain. Ned, who listens attentively to the foreman's story, is in tacit agreement with whatever Big Fellow might do to the landscape, and readers, too, see the value attached to the industrial process of changing Red Rock to Iron Ore. It is Ned's home landscape that Big Fellow excavates, and the child is depicted as excited by industrial change. Of course, even though Ned loves watching the workers and wants to ride on the steam shovel, he might not aspire to being a construction worker or a foreman like Bill. The narrative styles him as one who benefits from having a newly paved road, which enables him to better enjoy leisure pursuits like riding his bike or, someday, driving his car. In 1930, a year after *Big Fellow*'s publication, radical writer Mike Gold wrote that "we must teach proletarian children that they are to be the collective masters of their world, and that the vast machinery of modern life is to be their plaything."[21] Here, that call to action extends to children who play at management, suggesting the ambiguity of the child's position vis-à-vis labor, as potential proletarian, as blue-collar foreman, or as offsite engineer or architect on equipment design or building projects.

*Big Fellow*'s veneration of the machine and the knowledgeable labor force is echoed in picture books by Henry Bolles Lent, who created a series for Macmillan on trades and transportation. Lent's publications (not counting later books he wrote on the auto industry, newsprint, and aviation) include *Diggers and Builders* (1931), which he illustrated in awkward silhouettes (Figure 3.4). Three more books, more capably illustrated in black and white by Earle Winslow, include *Clear Track Ahead!* (1932), about the railroad; *Full Steam Ahead! Six Days on an Ocean Liner* (1933); and *Wide Road Ahead! The Building of an Automobile* (1934) (Figure 3.5). Lent dedicates *Diggers and Builders* to children who, like *Big Fellow*'s Ned, observe the world around them and stand a chance of becoming laborers or even engineers themselves:

This book is for

_____

who, like Henry Jr. and David,
(inquisitive little scamps!)
*must* know *What, How* and *Why!*

Lent writes for a deeply curious young audience, and his narratives demystify the work site, detailing men's pride and sense of purpose in their jobs. *Diggers and Builders* describes the day-to-day activities of six men doing mutually supportive work: Tony, the Steam Shovel Man; Sam, the Cement Mixer; Dan, the Derrick Man; Joe, the Steel Worker; Pedro, the Road Builder; and Bill, the Truck Driver. Lent, whose books with Winslow look substantially more polished, illustrates this one in crude silhouettes that effectively suggest a half-dozen Everymen. His characters' common names also signify ethnicity— Tony and Pedro's names suggest Italian American and Latin American heritage,

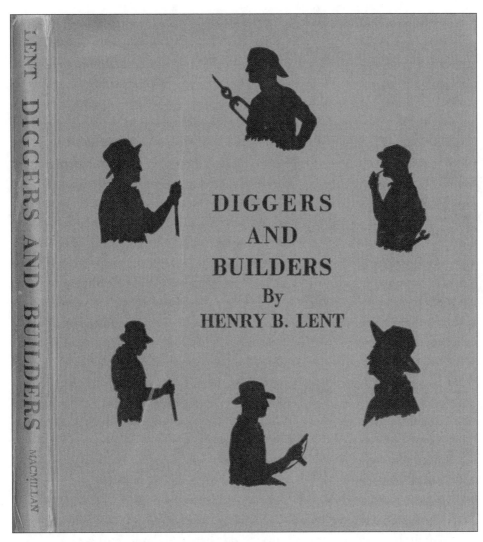

FIGURE 3.4. Henry B. Lent's *Diggers and Builders* (1931) represents its workers as silhouettes, suggesting anonymity as well as Everyman status for skilled tradesmen.

respectively—although in no case does he identify the characters beyond their first names and their shadowed bodies (each shown in distinctive headwear, from the steam shovel operator's slouching hat and neckerchief to the road-building foreman's broad-brimmed, eye-shading hat). Notably, five of the six men work as managers and complete difficult manual tasks too. Only steam shovel operator Tony speaks deferentially to his own boss, while planning to dig a large building's deep foundation. Afterward, all the other workers hurry to anticipate his needs:

click—click." Hear the little telegraph ticker? That is how the man in the signal tower away down the track tells Jack that the train has just left and that the track is clear again. Jack pulls the lever. Yes, it moves, and the green light flashes on. Bob opens the throttle, waves good-by to Jack, and the train starts on its journey again.

On some railroads the signal lights are automatic. It is very interesting to watch automatic signals work. When the track is clear the signal is green. Along comes a train. Overhead the signal changes to red, just like a traffic light, as the train passes under it. As soon as the train reaches the next section, or block, the first signal changes to yellow. This is a warning to trains that may come that there is still a train in the block ahead.

[ 43 ]

*Jack the signal-tower man.*

FIGURE 3.5. The informational *Clear Track Ahead!* (1932) clarifies the mysteries of the railroad for contemporary passengers.

Tony walks up to the foreman. "We're ready to move, boss," he says. "If your men will give us a hand, we'll soon be out of here." The men carry heavy timbers over to the steam shovel. They lay them down close together so that they make a plank road leading right up to the steep runway that the trucks have been using. Everything is ready. Tony climbs back into his steam shovel. Now then, everybody must get out of the way!

What a puffing and snorting as the steam shovel starts to climb up, up, out of the hole! Sometimes it slips back a little, but Tony opens the throttle, turns on more steam, and it keeps on moving. (10)

Through the generic Tony, Lent provides useful information about steam shovels, the building process, and the negotiations among the laborers. He enables spectators at a work site to predict what will happen as building progresses, and he valorizes the men's skilled efforts, each worker going about his tasks with confidence.

Lent excitably describes easy-to-visualize step-by-step processes, using

exclamation points to emphasize the workers' ingenuity. The next man on the
job mixes cement, then pours the foundation's floor and basement walls: "Walls
are much easier than floors to build. The carpenters merely board up the sides
of the excavation. This is called building a 'form.' The men move the chutes
so that the cement which pours from the mixer dumps right into the forms.
Then they leave it until it becomes hard. When the wooden forms are removed,
there is the cement wall!" (22). Next to arrive is the derrick man, who hoists
the building frame into place, and a "sure-footed" steelworker who works high
above the ground to hammer hot rivets into the girders (46). Lent describes
the men's strength and the noise of their job, then considers their labor in terms
of technological change by speculating, "Perhaps, some day soon, the clattering
rivet 'gun' will be a thing of the past. . . . For men who know all about new ways
of building say that it is possible to weld steel girders together at the joints, just
as you make a candle stick to its holder by melting some of the wax. . . . People
who are annoyed by the clatter of the rivet 'gun' will be glad, for welding makes
no noise" (46). The text acknowledges obsolete techniques, updated tools, and
the city's expansion: "Out beyond the apartment building, at the edge of the
city, Pedro and his crew of road builders are tearing up a long stretch of old
road so they can build a smooth wide highway for us to drive on." The road-
building team's compressed-air drill lets them do what "five or six men would
ordinarily do with only a pick, a hand drill, and a sledge hammer" (53), and they
apply layers of sand, gravel, and tar to create a modern road of asphalt rather
than old-fashioned concrete. The final man described is the truck driver, who
hauls materials and makes deliveries for the other five workers. Lent's prose is
hackneyed at best, yet the public responded favorably to this basic information.
After its June 1931 publication and a December reprinting, *Diggers and Builders*
was reissued annually from 1933 through 1941. Like *The Story of Transportation*
and books in the Harper City and Country series, *Diggers and Builders* urges
readers to notice and appreciate the modern city's men and machines. The informed reader becomes aware of a work crew's practical knowledge and learns
that older building techniques cede to contemporary approaches using more
convenient, quieter tools.

   Children are not yet cultural producers, so they initially take up a marginal
position in regard to modern technology. Because they belong to the nursery
and the domestic realm, they are affiliated with a private, not public, space of
maternal comfort. But with access to allowance money, leisure time, and the
sights of residences and businesses being built, American children are poised to
become consumers, intimately involved in the exchange of marketable goods and

the inevitable transformation of landscape and living space brought about by this circulation of commodities. Texts such as *Big Fellow* and *Diggers and Builders* celebrated technology and claimed to give 1930s children insider knowledge of the industrial world and the modern wonders they encountered every day.

American picture books and illustrated texts respond to cultural uncertainty with the fairy tale of modernity, which represents diverse attitudes toward childhood and includes everything from historical fiction, like *Little Blacknose*, to documentary-style, global-scale explanations, like *The Picture Book of Transportation*. Road-building equipment can be pictured in service to human beings, as in the Petersham Story Book series, or deemed lifelike and monstrous, as in the novel *Big Fellow*. Tales of dynamic machines empower the commodity and alienate the sentient human amid the spectacle of modern life; they tend to demystify mass production to show humans and machines working as intimate partners, or to introduce uncanny machines operating solo but doing beneficial deeds. These texts counsel readers by giving a pragmatic view of machines as operated by skilled workers. Tales of the machines implicitly recommend changing with the times and adapting to the latest technologies, and are as much about adult creators' anxieties for the future as about children's actual environments.

## HAUNTED MACHINES: MECHANICAL ORGANISMS
### IN THE POSTINDUSTRIAL WORLD

Didactic texts highlight humans' role in technological invention. They also establish humans' debt to, and fragility in comparison to, the volatile powers that feed mechanical devices—the "giant Steam," "giant Electricity," and "giant Gasoline" of Eaton's 1927 *Story of Transportation*. As domesticated animals became obsolete (for work, though not for food), machines began to be treated as independent-thinking entities in texts for young readers.[22] Joseph Schwarcz has recognized a "benign image of dehumanization" common to twentieth-century children's "stories about man-made objects that are represented as 'naturally' active, autonomous in their actions, co-existing with the child on a basis of equality and even, on occasion, being superior to him."[23] Although Schwarcz does not historicize or contextualize machine stories, pulling examples from various decades and social contexts, he calls it "only natural that gadgets and machines should loom prominently in children's books in an era and a society that is, in fact, based on technological development." Yet he aptly cautions, "The machine . . . aids to prepare children for . . . the functional cooperative anonymity

So the Angel Gabriel Flew very fast, and he came to Earth, and he took some of the milk that was all fixed for the Queen to take her bath in.

And the Angel Gabriel went to the house of the little girl, and he built up the fire, and he warmed the good milk, and he prepared some cereal for her, and when she had eaten he sang her to sleep.

PLATES 1 AND 2. Lauren Ford's *The Little Book about God* (1934), a digest version of the Old and New Testaments, is painted in the style of an illuminated manuscript. The book concludes with a present-day visit from the Angel Gabriel to a child in need, suggesting the desperate poverty of the Depression in America.

And he carried the little girl to the place that her mummy and daddy had fled to because of the war. And he gave her to her mummy.

And the Angel Gabriel came back to God, and he said: "Surely we can show these poor people how to behave to each other, they are very nice when they are little."

Then God said: "If My first people had not disobeyed Me about that fruit there would be no lazy and no stupid people."

PLATES 3 AND 4. C. B. Falls's
first A-to-Z compendium,
the *ABC Book* of 1923, mimes
a turn-of-the-century block-
print style and features elegant
compositions of animals.

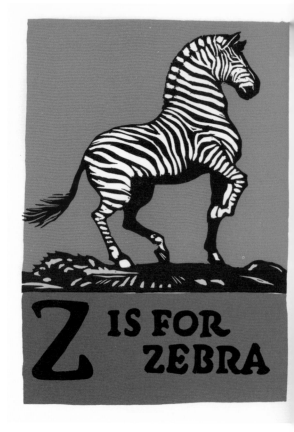

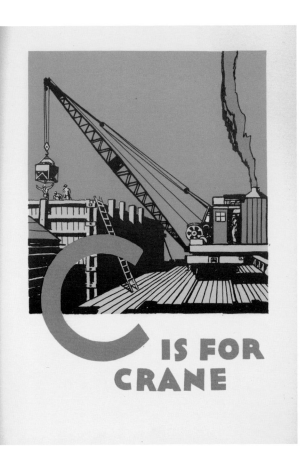

PLATES 5 AND 6. C. B. Falls eliminates borders, tilts letter forms, and pictures industrial machinery in *The Modern ABC Book* (1930).

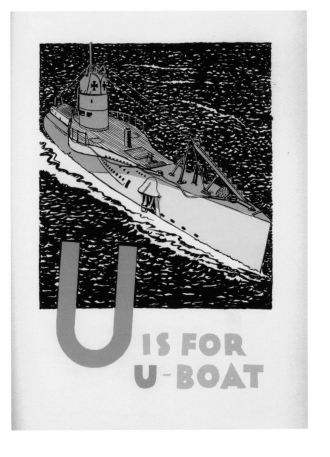

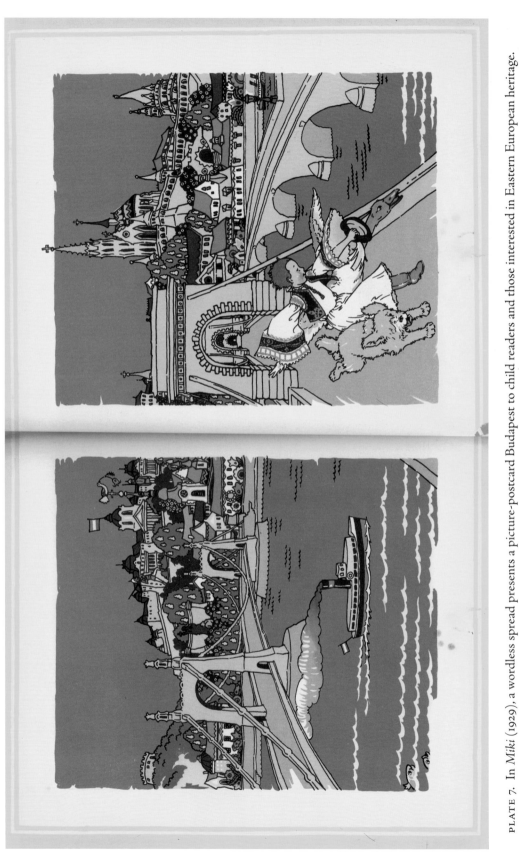

PLATE 7. In *Miki* (1929), a wordless spread presents a picture-postcard Budapest to child readers and those interested in Eastern European heritage.

PLATES 8 AND 9. Walter Cole
unapologetically goes from
"A is for Arab" to "Z is for Zulu"
in *The ABC Book of People*
(1932), an anachronistic listing
of ethnicities and nations.

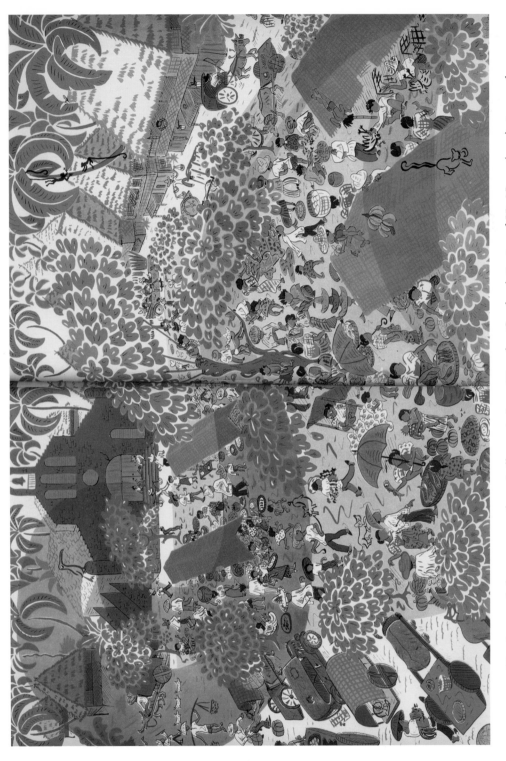

PLATE 10. Simultaneously homespun and tropically exotic, Lucy Herndon Crockett's *Lucio and His Nuong* (1939) gives readers a wordless, bird's-eye view of a marketplace in the Philippines.

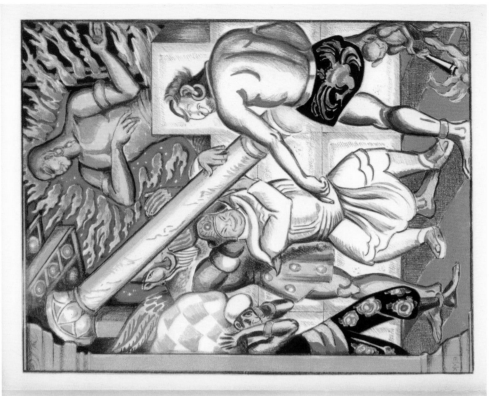

PLATE II. A fantasia of Islamic designs, a Moorish genie, and a South Asian carnival of colors suggest global but unspecific inspirations behind Elizabeth MacKinstry's 1935 version of "Aladdin."

THIS IS
BORA BORA

PLATE 12. Armstrong Sperry, who left a career in advertising and traveled in the South Seas, drafts a pristine Bora Bora lagoon and village as his introduction to *One Day with Manu* (1933).

JAMBI TAKES HIS SHOWER-BAT[H]

PLATE 13. The child hero of Armstrong Sperry's *One Day with Jambi in Sumatra* (1934) has wild animals as playmates and protectors.

PLATE 14. George Bock reveals the aesthetic and practical aspects of modernity in this streamlined exterior image and exploded view of a locomotive, from *What Makes the Wheels Go Round* (1931).

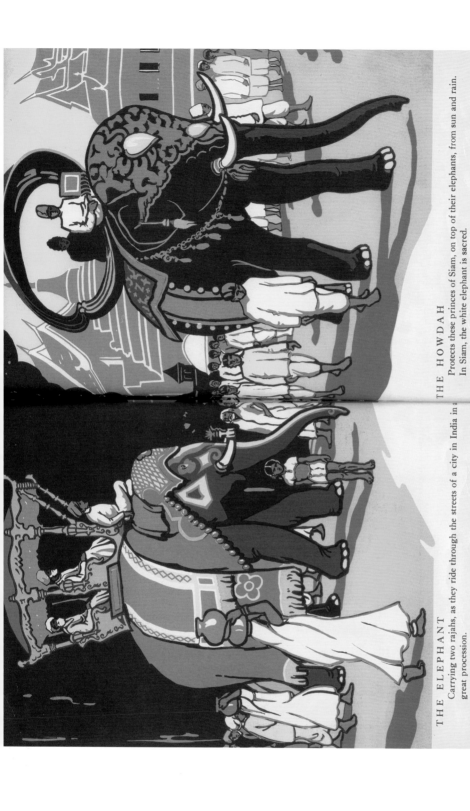

THE ELEPHANT

Carrying two rajahs, as they ride through the streets of a city in India in a great procession.

THE HOWDAH

Protects these princes of Siam, on top of their elephants, from sun and rain. In Siam, the white elephant is sacred.

PLATE 15. Berta and Elmer Hader's *The Picture Book of Travel* (1928) focuses on ethnographic curiosities and impractical modes of transit in Siam and India. A pictured child faces the reader, whereas adults do not meet the observer's gaze.

PLATE 16. Panama residents flee as a Panama Canal towing locomotive breaks free of its tracks, leaves militarized U.S. territory, and explores the city and jungle in Enid Johnson's *Runaway Balboa* (1938), illustrated by Anne Merriman Peck.

required by industrial society."[24] It is this metaphorical treatment of alienated labor that most closely pertains to the fairy tale of modernity and the sentient machine of the 1920s–1940s American picture book.

Before the turn of the century, the human operator could be seen on horseback, in a carriage, in a wagon, in an omnibus, or upon a then-faddish mode of transportation, the bicycle. People could go as fast as they could turn their bicycles' pedals or as quickly as their animals could pull them. Locomotive engineers had the regular experience of self-propelled motion, yet for railway passengers looking out a train window, the landscape was blurred and defamiliarized, and the velocity of travel was unprecedented. In the modern era of machines and warfare, Walter Benjamin writes, "A generation that had gone to school on horse-drawn streetcars now stood under the open sky in a landscape where nothing remained unchanged but the clouds and, beneath those clouds, in a force field of destructive torrents and explosions, the tiny, fragile human body."[25] Today, it is difficult, if not impossible, to imagine the state of shock Benjamin describes. Jaded jet travelers are unimpressed by quaint literary images and media impressions of earlier modes of travel. Yet, in 1896, Stephen Crane reported with amusement on "New York's bicycle speedway" along "the Western Boulevard which slants from the Columbus monument at the southwest corner of Central Park to the river."[26] Crane noted that outside this route, a bike-riding "wheelman" (or -woman) confronts a horse-driving

> truckman with a fiend's desire to see dead wheelmen. The situation affords deep excitement for everyone concerned.
>
> But when a truckman comes to the Boulevard the beautiful balance of the universe is apparent. The teamster sits mute, motionless, casting sidelong glances at the wheels which spin by him. He still contrives to exhibit a sort of sombre defiance, but he has no oath nor gesture nor wily scheme to drive a three-ton wagon over the prostrate body of some unhappy cyclist. On the Boulevard this roaring lion from down town is so subdued, so isolated that he brings a tear to the sympathetic eye.[27]

Crane's arch remarks illustrate the clash between representatives of the old and new centuries while still focusing on the human personalities that drive familiar technologies. In his account, the cyclist taunts the wagon driver, a bicycle policeman pursues fast-riding "scorchers," and "the girl in bloomers . . . steers her steel steed."[28] But a quarter century later, and despite ongoing protests against factory routines and the mechanization of life in general, actual beasts of burden had been marginalized and most horse-driving truckmen displaced to alternate lines of work. Old machines ended up in junkyards—or, in special cases, museums—becoming memories for the aging adults that had used them and objects of whimsical fascination for the children of the next generation. These machines became fodder for nostalgic picture-book creators, from Hildegarde Hoyt Swift and Watty Piper to Virginia Lee Burton and Hardie Gramatky. But with the actual machines went familiar ways of life for the people who once depended upon them.

Cinematic production of this time echoed this shift. Early animation effectively foregrounds the mechanical apparatus, optical trickery, and a disconcerting awareness of artifice. Where some early animators borrowed from the print media, photographing individual drawings on paper to create a sequence of cels, and retelling well-known tales, the producers of print media in turn used metaphors of animation to explain the interplay of words and pictures on the page. The moving images of a film and the sequential still images in a picture book stand in different relations to time, because under ordinary conditions a film cannot be halted, reversed, or hastened to a close in the way a book can. But as modes of production that developed in parallel, animation and the picture book share similar subject matter and a focus on sequentiality that became possible with changed technical standards in cinema technology and printing. Animation and picture books also share a fascination with the mechanized body and assembly-line automation that resonated with people's personal experiences. Workers in the trades were intimate with technical practices, and they could see this analogy between technology and the organic body played out in onscreen comedy and in the pages of picture books.

In 1928, Walt Disney and Ub Iwerks debuted the animated cartoon *Steamboat Willie*, an early appearance of Mickey and Minnie Mouse that provides an excellent example of how mechanical and living beings were represented in art in the twenties. Disney and Iwerks's treatment of the animate creatures and inanimate objects in the cartoon shows the prevalence of organism-and-machine hybrids.[29] The black-and-white sound film opens with a steamboat churning along a river, its waterwheel clacking and its smokestacks extending and collapsing, accordion style, to puff steam. Mickey is at the helm. When he pulls a cord, the film cuts to three cylindrical whistles atop the boat. The whistles resemble heads wearing hats; each one has a semicircular, frown-shaped cut, which opens wide like a mouth when it blows. When the shortest and stoutest of the three whistles fails to produce a sound, a taller whistle kicks it and startles it into making noise. All three seem alive. Later in the cartoon, a goat eats a ukulele and a pile of sheet music for "Turkey in the Straw." Mickey and Minnie capture the goat and turn its tail like a Victrola crank, and the tune blasts out of the goat's mouth. At this, Mickey grabs other animals and turns them into make-shift musical instruments too. By stretching and squeezing a duck's neck and by tapping a cow's xylophone-like teeth, he joins the tune issuing from the goat. Such blurring of boundaries between animal and object in animation presages Erwin Panofsky's 1934 remark that, in an animated or live-action film,

> no object in creation, whether it be a house, a piano, a tree or an alarm
> clock, lacks the faculties of organic, in fact anthropomorphic, move-
> ment, facial expression, and phonetic articulation. Incidentally, even
> in normal, "realistic" films the inanimate object, provided that it is
> dynamizable, can play the role of a leading character as do the ancient
> railroad engines in Buster Keaton's [The] General [1927]. . . . How the
> earlier Russian films [including Dziga Vertov's Man with a Movie
> Camera (1929)] exploited the possibility of heroizing all sorts of ma-
> chinery lives in everybody's memory.[30]

Thanks to advances in filmmaking techniques, sedentary commodities (appli-ances, furniture, toys) appear to participate in the natural world.[31] The same mobility infects the dolls (Hitty, the Little Wooden Doll, Clever Bill) and stuffed animals (Winnie-the-Pooh, the Velveteen Rabbit) of popular 1920s children's books. Modern children's literature reflects a changed human rela-tion to the newly dynamic commodity.

Children's literature thus borrowed the literary and artistic modes of rep-resenting change and progress. Machines could be conceived as enjoying work and fearing the junkyard. Human beings might be imagined as the delicate guts and minds of an engine, and the machine might be perceived as an extension of or substitution for flesh and bone. Human drivers' intentional movements were translated into machinery's animal-like motion as old buildings were torn down, cities went up, tunnels were dug, and bridges spanned rivers. In heart-warming stories, machines demonstrated lifelike characteristics, and children were given to wonder at their deeds. An urban spectator, who had trouble ob-serving the operators and innards of mechanical equipment, reasonably could conceive of the machine as an extension of the organic body, perhaps even capable of knowing physical or emotional pain in an animal way.

At this time, as Benjamin remarks, "Haptic experiences [like the pressure of a finger to snap a picture or dial a telephone] . . . were joined by optic ones, such as are supplied by the advertising pages of a newspaper or the traffic of a big city. Moving through this traffic involves the individual in a series of shocks and collisions. At dangerous intersections, nervous impulses flow through him in rapid succession, like the energy from a battery."[32] Benjamin depicts a person constantly on the alert, aware of the fragility of the human body and amazed at the dynamism of the urbanizing world. This sensational impression partly accounts for the long-standing popularity of the locomotive as a subject for children's literature, films, and other mass arts of the time.[33] The omnipresent train engine is cold and inorganic, relentlessly forward-moving, eyeless and senseless unless guided by its human crew, and quite hazardous to street traffic at railroad crossings. As Viviana Zelizer explains in *Pricing the Priceless Child*, which includes an extensive survey of child deaths and the cost of child insurance in that era, people of all ages were in mortal danger from trolley cars, railroads, and other moving equipment on city byways. Yet children's texts bring the engine (though not necessarily its operators) to a companionable level. Alice Jenkins, borrowing Michel Foucault's concept of the heterotopia as a space resembling but apart from the everyday, writes, "Long after it vanished from the landscapes of the real world as a functional means of transport, the steam train in particular continues to feature ·in works of fantasy aimed at children, operating by laws often unlike those of the realms through which it passes, and providing a space for the dramatization of spiritual and emotional adventure."[34] Train travel, Jenkins adds, allows the passenger to make a transit "through various 'zones,' either geographical areas, spiritual states, or different kinds of reality, but by enclosing the traveler in a bubble with its own internal logic and physical or magical laws, it shields the passenger from the logic and laws of the places it passes."[35] Metaphorically, the railway journey is analogous to an ahistorically defined childhood, yet the child body itself will metamorphose into something bigger, newer, and faster—the historically defined adult, worker, and soldier—in a matter of a few years.

To account for outsized, unwieldy new inventions that look unfamiliar and even hostile, texts about locomotives often feature a near-obsolete, weak machine that admits defeat to newer technologies but departs with a gesture of rebellion. In a sense, this version of technological change mimics the transition from childhood to adult maturity, and therefore serves as a prime fairy tale of modernity. Cornelia Meigs's *The Wonderful Locomotive* (1928), illustrated by Berta and Elmer Hader, presents this kind of equivalence. *The Wonderful Locomotive* is too text-heavy to be a true picture book, but its beautifully designed

*Peter was quite certain this must be New York.*

[ 35 ]

*"Go it, 44!" shouted Peter.*

[ 96 ]

FIGURE 3.6. A rusty train engine, old Number 44, revives and carries its wide-eyed boy engineer across modernizing America in Cornelia Meigs's *The Wonderful Locomotive* (1928), illustrated by Berta and Elmer Hader.

pages attest to publishers' willingness to experiment with hybrid literary forms at a time when "juveniles" were popular and selling well, especially to libraries and schools building their children's collections (Figure 3.6).

In *The Wonderful Locomotive*, a boy named Peter anthropomorphizes locomotives, whose "voices" he hears from his bed at night. When he listens for an approaching train whistle, "he heard, far away, a little sleepy voice answering, 'Toot, toot, toot.' / It was the small pusher engine that lived in the roundhouse and only came out when a train needed to be helped" (2–3). Peter visits the railroad switchyard by day, where he feels a particular fondness for a rusty, retired train cab, Number 44: "Here all the engines could be seen at once, puffing and spouting out steam, pushing cars here and there, swinging about on the big turntable, or standing quietly in their stalls at the roundhouse, resting from a long run and waiting to set out again for New York or Baltimore or Chicago. . . . Peter used to wonder whether poor old 44 did not feel unhappy as it stood among the weeds and looked with its dull headlight, over at the clouds of smoke, and heard the roaring and the grinding of the locomotives in the roundhouse" (4–5, 11).

*The Wonderful Locomotive* begins in a contemporary world but digresses into a fantasy in which Peter drives Number 44 cross-country. Meigs aligns the small child with the obsolete equipment of history. Emotionally charged stories of old or tiny trains, young tugboats or silly steamboats, and juvenile robots equate machines—either in their infancy or in some harmless, weakened condition like Number 44's—with flesh-and-blood children, who use them as the basis for adventure. The animate machine temporarily suspends time and reality, even as the form and content of the text attest to the inevitability of technological and temporal change; for example, it is not quite clear whether *The Wonderful Locomotive's* Peter is dreaming or awake, although he must come to the end of his overnight ride.

Reviewers and booksellers were enthusiastic about Meigs's book. In an article about the Haders for the *Horn Book Magazine*, editor Louise H. Seaman reported, "When the sales conference saw the [book] dummy, with the little old 44 puffing away, they voted to double the edition. AND when the artists sent in the pictures, there were a third again as many as either contract or publishing plan would allow. But who could leave out one of them[?] . . . Pennies must be counted again, and every picture fitted into its perfect place."[36] The Haders enthusiastically supplied extra black-and-white images for what was intended to be a conventionally illustrated chapter book, and the publisher's marketing department was won over, twice. Seaman details the irresistibility of the words and pictures, suggesting that *The Wonderful Locomotive* provided a fairy tale of modernity—both a persuasive definition of nostalgia and a wistful example of counsel—that modern readers clung to in 1928. The book's fanciful words and images about a boy engineer and his rejuvenated train suggest how much 1920s enchantment relied on mysterious, marvelous machines and granted children communion with unnatural wonders. Texts such as *The Wonderful Locomotive* imply the melding of human and automaton into a kind of machine consciousness and capture the national American imagination at the height of the twenties.[37]

Yet aspects of this national imaginary would shift with the Depression. From 1919 until 1929, picture books were an economic success, whether perpetuating a vision of the Romantic, leisurely child or informing the here-and-now young citizen with civics lessons. Publishers had devoted departments and resources to juveniles publishing; cylindrical presses had been improved for better printing; absorbent papers and fast-drying inks allowed for more exacting color and duotone printing; and new periodicals, book fairs, and annual awards helped bring children's literature to public attention. After 1929, however, library and home sales were threatened, leading companies to decline book contracts to prolific author-illustrators and to lay off pioneering children's editors.[38] Doubleday editor May Massee was laid off and moved to Viking Press; Virginia Kirkus lost her editorial job at Harper's and launched the editorial service *Kirkus Reviews*. Publishing companies cut costs by turning to their backlists and offering reprints of classics, without losing sight of visual-verbal experimentation.[39]

Although children's publishing recovered quickly, especially in sales of inexpensive series books, and was strong by 1937, economic hardship and disillusionment are detectable not only in the material manufacture of picture books and illustrated texts but also in the narratives common to them. Socioeconomic crisis forced a reconsideration of childhood as an ageless, classless zone (although sentimental accounts of youth were far from extinct). Where 1920s and early 1930s picture books such as *Miki* revived folk history, books like *The Wonderful Locomotive* resorted to magic to save the day, and still others, like *Today's ABC Book*, venerated up-to-the-minute technology, many 1930s originals acknowledge the dilemmas of labor, obsolescence, and a loss of affect in a political and sometimes nationalistic way. Picture books of the mid- to late 1930s subtly acknowledged that the book industry and children themselves were undergoing troubled times. According to Anne MacLeod, children's texts "transmit the emotional tone of their culture. Twenties books conveyed the nervous energy of a society whose hopes were for success and achievement in the material world, whereas thirties fiction reflected a society hunkered down to wait out hard times, returning for reassurance to family and community, taking what comfort it could in human warmth, and enduring, on the whole, with tolerance and good humor."[40] Depression-era children's texts urged a spirit of community.

Although these books gave a sunny and not necessarily pessimistic account of present and future, they acknowledged adversity, validated labor, and glanced with longing on those machines that were going out of production—among them the coal-burning locomotive, the steam shovel, and the antique fire engine—all popular topics. This cultural climate, and the circulation of the national imaginary around its pet machines, is perceptible in E. B. White's bittersweet 1936 epitaph to Henry Ford's paradigm-shifting Model T.[41] White opens with a reference to another cultural icon, itself a sign of the decline of the small-town general store:

> I see by the new Sears Roebuck catalogue that it is still possible to
> buy an axle for a 1909 Model T Ford, but I am not deceived. The great
> days have faded, the end is in sight. Only one page in the current cata-
> logue is devoted to parts and accessories for the Model T; yet everyone
> remembers springtimes when the Ford gadget section was larger than
> men's clothing, almost as large as household furnishings. The last
> Model T was built in 1927, and the car is fading from what scholars
> call the American scene—which is an understatement, because to a
> few million people who grew up with it, the old Ford practically *was*
> the American scene.[42]

Not only is the frontier era finished, says White, but the industrial era is on its way out. The assembly-line product, once a sign of the loss of community, has become a source of national yearning to "a few million people who grew up with it." White waxes nostalgic about the creative work of keeping his car roadworthy: "Gadget bred gadget. Owners not only bought ready-made gadgets, they invented gadgets to meet special needs. I myself drove my car directly from the agency [the point of purchase] to the blacksmith's, and had the smith affix two enormous iron brackets to the port running board to support an army trunk."[43] White salutes the old-fangled spirit of ingenuity, showing that a new car owner of 1909 had the wherewithal to make alterations to a mass-produced good without pausing to consider its resale or trade-in value. As artisanal labor was replaced by the assembly line and reproducible goods easily replaced broken ones, the thought of altering one's belongings with nonfactory widgets fell by the wayside. Older machines ended up in junkyards, becoming corroded objects of whimsical fascination for the children of the next generation. With those machines went ways of life for the laborers who had depended upon them.

Writer May McNeer and illustrator Lynd Ward's prescient picture book *Stop Tim! The Tale of a Car* (1930), which predates White's essay, likewise leavens Depression-era melancholy with peculiar humor in its portrait of a ragtop Model T. *Stop Tim!* appeared shortly after Swift and Ward's *Little Blacknose* (and twelve years prior to their 1942 *The Little Red Lighthouse and the Great Gray Bridge*), anticipating a bumper crop of picture books on obsolete machines and their out-of-work operators. *Stop Tim!* also represents a development of picture-book graphic conventions, with its variety of horizontal landscape layouts, page-turning momentum, and typography incorporated into visual compositions (Figure 3.7). It parallels the publication of Ward's melodramatic wordless novels, including *God's Man* (1929) and *Mad Man's Drum* (1930), and, like these two graphic narrative sequences, its pictorial narrative features visual play with a perceptible level of menace.[44]

Ward's visual style also echoes Harlem Renaissance painter and graphic

FIGURE 3.7. *Stop Tim! The Tale of a Car* (1930) describes a jalopy's desperate quest for the speed attained by newer automobiles.

artist Aaron Douglas's easel-scale and mural-size images of African American laborers, which feature similarly transparent layers of color. Lithographed in shady gradations of charcoal black and teal ink, *Stop Tim!* follows an exultant Art Deco aesthetic. Its cover and endpapers are printed in a kaleidoscopic pattern of columns that imply looming city buildings and steep mountains, which the tenacious Model T climbs. The book's large, upright sans-serif typeface likewise implies modern design, and McNeer's economical words are typeset to frame and complement Ward's images. Some four-stage spreads, which balance a vertical text panel, a vertical image panel, another vertical image, and more vertical text, are reminiscent of Wanda Gág's picture-book layouts.

The title character in *Stop Tim!* is a creaky but still lively jalopy who wants nothing but to "run faster than ever car ran before," a phrase the antic narrative repeats with intense conviction. With the addition of one letter, *the* title of the book could be misread as "Stop Time!" which the car might gladly do if it could enable him to overcome corrosion and achieve the speed of light. Tim resembles *The Wonderful Locomotive*'s resurrected Number 44, but without the latter's unspeaking gentleness and without the need of a child to spark his aging cylinders. Like Number 44, too, Tim makes a mythic cross-country excursion in the text's surreal conclusion.

*Stop Tim!* opens calmly with a farm at sunrise. A rooster crows and Tim, wide awake, awaits his driver. McNeer describes Tim with human rather than mechanical traits, and Ward gives Tim's headlamps a watchful look: "Tim's two round eyes were always open. His brass nose was shiny. His four rubber shoes stood firmly." The literary-visual imagery encourages the reader to see the ordinary car as live, unsleeping, and ever-alert as it (or he) awaits the driver, a mailman named Angus who calls "Good morning, Timothy." "Let's go! Let's go!" responds Tim. "'Not too fast,' warned Angus. / Tim snorted. He rattled. He shivered to be off." For all the anticipation, Tim and Angus live a life of placid routine. Sequential sentences and images picture them proceeding along a country road "as slow as a tired turtle," stopping at labeled mailboxes. Tim bucks and behaves like an impatient horse, albeit one that talks to its owner.

The narrative takes a superstitious turn with a revelatory and "queer secret about every hill. / Inside each hill and mountain that Tim came to lived two fellows, two great fellows with bristly hair and arms as strong as the North Wind. Twin brothers they were, but more unlike than ever brothers were before." The animism of "the hill brothers" recalls Carl Sandburg's *Rootabaga Stories* of 1922, which metaphorically mourned the industrializing agricultural landscape of the Midwest; *Stop Tim!* pits a living and malicious nature against the mechanical device that lumbers up and rolls down hills. Nature is of two minds about the automobile; the uphill brother slows Tim down and the downhill brother speeds him up. Whereas the Little Engine That Could—an invention of the same year, 1930—famously chugs, "I think I can! I think I can!" while climbing steep hills, Tim "pushed and puffed . . . [because] one of the brothers was holding him back with his great hand on Tim's bumper." On the down slope, Tim feels "a large push on his back bumper," but his driver, Angus, engages the brake, which has a personality of its own, laughing, "Ha! Ha! Not too fast." Tim is mocked by newer-model cars too, which slip past him in a blur. For all his successful battles with the mischievous hill brothers, Tim is quite literally over-the-hill compared to the latest automotive designs, and certain to lose any race. And although Virginia Lee Burton's *Choo Choo: The Story of a Little Engine Who Ran Away* (1937), with its imitation of train sound, has been credited as "apparently the earliest important children's book where printed language is consistently used for both visual and acoustic purposes. . . . [demonstrating] the visual representation of sound,"[45] McNeer and Ward experiment with onomatopoeia and the space of the page when Tim challenges streamlined new cars, which taunt him with "long hoot[s] of laughter":

"I can run faster than ever car ran before," rattled Tim to a big sleek green car.
"Hoo-o!                  Hoo-o!
           Hoo-o!                 Hoo-oo-oo!"
cried the big green car through his musical nose.

The "Hoo-o!" honks of the passing car, extended across the space of the page, imitate and invite the playful imitation of sound.

An old car cannot grow and mature as a readership does, and the driver Angus is an old-fashioned person who prefers reduced speeds; Angus might even be an out-of-work farmer, delivering the mail rather than harvesting his once-productive land, and lacking the wherewithal to purchase a new vehicle. Whatever the case, McNeer and Ward seem unable to resolve this comic story by nonmagical means. Instead, Angus loads Tim with suitcases and they embark on a long drive without an apparent destination, visiting a skyscraper-studded, *Metropolis*-style city and a vast plain. When they come to a mountain and begin to climb, Tim's "rubber shoes twirled wildly. His body rattled madly. His nose grew hot. His round eyes glared" until "He gave a last jump. He was on top." After a vertiginous glance down the other side, "Tim plunged. / . . . But he felt the brake rasp and catch his wheels a little. / 'Ha! Ha! Not too fass-ss-ss!' The hoarse voice ended in a groan. The brake let go. Tim felt his rubber shoes whirling faster and faster and faster. He felt his nose racing along the road."

Tim blissfully achieves his goal—reaching the top of the mountain—but the machine's desires are opposed to the man's. As Tim goes out of control on the downhill side, the situation turns nightmarish rather than pleasurable: " 'Stop, Tim!' roared Angus. But Tim's wheels were spinning. His crank fell out. His little round mouth drank the wind. He was running faster than ever car ran before!" Tim's momentum is such that he coasts up and down another mountain, "And with the brake broken there was nothing to stop him. And so he is still going. And so he will go on forever." This "forever" implies the Model T's fond status in cultural memory but admits its increasing absence from the American scene. The narrative ends on a "Legend of Sleepy Hollow" note, with Tim turned dynamo and Angus on an unwilling, endless journey. McNeer's closing page implies humor but evokes a grim threat and a nighttime setting as well: "When you are riding along the wide smooth road you may, perhaps, see Tim whizz past in the dark. . . . And if you have time to look, and to listen, you may see the long legs and flapping elbows of Angus. And you may hear him cry, 'Stop, Tim!' "

This description of a trapped Angus recalls Washington Irving's foolish Ichabod Crane, just as the invocation of the hill brothers resonates with Irving's unpredictable Hudson Valley. As Judith Richardson contends in her book *Possessions*, Irving's mid-nineteenth-century stories of hauntings "were linked to contingencies of local geography and experience and to a problem of historical memory amid progress, which had peculiar salience in the Hudson Valley, but which resonated with American cultural anxieties and desires more broadly."[46] Richardson explains, "Ghosts operate as a particular, and peculiar, kind of social memory, an alternate form of history-making in which things usually forgotten, discarded, or repressed become foregrounded, whether as items of fear, regret, explanation, or desire."[47] Rather than posit ghosts of a human past, picture books such as *Stop Tim!* treat uncanny machines as the ghosts of a bygone era of technological progress, relegated to the junkyard yet haunting the imagination. Tim's rambunctiousness suggests the freedom and uncertainty of the open road (not to mention the possibility of engine malfunction or brake failure) that automobile owners had experienced since the turn of the century. With more reliable cars and improved roadways coming on the scene, mountainous national parks and other remote destinations were within reach, giving bold family adventurers access to previously inaccessible landscapes. Strangely enough, the America envisioned by McNeer and Ward is haunted not by the usual folktale phantoms—the troubled ghosts of displaced Native Americans, of slaves, or of settlers and soldiers—but by the tragic specter of an outmoded car and its driver.

Based on its rarity today, *Stop Tim!* did not capture readers' attention to the degree that other tales of uncanny machines did. It lacked the sugary sweetness of *The Little Engine That Could,* and it might have frightened readers with its frenzied dynamism and the spooky ambiguity of its conclusion. Tim is obsessed with speed, his operator Angus holds on for dear life, and playfulness descends into madness. Yet *Stop Tim!* is an innovative example of the 1930 picture book and the fairy tale of modernity. In hindsight, its mechanical and natural animism tellingly evoke the anxieties of Depression-era culture, marked by uncannily lifelike machines and industrial processes that posed a challenge to, and were sometimes undone by, potent natural forces.

The Depression era also saw a surge in texts that focused on the role of craftspeople (particularly male artisans) in the modern metropolis. Among these, Wilfred Jones's *How the Derrick Works* (1930) features elegant prints in warm denim blue and coal-black ink on a white ground (Figure 3.8).[48] Jones worked in advertising as well as children's publishing, and he approached the single pages and the spreads of the book with rigor and a keen sense of design. Bertha Mahony and Elinor Whitney noted, "Through his advertising he has become thoroughly interested in book make-up and typography, and therefore, it is not surprising that he is able to lay out both his hand-lettered title pages and the text of his books so successfully."[49] Jones's stylized compositions balance hard-edged architectural shapes, graceful machine and human figures, and harmonious areas of negative space. He designs the title page in heavy, angular capital letters, drawn with a steady, borderline-mechanical hand. Monumental rectangles and ziggurat shapes reflect a modish Art Deco style.

With its precisely labeled diagrams and images of heavy equipment operated by muscular, strong-jawed men, *How the Derrick Works* instructs readers in builders' equipment and the stages of building a skyscraper. In a typical diagram, a small-scale man is pictured at the lower left to indicate how a human operator guides thick, steel-wire lines that are capable of lifting several tons of material. The human being sits at the controls, but a note calls steel wires "the muscles of the derrick," because the crane is much too unwieldy to be handled by fleshy muscle alone. Meanwhile, the pared-down black-and-white design of the pages suggests a functional simplicity, an ease of operation. Jones creates diagrams of pulleys and counterweights used to lift girders into the sky, while calling attention to the human job of putting rivets and beams together. The

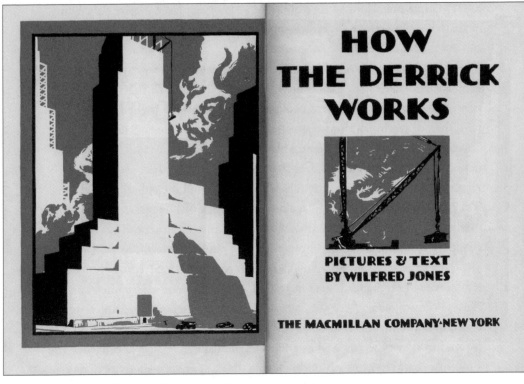

FIGURE 3.8. Elegant blue-and-black compositions detail a commonplace urban vision, the building of skyscrapers, in Wilfred Jones's *How the Derrick Works* (1930).

man is the brains but not the bodily strength of the oversize, animalistic machine. The text encourages readers to imagine construction as a harmonious and masculine occupation combining grace, heady power, and worldwide travel opportunities:

> A few inches of girder to stand or walk upon—hundreds of feet of empty space below. Dangerous-looking work, you think, as you see the man on the beam far above you.
>
> His work may take him to the south or west, or even to Russia and the Far East, there to build bridges or skyscrapers. Wherever American engineers go, these skilled workers follow, turning blue-print prophecies into reality.
>
> But the man up there is very much at home. Hundreds of feet above the earth, or a few stories—it is all the same to him. (1)

Jones's respectful narrative indicates that the worker is one who "follow[s]" American engineers all over the globe. The laborers' incursions into "Russia and the Far East" betoken a curiosity for faraway countries and envision these exotic locales as sites for future skyscrapers, twentieth-century symbols of U.S.-style capitalism and know-how. Further, the generic worker is described as "at home" in the unnatural environment, as though merging his own flesh with the metallic tools that he uses.

In unadorned language, Jones makes sense of scenarios that a child or adult might witness in an American city of 1930. In the image titled "Ballast," Jones foregrounds a seated worker perched on a partially completed building frame. The man's uniform, the blue sky, and the blue of the steel girders are in harmony, and two side-by-side skyscrapers rise in the distance, one with a flag fluttering on its pinnacle. A matching caption on a nonconsecutive page explains:

> Straddling the beam is a steelworker—one of the men who make tall buildings possible. He is counting his stock of bolts and nuts, which he carefully puts on the beam before him. To do this he has taken off his leather gloves, and tucked them under his belt. . . .
>
> Beyond, in the distance, are two skyscrapers. One has just had its last piece of steel riveted in place, and the flag is running up the halyards, to celebrate the event. Since the other still has a derrick at work, we know that it is going higher. (38–40)

Jones explains how much "we know" about the construction process from reading this book and observing the work of steel-lifting derricks. For the ground-level spectator, the derrick signifies humans' "going higher" in a literal and metaphorical sense, and the flag atop a building sends a triumphant sign of completion. Of course, the higher humans go, the tinier they appear in the grand scheme of things, as is evident in an image of workers attaching girders to a huge hook, to be hoisted by a derrick (13). Jones explains that pedestrians on the street below sometimes see the laborers far above: "Then the men seem like mere insects compared to the height of the derrick" (41).

Jones brings attention to issues foremost on the minds of post-1929 readers who had witnessed restructurings of material social space and of the social imagination in the century's early decades. In the workplace, laborers received different training and assignments based on heritage and race, creating pools of skilled and unskilled workers. Assembly lines allowed managers to "control every detail of the worker's energy and time in the factory,"[50] a restrictive system parodied by Charlie Chaplin's alienated workman in the film *Modern Times* (1936). Working-class and immigrant neighborhoods, churches, and social clubs kept a diversifying population from having as much face-to-face contact in the urban environment as had been possible in the nineteenth century; corporate technological structures did the same. Strikes and labor parades, race riots, and street demonstrations in response to business and government policies were vestiges of urban boulevard culture in an increasingly automobile-centered, pedestrian-unfriendly United States.[51] People learned to interact in prescribed manners, with others of their ostensible kind, based on their time- and machine-related rituals; this reinforced racial, ethnic, and class distinctions while preventing direct clashes—or chances for improved communication—among groups founded on perceived difference. *How the Derrick Works* and other children's texts on labor describe these commonplace separations, generally from the viewpoint of upper- and middle-class cultural producers. These same texts show the automobile (as well as the clamshell dredge, steam shovel, and derrick) gaining the status of an admired, reliable friend to Americans.

In the last section of *How the Derrick Works*, titled "Finished," Jones compares the skyscraper to an ancient wonder of the world:

> The last beam is in place, the last rivet is driven home. The steelwork
> on the big skyscraper is finished.
>     Though it is much larger than a pyramid of ancient Egypt, the
> great modern building needs no army of slaves to help its growth. (43)

Jones implies that great social progress has been made. It is not clear whether the author refers to the past enslavement of laborers, who now receive pay for their physical contributions (slavery, in 1930, was only some sixty-five years past), or to the metaphorical enslavement of the functional machine, which does not complain about how it is used and enables the relative freedom of working people. *How the Derrick Works* does not anthropomorphize the machine like some children's texts of its day, but neither does it introduce any working person with whom a reader can identify or sympathize. There is "no army of slaves," but there remains a sort of army of fit laborers, albeit troops that earn wages in exchange for productive efforts. This picture book implies that the modern child inhabits a world of spectacular human artifice but one in which the laborer is anonymous, fearless, male, and secondary to his equipment.

Humans and machines are extensions of one another, and the distinction between their labors is blurred.

Two years after the publication of *How the Derrick Works*, labor activist and photographer Lewis Hine presented a volume of his photographs of the Empire State Building as it was being built. *Men at Work: A Photographic Account of Men and Machines* (1932) is a pep talk on labor; it glorifies the death-defying laborers and focuses attention on labor issues without using overt political terms; Hine's populist rallying cry reads today as pro-city, pro-U.S. propaganda, with cautionary overtones regarding the common man.[52] As its title suggests, *Men at Work* is concerned more with the hand labor and less with the skyscraper and derrick technology that fascinate Jones. In his foreword, "The Spirit of Industry," Hine writes,

> Cities do not build themselves, machines cannot make machines, unless back of them all are the brains and toil of men. We call this the Machine Age. But the more machines we use the more do we need real men to make and direct them. . . .
>
> I will take you to the heart of modern industry where machines and skyscrapers are being made, where the character of the men is being put into the motors, the airplanes, the dynamos upon which the life and happiness of millions of us depend.
>
> Then the more you see of modern machines, the more may you, too, respect the men who make them and manipulate them.

This introduction reinforces a belief that machines are the products of human ingenuity and that the "men," not the machines, deserve respect. This is in line with Hine's humanist vision, conveyed through the camera apparatus. Throughout his career, Hine deliberately let the camera mediate between the photographic object—whether an immigrant at Ellis Island or a child mineworker or weaver—and a middle-class viewing audience, for the purpose of arousing sympathy and empathy. Further, Alan Trachtenberg calls Hine's text a "teaching tool . . . not just on 'the dignity of labor' but on a way of seeing, on what to look for and what to see in the city's angular lines and crowded streets."[53] *Men at Work*'s photographs, intertitles, and captions attest not only to the builders' commitment to their craft but also to one photographer's daredevil experience atop the girders. Hine becomes a star loiterer, watching the construction from his unique vantage and then sharing that perspective with a distant readership.

Like *How the Derrick Works*, Hine's *Men at Work* represents the small human body in relation to the large-scale machine and to mass-produced products, helping normalize that partnership. Yet, as Trachtenberg points out, this normalization has its paradoxes: "The pictures bracket the constructive heroism of labor in a way which isolates the making of the building from its context, both the economic context of the 1920s building boom, the grandiose (and in many minds, anti-civic) ambitions of real estate speculators, investors, and developers, and the cultural context in which the building functions as a commercial temple celebrating (or worshipping) empire."[54] Hine celebrates labor as individual human actualization and praises the bravery and skill of the anonymous male workers, without dwelling on such concerns as class and race, hiring practices, and eventual business to be done within the structure itself.

Another photographic text of the decade, *SKYSCRAPER* (1933), provides another account of construction work and of job site politics.[55] In this oversize, eighty-page volume of heroic poems and photographs, progressive educator Lucy Sprague Mitchell, researcher Elsa Herzfeld Naumburg, and poet Clara Lambert focus on the construction of the Empire State Building in 1930, and echo *Men at Work* by using many of Hine's plates. Their collaborative photo book also indicates that big structures were going up all over the United States, and approaches scenes of building with a sense of wonder and entitlement: "Pittsburgh has its skyscraper university—called the Cathedral of Learning," Mitchell trumpets in her introductory overview of architecture, whose title, "Skyscraper Is Born," implies that the building was from the start a living presence in the world. The title, *SKYSCRAPER*, always appears in small capital letters that set it off from the page and lend an individual punch beyond that of a generic descriptive word.

Lambert's unrhymed verse, laid out in a squared-off Art Deco fashion that complements the photos and the Empire State Building's sleek design, celebrates the tools of labor and presents the laborer as an indispensable cog in a larger machine. Her first poem, a call to action titled "Summon the Workers," exhorts not people but machines:

Come, monster gasoline engines,
> Crawl on your caterpillar treads; let your mighty jaws
> open and close on the shattered rock; let the procession
> of trucks come down the ramp to carry away the scattered schist
> for *SKYSCRAPER* is to be built! (9)

In a thunderous biblical register, Lambert sings of behemoths that "crawl" and open their "mighty jaws." With gusto, she describes metal, rock, architectural planning, and the laying of a skyscraper's foundations. Her images of gas-powered shovels resonate with *Big Fellow* and the later *Mike Mulligan and His Steam Shovel* (1939).

In awe-filled prose passages that serve as transitions between poems, Mitchell calls attention to the men who lay the groundwork for the larger machinery and then put each piece of the skyscraper in its proper place:

> So the "common labor" comes—the unskilled men, the general
> helpers to different gangs who themselves belong to no special
> gang. Hard, heavy work is theirs. Only strong men can be common
> labor! Powerful negroes, stocky, broad-shouldered workers from
> the orchards of Italy or work shops of Germany, all glad of a job in
> SKYSCRAPER's pit....
>
> Drill and powder gang, common labor, shovels and trucks. All are
> working in the pit. Noise and movement everywhere. But no confu-
> sion. Everything planned. Everything moves in sequence. No one has
> to wait.... The speed with which the work must progress is worked
> out in an elaborate time table which covers weeks and months; for
> SKYSCRAPER must be completed by a certain date. (18)

The blurry black-and-white photographs of "common labor" picture men with shadowed faces, leaving their hats and clothing to signify their ethnic backgrounds. Indeed, Mitchell emphasizes the racial and ethnic divisions among the workers, indicating that men of African, Italian, and German descent rank among common labor, which is separate from skilled gangs. While insisting that there is "no confusion" among these segregated specimens of brawn and brains, Mitchell gives unskilled workers second place in a list that includes a practiced "drill and powder gang" and "shovels and trucks." The "common" men occupy a halfway point between educated workers and inanimate tools, and the notion that there is no confusion implies that they accept this place without question. They do not aspire to jobs like riveting, which is described as more complex and dangerous than the work they do, and therefore is left to another kind (or, implicitly, another breed) of man: "The whole steel skeleton of beams and girders and columns must be riveted into one, if it is to stand the strain of the weight and wind. For this reason, the rivets must be put in wherever two beams intersect, and they must be put in red hot—no easy task. It is dangerous work and exhausting work. . . . It appeals to daring Irishmen and cool-headed Swedes. Dangerous work is well-paid work" (48). Although "only strong men can be common labor!" the "well-paid" riveters make better money than those in unskilled (but not undangerous) positions on the work site. "Daring Irishmen and cool-headed Swedes," described in terms of their mental sharpness and not in terms of their bodies, stand in counterpoint to the "powerful negroes" and "stocky, broad-shouldered" Italians and Germans, admired for their physical capacities. In addition, the more profitable work "appeals to" the Irishmen and Swedes in an ostensibly natural way.

Such a celebratory yet overtly biased documentary portrait is in keeping with the proletarian literature of the era, which outlined collective groups and their communities by marking ethnic and racial difference. Michael Denning calls ethnicity "the modality through which working-class peoples experienced their lives and mapped their communities. . . . The invention of ethnicity was a central form of class consciousness in the United States."[56] Machine culture and technology were modalities around which working-class communities were constructed, too. SKYSCRAPER, an up-to-the-minute picture book using photographs as opposed to block prints or lithographs, gives readers the keys to understanding 1930s class consciousness and segregation, even as it teaches about tools, construction, and a job well done. SKYSCRAPER recalls a period when laborers received different training and assignments based on heritage and race, creating pools of skilled and unskilled workers who developed traditions of handling certain types of equipment (from basic shovels and pickaxes to more complicated derricks).

In addition to pointing out intellectual and physical differences among the workingmen, SKYSCRAPER fetishizes the efficiency and aesthetic beauty of the muscular laborers and the machines. The common labor and the gangs work in perfect synchronicity while remaining discrete units; they operate heavy equipment smoothly, as though born to their tasks, and the machinery and skyscraper comply with their wishes. In a poem called "Derrick Gang," Lambert writes,

> Derricks swinging tons of steel
> > suspended on swinging ropes
> > swaying upward floor by floor.
> Derricks run by man to do his bidding,
> > to pile steel into a form. (39)

The machinery is "run by man to do his bidding," so that "man" takes on a godly role in the enterprise, yet the men described here work like bees in a hive. "SKYSCRAPER is a little city," (66) Mitchell writes. "Everything works like parts of a great machine. Organization; planning!" (56–57) The coauthors fixate on timetables and on the terms "organization" and "planning," and draw analogies between the natural world (human physiology and trees), the precision time-piece, and the object of solid steel. The unfinished building's vertical I beams form a "forest of two hundred columns" (36), and a "steel skeleton" supports the metaphoric body of the structure. Jones, in *How the Derrick Works*, also employs the metaphor "skeletons of steel" and describes "men controlling the movable arm of the derrick, swinging it out like an elephant's trunk over the street hundreds of feet below" (32). The skyscraper and equipment are likened to sequoias and elephants. Compared to these metal and concrete behemoths, which imitate nature and go it one better, the single human being is tiny and fragile, and the real blood and sweat of the enterprise tend to get overlooked. Cecelia Tichi comments that "the mix of American flora and fauna with pistons, gears, and engines indicates that the perceptual boundary between what is considered to be natural, and what technological, is disappearing. The world of the pastoral, the primitive, the edenic, the agrarian is fusing with that of machine technology."[57]

Humans are imperiled by the gargantuan tools of their trade, and Mitchell's exposition for SKYSCRAPER does carry a subtext about physical danger and itinerant labor. Men are "glad of a job in SKYSCRAPER's pit," but they can come to harm: "Each man is insured according to his trade; i.e., if he is injured he will be paid a definite amount. This means very elaborate bookkeeping for the timekeeping department. More organization; more planning" (66). Accidental injury becomes a financial consideration and a headache "for the timekeeping department." As in *How the Derrick Works*, the healthy human being—generically male, brave, and anonymous—occupies a heroic but treacherous place in the capitalist urban landscape of the postindustrial United States.

Picture books such as SKYSCRAPER and *How the Derrick Works*, designed to educate and entertain, acquaint the young reading subject with exciting urban space and with human achievement with machines. They also carry evidence of bustling and yet individually isolated fields of laborers; a crowded, competitive work environment open only to those with specialized physical and mental traits; an alienated, segmented workforce that runs important machinery; and distinct racial and ethnic divisions among workers themselves. Further, the picture book itself, a material object, provides an example of the narrative production and efficient money making of the white-collar publishing and bookselling industry, and the ongoing efforts of the blue-collar print shops and distribution channels throughout America.

## MECHANICAL SUBJECTIVITY

Picture books that focus on humans' relationship to mechanical equipment signal the complexities of their own reproduction as well as the social concerns of adult producers who envision a technological future. In addition, these texts signal a change in reading subjects' awareness of themselves as spectators and as parts of the grand modern spectacle. These texts take for granted that young readers readily imagine the machine or commodity exchanging a glance with them and being capable of feeling happy or hurt. Children are given to imagine that Swift and Ward's Little Blacknose or McNeer and Ward's Tim the car fears the junkyard, and that a little boy can befriend Number 44 or Big Fellow. The machine—and even the text itself, a commodity affiliated with its child owner—aims to fulfill a sort of partnership, becoming a substitute for human or animal presence in the life of the reader who interacts with it. Not only does the sentient-machine narrative propose that toys and tools "come alive," to cite Lois Kuznets's *When Toys Come Alive,* but also this trope implies that sentient commodities can feel and die, and places mortal, flesh-and-blood beings in an altered relationship to their mechanized equipment and household commodities. The fairy tale of modernity cannot account for how the machine, once awakened, can return to its insensitive, sleeping state. In place of the magical broom that may be silenced without its user's guilt (for example, in Gág's translations of traditional Grimm tales), picture books, illustrated texts, stop-action cinema, and animated cartoons bring the object to life with the understanding that to break it is to kill it.

The popular modern conception of the sentient machine has implications for understanding empathy, sympathy, and affect generally in an industrializing and postindustrial nation. No one mistakes a machine for a living animal, but the fantasy of treating machines as animals raises ethical concerns in how modern subjects, and their inheritors, come to imagine organic versus technological consciousness. Hal Foster, commenting on surrealism and the uncanny, writes, "In the premodern instance the machine is thought to mimic the organic movements of the human (or animal) body that is its model (residual, say, in the description of the early train as the 'iron horse'); the machine remains a tool, suited to the craftsman and subservient to him. In the modern instance, however, the machine becomes the model, and the body is disciplined to its specifications. . . . As the worker resembles the machine, it begins to dominate him, and he becomes its tool, its prosthetic." Foster asks, "Might the very apperception of the uncanny, in Freud no less than in surrealism, depend on the historical development of reification, of the ghostly doubling of the human by the mechanical-commodified, by *the thing?*"[58] Depending on the era, the uncanny emerges around different anxieties; for instance, the Industrial Revolution and the existence of slavery produced particular narratives of vengeful ghosts. A specifically modern anxiety attributes life to the store-bought commodity and the commonplace machine. An urge to vivify those tools that help people work and to breathe feelings into desirable market goods suggests an oblique awareness of the alienated, exploited labor that produces items for consumption, the violence that drives empire and capital, and the immense demands placed on the docile, fragile human body under twentieth-century conditions of industry and war.

This concern arises across the work of the historical materialists of the early twentieth century, predicting the rise of fascism; the Dadaists and surrealists, responding to war and censorship; the midcentury critical theorists, looking back with pessimism on the soldier's body and the assembly-line worker; scholars of postmodernism, globalization, and cultural studies, investigating alienated production under late capitalism (notably Donna Haraway's 1980s theories of the cyborg and science fiction); and, more recently, critics, writing on the object-thing dialectic.[59] The anxieties expressed indirectly in picture books of the 1910s–1940s reflected and shaped the storytelling practices of those growing up between the wars.

Modern perception differed definitively from that of the premodern era. Even if adults had difficulty adjusting, this altered mode of perception was naturalized in children.[60] A revised understanding of the gaze, based on changing relations to the human community and to technology, had been emergent since the nineteenth century, when rural-born arrivistes in the teeming city and industrial spaces tried to make sense of their individual subjectivity in the new urban collectivity. Changing social attitudes, combined with changing technical standards, enabled changes in the creative process and in expectations about the quality of human experience. Walter Benjamin wrote, "*Just as the entire mode of existence of human collectives changes over long historical periods, so too does their mode of perception. The way in which human perception is organized—the medium in which it occurs—is conditioned not only by nature* but by history.... And if changes in the medium of present-day perception can be understood as a decay of the aura, it is possible to demonstrate the social determinants of that decay."[61] Benjamin sought the social causes for this change in perception in the artifacts of the past and present, and saw a potential "revolutionary consciousness" in children who grew up accustomed to new ways of perceiving. The picture book, an outgrowth of multiple media including newspaper illustration, comics, advertising, and children's entertainment, developed in parallel with modes of production including mass-produced magazines and cinema, and Benjamin saw the political promise of redemption (not a dispersed postmodern schizophrenia, as Fredric Jameson later argued) in that increase in mass reproducibility.

New understandings of subjectivity thus arose in the late nineteenth and early twentieth century, brought on by the alterations in reproducible technology, the experience of social space, and unfamiliar demands upon human faculties of perception. A discomfiting comprehension of seeing and being seen, by others who likewise saw and were seen, developed in the nineteenth century and was in place by the time the first generations of the twentieth century were born. Representation of the perceived dominant culture and marginalized social groups posed a challenge to middle- and upper-class cultural producers, assigned with whether or how much to acknowledge a shared gaze. As picture books, illustrated texts, and related forms such as animation indicate, this uneasy modern gaze extended to inanimate objects.

Individuals' evolving relations to the urban throng, popular media, and indifferent machines—including everything from factory equipment to the camera apparatus—hastened an internalization of the gaze, a sense of watching and being surveyed not only by living entities, like people in the crowd and domestic animals, but also by judgmental commodities and objects that seemed to move of their own volition. The handmade doll had a personality all its own, granted by its known maker, but so did the mass-produced teddy bear and assembly-line products like the Model T. By the early twentieth century, people felt that when they looked at something, the object of their gaze had the capacity to react. Consequently, they had a sense of their own subjectivity inestimably different from that experienced by people of a century before. They now perceived the distance of their neighbors (particularly in block housing or the cell-like apartments of a city building), their uncertain relation to coworkers (often of diverse ethnic backgrounds and religious or political beliefs), and their relation to members of remote communities and nations all over the planet. They often looked not into human or nonhuman, animal eyes but into the eyes of a photographic or cinematic representation, the camera lens, the double headlights of oncoming cars, the lit windows of a skyscraper, or the steel "face" of the steam shovel or bulldozer; they had conversations over the telephone and heard disembodied human voices (to which they could not reply) over the radio and through the phonograph. And they transmitted this experience into the stories they told and the pictures they drew for up-and-coming generations.

An ideal example of this sensual intimacy with the urban world is writer Margaret Wise Brown and illustrator Leonard Weisgard's *The Noisy Book* (1939), which describes a blindfolded poodle named Muffin who listens to city sounds. Brown and Weisgard effectively recognized and responded to changes in technology and perception.[62] With its sidewalk setting and abundant machines, *The Noisy Book* combines here-and-now concerns with literary and visual allusions to modern living (Figure 3.9). Brown strives to imitate the everyday noises of a city street (the "Awuurra" of a car horn has lost its currency) and encourages readers to share Muffin's experience. *The Noisy Book* spawned many sequels, including *The Country Noisy Book* and *The Indoor Noisy Book*, and each time Muffin is in a box or is otherwise deprived of a wide view, hearing sounds without seeing their sources. In the country, for instance, katydids' songs and hogs' grunts are unfamiliar to him. In every book, Brown prompts guesses from listeners by repeatedly asking, "What was that?" and she proposes absurd, unlikely answers to which readers can object. The Noisy Books are like onomatopoeic detective stories, asking questions and prompting playful reader interaction.[63]

Weisgard models his boxy, postcubist illustrations of fire trucks and shop fronts after the stencil-and-collage paintings of Stuart Davis. He pursues a jazzy, avant-garde aesthetic, and he presents his flat, stencil- or stamp-style illustrations in a limited, mainly primary-color palette. Weisgard's sharp angles and tilting shapes are an affront to the delicate line and pastel inks of classic, golden-age children's literature in the Edmund Evans mode, and indicative of modern definitions of visual pleasure. *The Noisy Book* and other experimental modern texts suggest how new generations grew up accustomed to stimuli that shocked a previous generation's senses. They incorporate these unfamiliar elements into the comparatively cozy format of the shared picture book.

Benjamin believed that intimacy with nonhuman objects, such as the camera, the train, or the automobile, increased the likelihood of granting them the capacity to return the gaze. "Experience of the aura arises from the fact that a response characteristic of human relationships is transposed to the relationship

Then Muffin went down the street on his way home. «Poor little Muffin,» said the people on the street. «Muffin has a big white bandage over his eyes and he can't see a thing.»

But
Muffin could hear.

Muffin pricked up his ears and heard all the noises on the street.

First he heard the big noises

**MEN HAMMERING**
Bang bang bang

**AUTOMOBILE HORNS**
Awuurra awuurra

**HORSES HOOFS**
Clop clop Clop clop

**ANOTHER LITTLE DOG**
Bow wow wow

FIGURE 3.9. Leonard Weisgard mimes Stuart Davis's jazzy artwork in Margaret Wise Brown's *The Noisy Book* (1939), which describes a dog's aural experience of a busy city.

between humans and inanimate or natural object and man," Benjamin noted. "The person we look at, or who feels he is being looked at, looks at us in turn. To experience the aura of an object we look at means to invest it with the ability to look back at us."[64] The object does not look back literally, but its audience intuits its gaze all the same.[65] In this sense, the reproducible picture book is yet another inanimate thing that returns the gaze. It "looks back" at its rapt audience with a semblance of affection; for an individual reader, especially a young reader without a critical understanding of reproducible objects, it could be said to possess auratic status as an item for contemplation and pleasure. Consequently, the picture book takes on a reciprocal relation to the child that mimes the symbiotic relation between, say, a machine and its doting driver, and its audience is invited to respond to it not as a disposable commodity but as a living, valued entity. Although there is no eye-to-eye connection between the reading subject and the inanimate text, the reader transposes the deep, sentimental sense of communication and recognition (self-awareness, sympathy, or imagined empathy) that he or she typically experiences when exchanging a glance with another human being. The child identifies with the book itself. Likewise, the picture book normalizes the ways that contemporary child subjects interact with technology, and the ways that technology and alienated labor mold contemporary subjectivity. Should people, practically from birth, be seduced into imagining a human relationship with the camera, commodity, machine, or book, they might lose some of their ability to relate genuinely to humans and nonhuman animals. A metaphysical belief in the artifact's lifelike animation increases the probability of alienation in the social sphere and enables people to place the inanimate object on equal footing with animate, organic beings (especially those of marginal status, including distant, international others who perform cheap labor). Such is the ethical dilemma raised by contact with the picture book as a marketable commodity and as a meaningful, content-driven narrative of persuasive words and images.

## FOUR

# Murals in Miniature:
# Regionalism, Labor, and Obsolescence

### "NO STEAM SHOVELS WANTED": VIRGINIA LEE BURTON'S FAIRY TALES OF ALIENATED LABOR

The demise of machines and, with them, human livelihoods served as a sentimental favorite topic for nostalgic picture books and other media, including murals and public art. Whereas picture books of the 1920s show an uneasy consciousness of the scrap heap (for instance, Mary Liddell's *Little Machinery* describes a robot made of salvaged parts), picture books of the Depression-era 1930s reinforce an analogy between the junkyard and de-skilled labor.[1] In the thirties, New Deal murals were being painted in an effort to valorize small-town lives, muscular work, and regional identity—often in multiple panels interpretable as facets of a proud national story or collective image of American progress. At the same time, popular picture books venerated the partnership between technician and technology in a sequential mode, too. In a sense, the picture book might be described as a mural in miniature, calling attention to alienated labor and warning of a threat to American community values. Although the picture book is a small-scale narrative to be read spread by spread rather than wall by wall, thirties picture books shared murals' regional ideologies, cautionary themes, and sequential readability.

Thirties picture books tend to feature working-class machines or structures that are either dissatisfied with the unglamorous repetitiveness of their jobs or horrified they will be phased out in their prime of life. Such stories evoke pity for their outmoded protagonists, and the affective fallacy (which attaches to the unfortunate machine) extends to the worried members of the working class who no longer possess the up-to-date tools required by coldhearted, profit-driven management. If post office murals served to remind people of community over corporate interests, picture books likewise reinforced this civic concern.

Picture books about aging machines address public concerns about labor, technology, and consumer society. They indicate an increased distancing (à la

Crary's "technology of separation") of middle-class or white-collar workers from the sweat and blood of the laboring, working-class body. These books suggest, and in the best cases critique, "a logic of equivalence by which the bodily, the aesthetic, and the economic indicate each other, in a circular fashion, [conserving] the logic of market culture."[2] Through picture books for a young audience, some author-illustrators questioned the modern tendency toward models of convenience and away from the appreciation of manual human work. These creators recognized that, despite hard-to-shake sentimentality around childhood, actual children were not exempt from participation in the market, and that children's media acquainted the young with modern, and often cynical, perspectives on class and consciousness.

Virginia Lee Burton's picture books of the late 1930s and early 1940s explore the fairy tale of modernity while trumpeting the concerns of proletarian literature and American ambivalence about the labor economy. Burton's work suggests that the here-and-now city can be an inhospitable place for old-fashioned types or for those unwilling or unable to adapt to the latest technologies, and that the happy ending of any modern fairy tale does not mean closure for every character. Her picture books portray hardworking people and animal-like machines that are friendly, or at least indifferent, to humans. By filling her East Coast landscapes with images of busy steam shovels, locomotives, boats, and dredges, she pleases readers who are fascinated with motorized equipment, yet she also poses complex conflicts to capture readers' imaginations. Her texts, despite her evident fascination with machinery and its uses, urge extreme caution in inventing technology and altering the landscape too fast. This acknowledgment of ambiguity and multiple interpretations may account in part for her picture books' longevity and their beloved status across several generations.

Burton's *Choo Choo: The Story of a Little Engine Who Ran Away* (1937) and *Mike Mulligan and His Steam Shovel* (1939) address issues of labor and ethnicity, albeit in ways that may be more comprehensible to working adults than to leisure-time children. In illustrations with swooping curves and active vertical lines, Burton depicts New England landscapes of winding roads, rolling hills, small towns, crowded suburbs, and cities. Her words and pictures attest to the twentieth-century proximity of rural and urban settings, and the active human labor that it takes to build the houses and high-rises. Her stories, and the mass-produced books in which they appear, address timely social issues and suggest how machines from cars to trucks to trains close the spatial distance between human communities. Popular in their own decade and still in print today, these books suggest an ongoing adult desire to furnish the child with compendiums of machines, accounts of technological progress, and qualified reassurance of domestic comfort.

Burton's debut as an author-illustrator, *Choo Choo* features lithographs that appear hastily (though effectively) drawn with a lump of coal or a heavy stick of graphite; Burton biographer Barbara Elleman explains that the original book (although not its typeset reprints) featured an urgent, hand-lettered text (Figure 4.1). The tale gives a whimsical account of a small, female, coal-powered engine that follows a repetitive route:

> CHOO CHOO pulled all the coaches full
> of people, the baggage car full of
> mail and baggage and the
> tender, from the little
> station in the
> little town
> to the
> big station in the big city and back again.

Burton's funnel-shaped text mimics the shape of a locomotive's smokestack and implies the tightening sensation of increased speed. Its long, top line underscores a picture of a rural town, and the narrowest part of the funnel guides the eye to a tall, triangular city built around a central skyscraper. The eye scans down the skyscraper to the horizon and the conclusion of the sentence. Meanwhile, Burton's words indicate how the locomotive and its passenger cars make modern commuting possible, while admitting that the locomotive is not necessarily pleased with its back-and-forth routine. In addition, Burton informs readers about the salient parts of an older locomotive like her heroine: The tender is a small car just behind the locomotive, which holds coal and water. A fireman refuels the engine by loading it with coal. Consequently, Choo Choo requires three human operators: Jim, the engineer; Oley, the fireman; and Archibald, the conductor (who takes tickets). The three men play active roles in the story, but none serves as a true costar. Choo Choo is the main attraction.

By comparison to Choo Choo, the dual title characters of *Mike Mulligan and His Steam Shovel* "dug the great canals / for the big boats / to sail through . . . / cut through / the high mountains / so that trains / could go through . . . / [and] lowered the hills / and straightened the curves / to make the long highways / for the automobiles." The book opens with endpaper diagrams of a steam shovel, but in the narrative, Mike, the worker, and his machine, Mary Anne, are presented

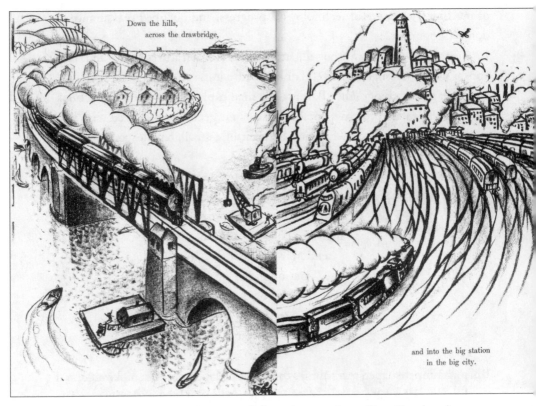

FIGURE 4.1. In these cacophonous side-by-side pages from *Choo Choo* (1937), evidence she had not yet mastered the integrated spread of her later work, Virginia Lee Burton visualizes the transition from suburbs to urban landscape.

as a team, enabling the rise of transportation and the city. In *Choo Choo*, and to a greater degree in *Mike Mulligan*, Burton chooses middle-distance views or long shots over close-up human and machine "faces," which keeps the small human body at a greater remove from the reader and gives more personality to the large, dominating machine presence. Nevertheless, Mike Mulligan—despite being an inch tall on the page—communicates his personality in grand gestures. In the opening image, he holds up his arms in a salute to Mary Anne, even if his tiny face is left to the imagination; Burton either trusts readers to fill this gap or leaves Mike to serve as a generic workman figure.

Burton begins both *Choo Choo* and *Mike Mulligan* by describing happy partnerships between the male workers and their equipment. On the one hand, each machine is described with a feminine pronoun or given a woman's name, and "she" responds to the working man's commands. On the other hand, the feminized machine is the source of the laborer's might and, potentially, his emasculation.

While the machine does not offer either a home or nourishment, it serves as the man's economic base, so that human and machine form a mutually dependent marriage of sorts. For instance, the title character of *Choo Choo* relies on her caretakers for her smooth operation: "Jim [the engineer] loved the little engine / and took good care of her. / He would shine and polish her till / she looked like new and oil all the / parts so they would run smoothly." In return, the locomotive ensures her engineers' jobs by serving the population well. The same goes for the "beautiful red steam shovel" that Mike keeps in excellent condition: "Mike Mulligan took such good care / of Mary Anne / she never grew old." But in both books, the considerate humans and their well-tended machines encounter dire situations. Times change, but the characters cannot. In *Choo Choo*, this is suggested by the locomotive's boredom and the machine's declaration:

> "I am tired of pulling
> all these heavy coaches. I could go
> much faster and easier by myself, then all
> the people would stop and look at me, just me."

The locomotive takes on human qualities, questioning her predictable duties. She wants to make a spectacle of herself. When her operators take a coffee break, Choo Choo leaves on her own. Astonished crowds point as she escapes to the city, chugging much faster than her human operators can run. But when she loses her tender and therefore her fuel in a magnificent leap over a drawbridge, she loses her chance at self-actualization. She runs out of coal and water along an "old old track that / hadn't been used for years. / Bushes and weeds had grown between the ties." Her panicked caretakers seek help from the engineer of a sleek electric Streamliner train, which has abundant power but conspicuously lacks the older locomotive's mischievous personality and feminine pronoun. Jim takes the controls from the Streamliner's engineer and pilots the sinuous new train down the tracks in search of Choo Choo.

They find the missing engine when an "old man, who used / to be an engineer / when he was young, / called out to them." He says the locomotive is hidden on "an old track / which hasn't been / used for well nigh / forty years." The disabled Choo Choo, the archaic railroad track, and the ex-engineer—all described as "old"—have been put out to pasture, as it were; they end up in the countryside, having outlived their usefulness, and Choo Choo rests amid a tangle of dead trees with handlike, grasping limbs. When the anonymous Streamliner tows the diminutive Choo Choo back to the switchyard, Jim, Archibald, and Oley dance "a jig together" and declare her "as good as ever." Despite Choo Choo's earnest promise to passively do her job from then on—"I am not going to run away again," she says—the flat ending of the story gives the distinct impression that the train has taken her last ride. After all, Jim has proved himself capable of driving a Streamliner. Meanwhile, Archibald and Oley wait for him in the railyard; the men may yet find work, even if their first passion is the older train.

Burton references a real innovation: On May 26, 1934, an actual stainless steel streamliner, the Pioneer Zephyr (introduced in the General Motors Building at the 1933–34 Chicago World's Fair), traveled the distance from Denver to Chicago, reaching 112 miles per hour and cutting previous travel times in half. *Choo Choo*'s title character "runs away" at the threat of this new technology, but, just as Choo Choo realizes her own outdatedness, the anonymous, personality-free Streamliner would soon enough become a relic.[3]

A similar situation arises in the better-realized *Mike Mulligan*, in which both the man and the steam shovel get displaced by improved industrial technologies. After all of Mike and Mary Anne's years of work together, "along came / the new gasoline shovels / and the new electric shovels / and the new Diesel motor shovels / and took all the jobs away from the steam shovels." Burton, who treats the shovel's digging mechanism as a dinosaur-like face, pictures the new shovels with their "chins" in the air and "eyes" closed haughtily. She shows Mike Mulligan hunched on a railroad tie, with his chin on his hands, and Mary Anne weeping; someone has painted "No Steam Shovels Wanted" on a wooden fence behind them. The next page pictures Mike and Mary Anne at the edge of a cliff, recoiling in shock from a pile of dead, broken steam shovels in the pit below. Burton pictures the junkyard as a tragic place where equipment perishes: "All the other steam shovels were being sold for junk, or left out in old gravel pits to rust and fall apart. Mike loved Mary Anne. He couldn't do that to her." Mike's bond with Mary Anne directly echoes Jim the engineer's "love" and care for Choo Choo, and Mike takes Mary Anne on the road in search of work. On their way out of the city, they pass all the things they have built: "They left the canals / and the railroads / . . . / where no one wanted them any more / and went away out in the country." Their contribution to history is effectively forgotten by society at large.

Ultimately Mike and Mary Anne reach the small town of Popperville, a traditional town that still has a general store, a one-room schoolhouse, and horse-drawn carriages and wagons (Figure 4.2). Fortunately, "the selectmen / were just deciding who should dig the cellar for the new town hall." Mike, recognizable by his red shirt, blue overalls, and cap, half-curtseys as he proudly offers the services of his steam shovel and promises to finish the job in a day: "Then he added, / 'If we can't do it, you don't have to pay.'" With this incentive, the town residents agree, and the morning sun comes up over the hill as Mike and Mary Anne set to work. When the thick black smoke from Mary Anne's stack startles the men of the Fire Department, they arrive on a by-then-primitive engine drawn by spotted horses, then stay to observe the event. The local schoolteacher calls "a long recess" so the distracted children can watch the spectacle. Readers know from the beginning of the story that "when people used to stop / and watch them, / Mike Mulligan and Mary Anne / used to dig a little faster / and a little better," and the two take heart as all the townspeople turn out to watch the digging. Like Choo Choo, Mary Anne and Mike enjoy being a public spectacle, and their urge to perform implies a pride in their physical presence that may well be disappointed; like an aging actor, they are no longer so young or fashionable as they once were, and they need this last big job desperately. As the day passes—represented by the sun moving right to left across the sky, contrary to the direction of the text—the suspense builds. Mike is just a blur in Mary Anne's cab, and a reader might forget who pulls the levers in the man and machine's relationship. Predictably, Mike and Mary Anne finish the job just in time, and take a bow from their position in the dirt bottom of the cellar. Their final performance seems triumphant. "Suddenly the little boy said, / 'How are they going to get out?'"[4] The answer is, they won't. The little boy suggests, and Popperville's residents gladly agree, that Mary Anne "be the furnace for the new town hall / and let Mike Mulligan be the janitor. / . . . / They built the new town hall / right over Mike Mulligan and Mary Anne." Mike gets paid and stays underground with his retrofitted steam shovel, now a furnace. The concluding page shows "Mike in his rocking chair / smoking his pipe, / and Mary Anne beside him, / warming up the meetings / in the new town hall."

This picture book entertains an imagined child reader with abundant pictures of machines and men at work or out of work. The loyal Mike remains faithful to his partner, Mary Anne, and finds them both new careers in an unwelcoming modern world. Yet their success is mixed. Mary Anne's treads have been removed and Mike's own mobility sacrificed. Both characters are fettered and planted firmly in the earth they used to shovel. The hobbled Mary Anne brings to mind the unrepaired, impotent gas shovel that shocks Ned in Baruch's *Big Fellow* or the rusted, ruined train engine that wins Peter's sympathy in Meigs's *The Wonderful Locomotive*. Mike and Mary Anne willingly settle down in order to go on existing in a modernizing world. Although Burton depicts the basement of the new town hall as a cozy place to be, her conclusion suggests

FIGURE 4.2. Unwanted in the modern city, Mike Mulligan and Mary Anne effectively attempt to travel in reverse, back to a small-town America untouched by massive construction projects, in Burton's *Mike Mulligan and His Steam Shovel* (1939).

that obsolescence and compromise follow the satisfaction of muscular labor. *Mike Mulligan* visibly attests to labor crises in an era when old technologies gave way to new ones and de-skilled human workers scrambled to find suitable occupations. *Choo Choo* and *Mike Mulligan* are fairy tales of modernity, both in their tangible materiality and in their representations of the modern landscape and the urban individual.

Burton's Caldecott Medal–winning *Little House*, too, is a fairy tale of modernity, with a "once upon a time" beginning. Like its predecessors, it signals a World War II–era shift to a new understanding of history, space, and time while evincing nostalgia for artifacts of the past. The Little House is built to last on a rural hillside. Days pass, seasons cycle, and years go by. Small and large changes are represented by an arc representing the sun's movement, a swirl of autumn leaves or snow, a parade of dresses and fashions, additional buildings on neighboring hills, and altering modes of transportation, from horse-drawn buggies to motor vehicles. Until the conclusion, Burton situates the house in the center of the right-hand page, with text on the verso, so that readers know where to find the house as the pages grow increasingly crowded. Ultimately, the countryside around the Little House is cleared away and urban sprawl fills the page, expanding onto the left-hand page where only text previously appeared (Figure 4.3). The Little House, falling into disrepair but "still as good a house as ever underneath," is surrounded by skyscrapers and shadowed by an elevated railway. Help arrives in the form of an ancestor of the original builder, who has the house lifted off its foundation and moves it by truck to a new rural location—the truck, a tool of modernity, making possible the evacuation and perpetuation of traditionalism. "Never had riverboat melodrama a maiden more grievously abandoned, a more precipitate rescue, a more sanguine end," writes Barbara Bader. "But easy as it is to mock *The Little House*, the book provides a magic-lantern look at modern city development before wholesale leveling blurred its lineaments. . . . For children it had and has the dimensions of legend, and every left-behind rundown frame structure on a city street is the Little House."[5] Other critics call *The Little House* "ahead of its time in speaking out against the encroachment of urban blight."[6]

In a discussion of "symmetrical, consonant, or complementary works," Maria Nikolajeva and Carole Scott provide a dehistoricized reading of *The Little House*, claiming, "The words tell us exactly the same story as the one we can 'read' from the pictures . . . [and] leave very little, if anything, to the imagination."[7] Yet this ahistorical, apolitical reading of the picture book neglects the commentary on modernity present in all Burton's books. Nikolajeva and Scott's semiotic, genre-driven approach avoids the ideological implications of *The Little House* and focuses instead on its

> charming illustrations and a simple, yet poignant plot. . . . It is also, if not unique, quite unusual in its use of an inanimate object to represent the child. Definitely unique in this book is its fixed point of view,

FIGURE 4.3. A Mary Anne–style steam shovel smiles at the Little House as road building commences, in Burton's *The Little House* (1942). Years later, the damaged Little House is rescued from the city and restored to a country hillside.

where the reader/viewer is placed in front of the house as if it were a theater stage. . . . [However,] everything that happens around the Little House in the pictures is extensively described in the text. There is little for the reader to discover beyond the words. Moreover, the text is built around the key word "watch": "She watched the grass turn green,'"She watched the harvest gathered," and so on. The text mainly describes what the Little House sees, although the pictures are better suited to this purpose. Further, the words suggest that we as readers share the Little House's point of view, while in the pictures we are situated in front of her. Thus while the story and the pictures must surely be enjoyed together, they inevitably create a mutual redundancy.[8]

Far from being needlessly repetitive, however, *The Little House* makes a case for mindfulness around the verb "watch" and the silent immobility of the stalwart main character, which may indeed be assumed to be a child rather than a patient entity of a nonhuman sort, representing the passage of time and unappreciated, long-ago human endeavors. There is redundancy in the words and pictures, but this is not a mere matter of clarity or denotation. Without this thick pileup of verbal and visual imagery, *The Little House* would be ineffective as a commentary on modern urban development and as a holistic example of picture-book composition. In addition, Burton's words do not describe her specific historical references as old-fashioned carriages and dwellings make way for updated architecture and technologies, including a Mary Anne–like steam shovel on a road-building project, hastening the Little House's grief.

Nikolajeva and Scott claim, "Spatiotemporal relations is the only area in which words and pictures can never coincide.... Conventional (verbal) signs are suitable for narration ... while iconic (visual) signs are limited to description."[9] This offers some clues to their limited reading of Burton. *The Little House* does participate in spatiotemporal verbal-visual relations, but as a sequence and not as atomized parts. The constant slippage between signifieds and signifiers in a sequential word-picture text can go unnoticed in a semiotic reading determined to effect a separation between written word and drawn image; Nikolajeva and Scott leave comics out of their assessment (because comic books "have a poetics of their own")[10] and thus dismiss picture books' direct relation to graphic narrative. In *Understanding Comics* (1994), a foundational work in comics criticism and one that includes picture-book artists Raymond Briggs and Maurice Sendak among its list of exemplary comics creators, Scott McCloud demonstrates how time may be communicated visually and sequentially, just as it may be described in words. Further, the static placement of the house, forever facing the onlooker, implies not just a "theater stage" but the house's inability to see what literally is on the horizon. The Little House has her "back" to the encroaching metropolis—implying, perhaps, that she still sees the past. Readers do not share the House's viewpoint because they witness the approach of the city and reflect on Little House's unwise, near-tragic curiosity about city life. The reader's relation to the House is one of alarm, raising awareness of what is sacrificed to urban development.[11]

Burton's texts are products of their era in their design, fabrication, and grasp of the social imagination. *Choo Choo* is the work of an inexperienced artist, including some chaotically juxtaposed pages of disconnected railroad tracks, looping and flyaway lines and angles, and few integrated spreads. By the time of *Mike Mulligan and His Steam Shovel* and *The Little House*, Burton had learned how to expertly balance type and pictures. As in a socially and critically informed mural sequence, Burton's words and images for *Mike Mulligan* and *The Little House* harmonize in every spread. The humped hillsides and smoothly curved shapes in *Mike Mulligan* represent Burton's growth as an artist and mirror the Very Old Man's path in Gág's *Millions of Cats* a decade earlier. Her balanced word-image layouts recall Gág's integrated designs, too. Her fine-tuned attention to pictorial sequence, her attention to time of day and season cycles, and her increasing ability to craft dramatic, action-filled spreads qualify her as a creator of murals in miniature—that is, on a picture-book scale. At a time when muralists sought to capture regional flavor, and often ignited controversy for their representations of politicized labor and small-town life, Burton's picture books sympathetically addressed national ideology and pressing personal concerns. As picture books, these were privately held commodities rather than public art, yet they commented on public life in an enduring manner.

Although Burton's visual style in *Mike Mulligan* is homespun and down-to-earth, with a repetition of motifs like the sunburst and smiling sunshine that become even more evident in *The Little House*, she incorporates an industrial dimension into her folksy tale.[12] "Underlining the basic story lies a concern for the changing times—both cultural and mechanical—that confront Mary Anne," writes Elleman. "Burton dealt with the changes visually: automobiles share the scene with horses and buggies, and faces reflect a diversity of age and economic status—an aspect not often found in picture books of the era."[13] Whereas Gág's bucolic scenes superficially ignore technology yet connote modernity—for instance, via German expressionist-inspired imagery—Burton's *Mike Mulligan* acknowledges the incursions of technology into country life and, according to Elleman, implies that "survival results from adapting to changes in life,"[14] in this case negotiating inevitable technological progress and the displacement of workers and old methods.

Based on the redemption offered by small-town or rural life in Burton,

Jon C. Stott and Teresa Krier note the temptation to place Burton's books "within the pastoral tradition, which is based on the tension between country and city life, between the purity and innocence and simplicity of the country, and the subtlety, complexity, and impersonality of the city." Yet, they contend, Burton does not produce pastorals, in which characters generally return to an urban way of life disillusioned with both the corrupted city and the destruction of the idyllic country. Burton's work, Stott and Krier write, "lack[s] . . . the irony" of the pastoral form. In Burton's books, "an element of the older, more sensitive life is displaced by progress and technology and somehow this character finds its way back into the country. . . . Unlike the pastoralists . . . Burton allows the progressive element to be defeated and consistently idealizes the rural life to which her characters return." They conclude that *The Little House* "is escapism" as well as "one of the great celebrations of an irrevocably past way of life that can be found in children's literature, if not American literature generally." They come to this conclusion by reading the ending of *The Little House* (and, to a lesser extent, *Mike Mulligan*; they do not mention *Choo Choo*) as "wish fulfillment."[15] But this is not quite accurate, given that the wishes fulfilled are not fond dreams but last-minute, desperate compromises, and the endings allow for ambiguity. Mary Anne the steam shovel is transformed into a furnace, no longer able to dig or go outdoors (a steam shovel's typical habitat); as a steam shovel, she is perceived as useless to everyone but Mike himself. Mike Mulligan accepts a new job title as janitor despite his evident enthusiasm for skilled excavation work; if he did not love his old job, why take "such good care of Mary Anne that she never grew old"? The Little House is resituated on a rural hill, but only after the lengthy text alerts readers to the way urban sprawl crowds bucolic space. Even Choo Choo—a noisy, dirty engine—is dragged home by an emotionless modern train and resigns herself to her route, which she formerly wished to escape; readers know Jim the engineer can drive a newer, bigger engine if his old one wears out. Burton's conclusions do not provide absolute closure, even if they provide their sympathetic heroes with temporary contentment.

Rather than consigning *Mike Mulligan* and *Choo Choo* to a nonspecific past, Burton's picture books focus on time's passage, changing modes of dress and transportation, labor needs, and the usefulness or uselessness of machines and skilled people. These texts are not entirely hostile to urbanization, yet they aptly question what happens to relics of the old ways, be those relics mechanical or flesh-and-bone. These picture books acknowledge that older, slower means of production—described in the feminine—are devalued and replaced by indifferent, ungendered, and faster means of production. Yet Burton herself was captivated by machines and wrote in an autobiographical statement, "An engine on the Gloucester Branch of the Boston & Maine is the heroine of *Choo Choo*.'Mary Ann[e],' Mike Mulligan's steam shovel, I found digging the cellar of the new Gloucester High School. *The Little House* was inspired by the moving of our own house 'into the middle of a field with apple trees growing around,' and *Katy* [the snow plow of *Katy and the Big Snow*, 1943] is the pride and joy of the Gloucester Highway Department. Each new book is an incentive to the artist to spread his roots—to reach out and add to his store of subject material from which he can draw."[16] Her illustrations attest to this careful observation of and interest in development, even if her deepest sympathies lie with laborers and obsolete equipment.

Despite upbeat language, appealingly curvy illustrations, sympathetic mechanical characters, and semihappy endings, Burton's texts attest to a creeping disillusionment in the United States that prior children's picture books refused at the level of content. Burton's stories show how the American countryside has diminished and allow that the modern child readily accepts the uncanny vitality of the machine despite maintaining a capacity for empathy with flesh-and-blood humans and aging machine bodies. Organic and inorganic characters alike exhibit signs of humanity and work together in sympathetic teams, implying if not producing a compassionate reader whose subjectivity is shaped not just by human interaction but also by a close relation to motorized and electric objects. In a technological present and future, the child lacks adult nostalgia and interacts daily with inorganic objects and media, including picture books, that signal the complexities of their own reproduction as well as the social concerns of their adult creators. Burton's picture books represent this human-machine intimacy as an inevitability and provide cautionary lessons in identifying too strongly with nonliving things.

## WORKING-CLASS MACHINES IN THE MODERN METROPOLIS

Such affectionate but shrewd picture books posit that the twentieth-century human's fate is tied—perhaps too tightly—to his or her machines. Adults and children alike had come to identify with motorized equipment and inanimate consumer goods by the mid-1930s, complicating the dilemma of alienated labor and valuation of the worker in capitalist America.[17] Writer Hildegarde Hoyt Swift and illustrator Lynd Ward's *The Little Red Lighthouse and the Great Gray Bridge* (1942) mines territory familiar to any reader of Burton. In both *The*

*Little House* and *The Little Red Lighthouse*, an indifferent city rises around a small dwelling or work site, threatening its autonomy, its joyful fulfillment of its function, and its future as a site of memory. In both cases, events transpire so that each diminutive character (the Little House and the Little Red Lighthouse) attracts attention and is redeemed to private and public memory.

Like the Little House, the Little Red Lighthouse is a small building, stuck in its one spot and addressing a limited function. (Where Burton's House is a "she," Swift and Ward's hero is a gender-neutral "it" that nevertheless thinks for itself.) With the arrival of the Great Gray Bridge—actually the George Washington Bridge, constructed in 1931—the Little Red Lighthouse seems to have outlived its purpose as a guardian on the Hudson River and can only wait to be slated for demolition. Yet it is not quite as sanguine as the Little House, who waits passively until she is noticed and removed. The heroic Little Red Lighthouse has a job to do. It recognizes the danger that a thick fog poses to ships sailing by, planes flying past, and motorists crossing the enormous bridge that has grown to overshadow it (Figure 4.4).

In grainy black, red, and blue illustrations, which also picture humans including the Lighthouse's elderly keeper and several bridge construction workers, Ward gives the Lighthouse eyes and a mouth. He suggests with pillars, lights, and openings that the Great Gray Bridge has a face too, and he anthropomorphizes even a long-bearded, humanlike fog that "trie[s] to clutch the boats one by one" on the Hudson River. On the evening of the threatening fog, the Lighthouse cannot warn ships as usual unless the lighthouse-keeper comes to turn on its light. As it waits in the storm, the structure becomes panicked when its human helpmate has not arrived. In other words, the danger is due not to mechanical breakdown but to human error. The man finally arrives in a hurry, complaining that his keys were stolen by "those boys. . . . This will never happen again!" When he arrives, the Lighthouse beams again and its bell rings out a warning to all boats (and—something that goes unsaid—to the people *piloting* the boats). Meanwhile, up above, the illuminated Bridge does its part to warn cars and "the ships of the air," airplanes, which in 1941 might have been understood as flying into and out of Newark International Airport, completed in 1928. The Lighthouse's suspenseful tale implies concerns of its present day related to commuting and the safe, efficient flow of capital goods.

The Lighthouse (less so its klutzy keeper) cooperates with the flood-lit Bridge to sound a warning and flash its signal lights. The Lighthouse and Bridge, like their operators and builders, are terrified that someone might be hurt in inclement weather. Thus, *The Little Red Lighthouse and the Great Gray*

FIGURE 4.4. In Lynd Ward's illustrations for Hildegarde Hoyt Swift's *The Little Red Lighthouse and the Great Gray Bridge* (1942), a Hudson River lighthouse looks askance at bridge builders. Later, anthropomorphized fog threatens river traffic, and the Lighthouse teams with the Bridge to light the way for human travelers.

*Bridge* reassures readers against any fear of mechanical inefficiency or any nefarious mechanical takeover of society. Machines and the structures in which they operate are gigantic. They require monitoring, manpower, and muscle to control, and they have a tendency to break down at inconvenient times. But in this book, the smallest to the very largest buildings watch out for their fragile human users. Picture books such as *The Little Red Lighthouse* reinforce the benevolence of machines in readers' memories, particularly emphasizing the way kindly machines worry about one another and their tiny human operators.

These tropes of machine animism and cultural memory recur differently in a certifiably weird piece of work, writer Enid Johnson and illustrator Anne Merriman Peck's unpaginated *Runaway Balboa* (1938). In this indirect acknowledgment of U.S. dominion over Central America, an electric-powered, canal-boat-pulling "Mule" (or traincar) named Balboa takes a vacation from the Panama Canal Zone. "It is high time I got out of my rut," Balboa decides before jerking free of his tracks. Then, "without so much a glance at the Keeper in the Tower Balboa kicked up his heels and scampered away as fast as his cogs could carry him." He rushes through an area called "Spotless Town," where the soldiers and sailors live, and careens into "the old Spanish Town where the natives live," less spotless than the American-operated area. He frightens the "brown-skinned people in cool white clothes," who are occupied with drinking coconut milk and eating papayas, then bolts for the "untidy" jungle, "very different from the spick-and-span Canal where everything stayed in its proper place" (Plate 16). Tormented by monkeys and parrots, who refer to him derisively as "Man-Made Thing," he regrets running away; eventually, the animals help him return to the Canal Zone, where he is cleaned off and received by the U.S. president. *Runaway Balboa* provides armchair travelers with a comical account of the Canal Zone, sidestepping any account of violent conquest and proposing that the segregated spaces for soldiers and natives, Spotless Town and Spanish Town, "mules" and monkeys, technologies and tropics, are sustainable divisions.

Other popular 1930s picture books demystify everyday transportation and blue-collar labor for a middle-class readership, but without the cautionary notes that make Burton's picture books memorable. Lois Lenski's Mr. Small series offers gentle accounts of a placid man driving his car (*The Little Auto*, 1934) and flying a personality-free plane (*The Little Airplane*, 1938). Lenski caters to the young reader who likes machines, but she does not question the infatuation as Burton does. Other artists—notably ex–Disney animator and *Fortune* magazine illustrator Hardie Gramatky—borrow Burton's anthropomorphism without her perceptive commentary on labor.

Gramatky, who moved from Hollywood to New York and watched Hudson River traffic from his studio, invented anthropomorphic machines that often act without apparent human intervention. His popular, unpaginated *Little Toot* (1939) tells the story of a boyish tugboat and its crotchety male elders, and reinforces the notion that machines lead lives of their own ("the river where Little Toot lives is full of ships"; "a tugboat's life is a busy, exciting one").[18] Like a kid, Toot loves to blow smoke balloons and make figure eights in the water, "although his antics annoyed the hard-working tugboats awfully" (Figure 4.5). (Gramatky leaves it to the imagination how a boat "grows up.") Little Toot gets in the way of his father, Big Toot, along with "a big tug named J. G. McGillicuddy, which was bound down stream to pick up a string of coal barges from Hoboken." (This tugboat's Irish name implies the *Mike Mulligan*-esque working-class identities of Little Toot and company, particularly given *Mike Mulligan*'s pie-baking character Mrs. McGillicuddy and a moment in *Little Toot* when "Oscar, the Scandinavian [cruise ship], rudely blew steam in his face.") Eventually, the other tugboats "began to make fun of him, calling him a sissy who only knew how to play," threatening his masculinity as one who will not work; the term "sissy" reminds readers that muscular labor is an admirable masculine pursuit.

Ultimately, Little Toot puts his smoke-blowing skills to use by skywriting an SOS for an ocean liner that has run aground during a storm, and afterward helps pull the liner to safety. "The people on board began to cheer," and Toot gains an

FIGURE 4.5. Disney animator Hardie Gramatky gives personalities to boats in his story of a baby tugboat, *Little Toot* (1939).

appreciation for the tugboat trade. Besides this quick reference to a ship's passengers, who are at the mercy of the weather and stuck on their foundering machine, people play a negligible role in *Little Toot*; the only other specific mention of humans refers to "crews who speak strange tongues" in port, and there is no suggestion that Toot or his paternal companions have captains (or female counterparts). In Gramatky's pictures, small human figures are visible on nontugs, which are noncharacter boats, but they're blurry and inconsequential. The drama takes place exclusively at the level of the young boat and his bravery.

Gramatky's tales of anthropomorphized, human-scale machines, whose central figures tend to be marginal or challenged in their size and strength and in clear danger of becoming obsolete along with their operators, belong to the late 1930s and early 1940s. Gramatky followed *Little Toot* with *Hercules* (1940), the unpaginated story of a horse-drawn fire engine from the time, according to the narrator, "when *your* grandfather was young." Hercules requires a crew of three male horses along with three bearded men: a fireman named Hokey, who "kept steam up in the big boiler," an engineer named Pokey, who "watched the gauges and connected the hose to hydrants," and a driver named Smokey. (Again, there is a close similarity to Burton's work; *Choo Choo's* Jim, Oley, and Archibald resemble Hercules' crew, and a horse-drawn fire truck appears in *Mike Mulligan and His Steam Shovel*.) One day, Hercules and his crew rush to a fire to find it has been extinguished by "a new kind of fire engine—an engine that wasn't pulled by horses at all. . . . Already one of these monsters was coming back from the fire. . . . Hercules met him face to face." In Gramatky's illustration, the horses, driver, and Hercules stare at a faceless fire engine, and a puff of black smoke forms a question mark over Hercules' antiquated chassis—the same question mark that appears in *Mike Mulligan* when Mary Anne realizes that she and Mike have not left themselves a way out of the cellar and may not get paid. The perkier Hercules has the same terrible epiphany, presumably shared by Hokey, Pokey, and Smokey. For Hercules, "Life was unbearable after that. The Aldermen and the Mayor solemnly decided that Hercules was 'obsolete.' He was too old—too slow. So they retired him." The three horses assigned to Hercules are farmed out too: "the black one to a riding academy, the dapple-gray to a junk dealer, and the white one to the police force. / And Hercules grew old like a soldier pining for the smell of gunpowder. / But Hokey, Pokey, and Smokey, because they loved the firehouse, stayed on. / 'Wait and see,' said Smokey, 'someday there's goin' to be a fire—the worst fire this city ever saw. An' we'll be there—with Hercules. There's things that Hercules and horses can do that those trucks can't do.'"

Unlike the nameless horses, Hercules has a mythic moniker; unlike Hokey, Pokey, and Smokey, with their rhyming names and triple effort (despite differentiated roles on board), Hercules is a singular entity. As the men predict, Hercules gets called back into service to fight a raging blaze the "horseless carriages" cannot reach. Hokey, Pokey, and Smokey never leave their post, but the reassigned horses valiantly hurry to the firehouse when they once again hear Hercules' "big brass bell"; one throws his rider, one leaves the junk cart, and one carries its rider to the firehouse. Yet it is Hercules who takes credit for saving the day: "And that was how Hercules got into the museum." At the museum, Hercules poses with a dinosaur skeleton, analogous to his own technology (Figure 4.6). In a second illustration, Hokey, Pokey, and Smokey sit in the background with a resting Dalmatian. They wear suits and ties, and three matching hats lie unused on the floor, as though the workers no longer have need for occupational uniforms. Everyone is out of a job except Hercules, who becomes a museum piece and a repository of American memory.

*Loopy* (1941), Gramatky's unpaginated story of a boyish "hedgehopper" airplane that yearns to be a skywriter, avoids human concerns and returns to the independent-machine narrative of *Little Toot*. Gramatky uses some of Burton's characteristic layout techniques, such as aligning printed text along a diagonal margin, but, unlike Burton, he includes wordless full-color spreads. Loopy, the title airplane, dislikes his job of "help[ing] the pilot teach flyers how to fly" and "imagined what it would be like to fly by himself, with no pilot to hold him in check and no heavy-handed student to horse him around." Loopy gets his wish when, guided by a careless pilot, he flies into a roiling black cloud. As the danger becomes evident, the plane's controls rebel and "glare" at the pilot, making "angry faces" like the Disney characters Gramatky animated. The inept pilot, having betrayed the dependable equipment, parachutes out, leaving "poor Loopy, harried by wind and dark and lightning, with no one to help him." As Loopy starts to spin, "he remembered the things he had planned to do if he ever was on his own. Instinctively he worked his elevators and suddenly realized he could check his fall." Loopy takes charge "instinctively," like an animal, and he outflies the storm with flocks of happy birds in his wake: "If the gas had only held out, he would have kept it up all day. But Loopy, wise airman that he was, knew it was time to go home" (Figure 4.7). Granted "airman" status, Loopy lands triumphantly: "Now he never bothers with students. He is a skywriter. . . . And from the ground you can always tell his work by the smooth, clear letters and from the fact he never fails to dot his i's." Unlike Burton's Choo

Today Hercules is in a museum. Had it not been for a wonderful act of courage—and a little luck—he never would have won such a fine place.

FIGURE 4.6. In *Hercules* (1940), Gramatky associates an obsolete fire truck with a mythic hero and a dinosaur while suggesting the smiling truck took pride in its work.

Choo, who is chastened for her escape and put back on her tedious route, Loopy requires no discipline and even gets a promotion.

*Loopy's* conclusion, however liberatory, signals the ridiculous limits of the sentient-machine tale. Barbara Bader approves of Gramatky's lively visual characterizations, pointing out that when Little Toot's "spirits soar, his bow sweeps up, his visor perks, his flag whips smartly behind; morose, even his smokestack sags; aghast, everything tenses. "In animating the inanimate . . . ," wrote Robert D. Feild in 1942, "[a Disney animator] must be able to feel exactly how the particular character would behave under all circumstances."[19] According to Feild, Gramatky succeeds. But "in subsequent books, Gramatky applied the same formula with less success, probably because it was a formula—the likes of Hercules the superannuated fire engine and Loopy the irresponsible airplane are not to be seen from any window."[20] Buoyed by such utopian depictions, moralistic Little Golden Books of the forties would reduce machines to

The dials on the instrument board glared back at him like angry faces.

The storm no longer frightened him.

FIGURE 4.7. During a storm, Loopy the airplane and his dashboard controls reject an amateur pilot in Gramatky's *Loopy* (1941).

harmless, misbehaving toys without human operators. Humans could coach machines to work or corral machines that acted irresponsibly, but humans no longer needed to operate anything. Gertrude Crampton and Tibor Gergely's *Tootle* (1945) features a locomotive like *Choo Choo* who jumps his tracks to race a wild horse and romp in a flowery field; Crampton and Gergely's *Scuffy the Tugboat* (1946) describes a toy who leaves his familiar bathtub and makes his way downriver to the sea, only to regret his adventure when he is caught in a flood.[21] Such accounts of the dissatisfied worker have parallels in 1920s studies of industrial psychology, a result of Taylorism and worker exhaustion.[22] Later picture books domesticate this anxiety in favor of amusement.

By the mid-1940s, possibly due to the overwhelming crisis of war, the mechanical, commodified machine body in picture books had been made cute. Even Burton's *Katy and the Big Snow* dispenses with human characters and labor concerns while preserving the femininity and helpfulness of the mechanical protagonist, a snow plow who cheerfully digs out her hometown after an enormous blizzard (no human operators seem necessary). As Burton's earlier work demonstrates, the demise of machines and human livelihoods belonged to the nostalgic picture books and media of the Depression. The fairy tale of modernity emerged and evolved to address timely issues of labor and obsolescence, in powerful contradiction to syrupy accounts of "timeless" children's fare. Texts such as *Choo Choo* and *Mike Mulligan and His Steam Shovel* resonate with the proletarian novel, Franklin D. Roosevelt's New Deal programs, the regionalist concerns of muralists, and cautionary films about industrialism that demonstrated the dehumanization resulting from contemporary modes of production and described people's failures to find gainful employment in the modern economy.

### "Z IS FOR ZEAL, AN AMERICAN TRAIT": ACCOUNTS OF DEMOCRACY AND PATRIOTISM

In 1939, artist James Daugherty, who had illustrated Stewart E. White's *Daniel Boone, Wilderness Scout* in 1927, published his own *Daniel Boone*.[23] Like Averill and Rojankovsky's version eight years earlier, Daugherty's *Daniel Boone* swarms with hale and hearty Kentucky pioneers menaced by bloodthirsty, kidnapping-crazed Native Americans (Figure 4.8). Boone is "the hunted fox of the wilderness with the red dogs in close pursuit" (57). The story reels with knife- and gunplay and depicts a slave-era fort as a "fantastic pageant" including "the black faces of African Negroes. . . . Around these wilderness outposts surged a drama of fierce passions and violent deeds" (54). *Daniel Boone* projects the exuberant visual styles of the late 1930s, reconstructs 1776 America prior to another war, and self-consciously asserts its brand of American ideology. Daugherty writes with passion and alludes to Depression-era economics in his account of the battles for American independence:

> Just as New England was starting on her own to make an independent
> nation of contrivers and inventors, of munition-makers and sermon-
> preachers, so over the mountains to the West another America was
> making its own kind of democracy, making war with rifle and ax and
> plow, wiping out the Indians and buffalo, destroying the great for-
> ests, and raising up green armies of tall corn in the valley bottoms.
> One was to be a nation of money-counters and machines, the other a
> barefooted rail-splitting, haranguing, horse-racing democracy of lean
> mule-drivers and land-poor, camp-meeting corn-huskers. One stood
> on the shoulders of black slavery, the other on wage slavery. . . . [They]

stood for two ways of life, two forces that pull and tug and say: "What price democracy?" (46)

Daugherty's rhetoric, with allusions to deforestation and industry, and comparisons of "black slavery" and "wage slavery," pleased the voting members of the American Library Association, who awarded it a Newbery Medal. Likewise, Daugherty's visual compositions—lithographs printed in browns and greens suggestive of unspoiled dirt and trees—impressed his audience.

Since the 1920s, Daugherty had been a muralist and a graphic illustrator, attentive to color combinations and the interplay of written text and heroic visual image. His populism and nationalist zeal were implicit in the words and images of his children's books, including *Andy and the Lion* (1938), which venerated tight-knit working- and middle-class American communities (Figure 4.9). According to Julia Mickenberg, Daugherty joined fellow artists including "Peggy Bacon, Crockett Johnson, Lynd Ward, . . . Syd Hoff, and Elizabeth Olds—[who] moved from producing socially conscious art to creating picture books for children."[24] Daugherty did both simultaneously, and in this he is remarkably similar to Robert McCloskey, whose 1940 *Lentil* and 1941 *Make Way for Ducklings* lament the decline of small-town America, albeit rather cheerfully. Although Daugherty's media and format differ as he shifts from murals to children's media, there is no divide between the ideologies of his wall art and of his picture books.[25]

For the Newbery award celebration, Lynd Ward wrote an admiring piece on Daugherty's mastery of picture book and mural: "Beneath this apparent disparity there exists a logical unity. . . . His work in each form gains sustenance from his experience in the other."[26] Ward compares Daugherty's prolific work as an author-illustrator to an eight-mural sequence the artist executed for Fairfield Court, a low-income residence constructed in Stamford, Connecticut, for the Federal Housing Project (1937). In the murals, "the broad theme of America's conquest of distance is given a boisterous setting of human and often humorous reactions to mechanical progress . . . ," Ward said. "It is a far cry from these twenty-five-foot walls to the nine-inch page of a book. But those who cannot live in Fairfield Court in Stamford will sense the same gay energy in any one of a dozen Daugherty-illustrated books."[27] *Life* magazine printed color images of these murals, captioned "The Iron Horse," in which a locomotive startles live horses; "Steamboat around the Bend," which idealizes a leisurely crowd of slaves and plantation owners; and "The Model-T Decade," in which a cheerful family waits while two men repair a broken-down car on the road to Weston, Connecticut (Figure 4.10). The festive images owe a debt to regionalist painters

FIGURE 4.8. James Daugherty's Newbery Medal–winning *Daniel Boone* (1939) is framed as a patriotic American epic during a period of international crisis, yet contains repellent caricatures of Native Americans that date it today.

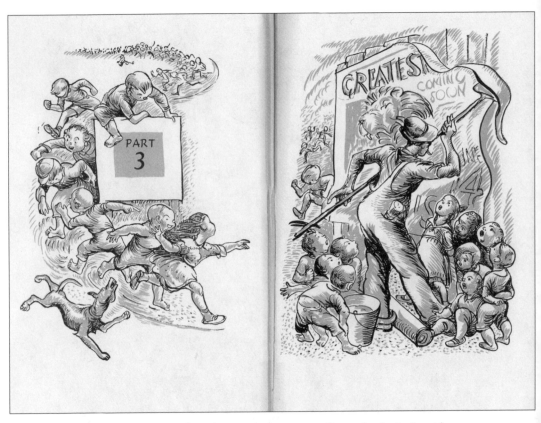

FIGURE 4.9. James Daugherty's experience as a muralist and colorist is evident in the regionalist style of *Andy and the Lion* (1938), which is printed in goldenrod yellow and black.

such as Thomas Hart Benton, who often took farming and agricultural laborers as his subjects. Daugherty's murals conjure an air of amusement and easy pleasure, casting scenes of technological and social change as quaint episodes in a not-too-distant American history—never mind the blithe insertion of languid slaves (or, at best, restful African American tenant farmers) in the celebratory landscape, which implies a respite from hard work.[28]

Daugherty's books and murals exemplify the overlap between verbal-visual storytelling across pages and across a thematically unified set of walls. Unlike a picture book, a mural presents everything at once on the picture plane yet must be perceived in concentrated pieces and at various depths. When a person scans one of several walls, additional details await notice and crowd the peripheral vision; foreground and background images compete for attention. Similarly, a picture book's turning pages reveal and conceal information by design.

"In sharp distinction to the technical form of the easel painting both of these media imply talking to a large audience and saying something to that audience that shall be both articulate and meaningful," Ward adds.[29] Ward does not dwell on sequentiality beyond noting "the interlocking relationship between word and picture that is the essence of [the picture book] technique,"[30] although he may have assumed his ALA audience grasped the finer distinctions between single-frame easel paintings, murals, and comics sequences. Ward's listeners doubtless knew his picture books and his wordless woodcut novels, influenced by Frans Masereel's graphic narratives.[31]

Daugherty's political ideals always were part of his narrative style, including his work for young readers. He responded enthusiastically to the 1913 Armory Show in New York, which led him toward "radical visual imagery" and "the depiction of rapid movement, inspired by Futurist dynamism."[32] Daugherty contributed modernist, full-color drawings to the *Sunday New York Herald*'s magazine section and befriended New York artists who admired the abstract color experimentation of Robert and Sonia Delaunay. In addition, Daugherty's World War I military service, camouflaging ships for the navy, required a practical application of his artistic ability to oversize spaces and "left him eager to work on enormous formats."[33] (According to Gertrude Stein, when Picasso first saw a camouflaged truck in the First World War, he exclaimed, "Yes it is we who made it, that is Cubism.")[34] Later, Daugherty's experiments in color synchronism and modernist abstraction led to his mainstream recognition in *Time*, *Life*, and the *New York Times*,[35] and he gravitated alternately to the public mural format and the domestic, intimate scale of the picture book.

As Ward suggests, Daugherty's murals and printed texts convey pride in U.S. history along with ideals of American cooperation. Daugherty's all-American reputation was carefully stage-managed, at least in the publishing industry. In 1929, *Publishers Weekly* saluted him in a profile that notes his "vigorous, nervous line, [with] the same luminous color as El Greco's, swirling in color designs as sinuous as the drawings."[36] The profile writer follows this mention of El Greco, referred to as "the Greek," with the qualifier that Daugherty's European-influenced art "is a plastic manifestation of Americanism, and the spirit that is responsible for it is as thoroughly American as Faneuil Hall"[37]— foreshadowing the American Revolutionary tilt of Daugherty's favorite themes. (Daugherty also illustrated an edition of Washington Irving's *Knickerbocker History of New York*, edited by Anne Carroll Moore, and Carl Sandburg's *Abe Lincoln Grows Up*.) Critics thus distance Daugherty's modernism from corruptive foreign influences and link it with the U.S. military and the domestic film

FIGURE 4.10. James Daugherty's nostalgic 1937 murals for the Fairfield Court housing project in his home state, Connecticut, celebrate mechanical ingenuity and the turn of the nineteenth to the twentieth century.

industry (his "camouflage painting came in handy in painting . . . vast murals in new movie theaters").[38]

Daugherty's Newbery acceptance speech, "Children's Books in a Democracy," connects modern mural art, picture books, and fervent expressions of American nationalism. This unreservedly patriotic talk foregrounds concerns for censorship and child citizens on the brink of another war. Obliquely alluding to his own achievements, Daugherty associates children's books with "national art . . . sponsored by a people's government": "From coast to coast one walks into public buildings whose walls are glowing with the ineffable beauty of significant mural painting. The theme of the pictures is not the silly goddesses and allegories of the Boston and Washington libraries, but the life of today in our America—the true art of democracy. . . . All this may not bear directly on children's books, but it has a lot to do with demonstrating that the spiritual and creative values of art can be achieved in democracy and express visually its meanings in books and pictures."[39] Daugherty separates murals' proletarian themes from children's literature, but his audience could make the connections easily enough. Ward, in his homage, feels that Daugherty's Newbery is "an act of long-delayed justice" for someone personifying the "'American spirit.' . . . Daugherty, like Whitman, is singing a song of America."[40]

*Daniel Boone*, a backward glance at a legendary American figure—one not generous to Native Americans or people of African heritage—complicates Daugherty's account of American community. Similar shortcomings may be seen in Hildegarde Hoyt Swift's *The Railroad to Freedom: A Story of the Civil War* (1932), a 1933 Newbery runner-up that Daugherty illustrated with images of Harriet Tubman, drawn with his trademark coiling and curvy lines. Swift's vernacular writing and Daugherty's stylized ink-line drawings mingle African American heroism with essentialism.[41] As in his nostalgic depiction of slaves at a riverboat race, Daugherty trades in American folk icons and a problematic vision of agricultural labor.

"Children's Books in a Democracy," like many statements Daugherty would make to organizations concerned with forties children's publishing, suggests a white, middle-class, populist vision and inflexible attitudes on the high-minded purpose of public art, children's literature included. He mocks "complacent oldsters satisfied with handing the rising generation a gas mask and a copy of *Alice in Wonderland* with which to tread the bomb-strewn path of childhood":

> I do not mean that the fall book list of juveniles should bristle with
> "Tom Sawyer Among the Okies," or "Snow White and the Seven

Dwarfs Before the Dies Committee," or "Pinocchio and the Trojan Horse," intriguing as they might be. But I do think that somewhere between sappiness and sourness children's books can go along courageously and frankly and gaily with the forward-marching masses of young people to tackle with imagination and good cheer the tough problems they may have ahead.

If it is true that the Horatio Alger books helped produce the industrial giants and economic royalists of today, and if our capitalistic system is only the triumph of Alger over Karl Marx, then certainly modern juvenile literature today and tomorrow can confidently challenge the Nazi Primer, the brutality and dullness of dictator propaganda as well as our own apathy and indifference, and in its own particular field help to realize the fullness and goodness of living that is the American faith.[42]

Daugherty sets an unambiguous political agenda for children's literature as politicized modern art. He wants to "challenge the Nazi Primer" with propaganda of his own creation. Such firm statements enable readers to reevaluate Daugherty picture books including *Andy and the Lion*, which revises the Androcles myth with a barefoot, overalls-wearing American farm boy and an escaped circus lion. In the context of Daugherty's speech, towheaded Andy becomes a healthy, energetic, literate child of sharecroppers or Midwestern farm laborers, representative of small-town American gusto. The three-part book and Daugherty's antic yellow-and-black lithographs mime a theatrical series of three acts, not unlike a dramatic mural sequence designed to play across multiple walls.

Karal Ann Marling describes the mural as "a frozen movie projected gratis on the post office wall," and details the controversies around the design and installation of murals, which required community consensus and frequently were brought down under charges of propagandizing.[43] Marling's mural-movie metaphor, in the context of Daugherty's commissions and movie-theater murals, indicates the diverse media available to spectators of the 1930s and 1940s and the provocative content of the regionalist mural, often conceived by creative artists with a progressive, if downplayed, political agenda. Movies, murals, and picture books are not equivalent media, but these coexisting technologies represent visible and modern modes of public storytelling. Daugherty, in his *Daniel Boone* and other children's work, imagined revolutionary potential in pictorial children's literature and the mural alike, and used both these formats to disseminate a problematic, but undeniably popular, account of American democracy.

Among Daugherty's contemporaries and fellow ALA honorees was the picture-book artist Robert Lawson. After catapulting to fame with his and Munro Leaf's *The Story of Ferdinand* (1936), Lawson produced memorable work including *Ben and Me* (1939), a humorous tale of Revolutionary War–era statesman Benjamin Franklin "as written by his Good Mouse Amos," and *They Were Strong and Good* (1940), an account of his pioneer ancestors. Lawson inserts ample political content into *Ben and Me*, including unflattering portraits of the "erratic temperaments" of Italian and Spanish mice (this in the era of Franco and Mussolini), admiration of "wild, uncouth" Russian mice, who fight viciously, and affirmative accounts of Swedish mice as "stalwart, steady, powerful warriors" (86–87). Lawson also describes Amos's radical associate, a reckless and doomed mouse named Red, who "had come up from Virginia with Mr. [Thomas] Jefferson—in his saddlebag. Like his patron, he was redheaded, a fiery revolutionist, and a great talker. Scarce had they arrived before Red began preaching Revolution to the mice around the Inn stables" (66–67). Red writes a mouse manifesto that Amos borrows and shows to Ben. When the manifesto becomes the humans' Declaration of Independence, Red "was in a fury and orated for hours about this theft of his labors, but we all thought it a rather good joke on him" (69). In effect, Lawson shows Benjamin Franklin exploiting the mice the way the British exploited the colonies, and smilingly accuses the Founding Fathers of plagiarism from rodents. Like Daugherty's *Daniel Boone* or Esther Forbes's novel *Johnny Tremain* (1943), albeit with comic and fanciful touches, *Ben and Me* participates in the tendency to retell Revolutionary War history at the time of World War II. It does not touch upon the more recent Civil War; an Amos type as General Grant or General Lee's sidekick would never have passed as comedy. Lawson ensures that revolutionary sentiment stands at a safe distance from the present day and styles it as solidarity among American colonists rather than among fellow denizens of his own Popular Front era.

By comparison, *They Were Strong and Good* mirrors the folksy patriotism of *Ben and Me*, but without the leavening humor. It presents an expansionist United States dominated by passionate Anglo-American Christians and suggests that white settlers triumphed over obstacles like hostile Native Americans on the basis of pure strength and goodness. Lawson's righteous title echoes that of John Steinbeck and Dorothea Lange's photo-illustrated political pamphlet *Their Blood Is Strong* (1938), about the fortitude of white explorers in dangerous territory that is rightfully theirs to conquer.[44] The solemn, high-contrast imagery of *They Were Strong and Good* conveys a stern, purposeful attitude toward Anglo-Saxon progress. And its achievement of the 1941 Caldecott Medal, surprising to anyone who scans its polemical content today, says much about the ideological, racially divisive climate of late thirties and early forties America, as well as about acceptable prewar expressions of U.S. nationalism. Lawson supports what Caroline Levander describes as an Emersonian belief in the greatness of Anglo-Saxon heritage among the Founding Fathers, specifically white settlers. Inherent in descriptions of this Anglo-Saxon love of liberty is a sense of superiority to races colonized by white arrivistes, even as the American colonists themselves felt enslaved by and broke from British rule in the Revolutionary War.[45]

The autobiographical narrator of *They Were Strong and Good* explains that his ancestors helped found the United States: "This is not alone the story of my parents and grandparents, it is the story of the parents and grandparents of most of us who call ourselves Americans. . . . Let us be proud of them and guard well the heritage they have left us." Lawson speaks to "most of us who call ourselves Americans," suggesting that some who called themselves Americans might not qualify. At a time when the international economic and political crisis was deepening, Europe was in the grip of war, and U.S. tensions around race and ethnicity continued to be volatile, Lawson asserted that "we" Americans must "guard well" an implicitly white, Protestant heritage.

*They Were Strong and Good* includes six minichapters, starting with "My Mother's Father," a Scottish sailor pictured with a caricatured black serving boy and a slouching, pirate-like Cuban man, and "My Mother's Mother," a Dutch immigrant living in Paterson, New Jersey. Lawson skillfully balances words and images, urging readers to appreciate industrialization and the years' passage by contrasting the smoky East Coast factories of 1940 ("The City of Paterson stands there now and looks about like this—") and a bucolic picture of a nineteenth-century farm ("But in those days it looked more like this—") (Figure 4.11). He explains how his grandparents met and moved to Minnesota, and then he leaves them behind to pen a new chapter, titled "My Mother": "When my mother was a little girl there were Indians in Minnesota—tame ones. My mother did not like them. They would stalk into the kitchen without knocking and sit on the floor. Then they would rub their stomachs and point to their mouths to show that they were hungry." In the image, a small child in a cotton dress watches while an African American woman in an apron waves a broom, shooing away a Native American man and woman. The Native people leave hastily, greedily looking at the pie they carry away. Although the caricatured black woman goes unmentioned, she establishes a servile, comic role for people of African descent among the "strong and good" white ancestors. The Indians have no language ("they would point to their mouths" when hungry) and no manners, despite the fact that they are "tame ones" and pose no physical threat. Just as nonwhite people are excluded from the foreword's "most of us," the non-white reader is the implied Other of the entire visual–verbal text.

Lawson's second section includes chapters on "my father's father," who "fought the Indians in the Seminole War . . . [then] decided to be a preacher and fight the Powers of Evil," and "my father's mother." Again, Native Americans are antagonistic, analogous to "the Powers of Evil" that the preacher battles. A brief chapter called "My Father" likewise takes a dim view of ethnoracial difference: "When my father was very young he had two dogs and a colored boy. The dogs were named Sextus Hostilius and Numa Pompilius. The colored boy was just my father's age. He was a slave, but they didn't call him that. They just called him Dick. He and my father and the two hound dogs used to hunt all day long." This passage—revised in later editions—places the slave boy second in importance to the hunting dogs.[46] Even if the boys' mutual participation in the hunt implies a grudging equality between them, Lawson's illustration depicts their actual, uneven relationship: the author-illustrator pictures a crouching white boy with a long rifle and a black boy walking behind him as his porter, carrying two dead rabbits. Yet slaves' inferior status passes without further comment; it is presented as natural. In a subsequent image of the "father's father" going "off to fight the Yankees," Dick and another slave cover their eyes as though weeping for sorrow. In this picture, the son with the rifle leans sadly against a tree, too. The remainder of the tale chronicles the boy's exploits during the Civil War (in a dangerous country "filled with deserters and runaway slaves"). Lawson explains that at the end of the war, "Numa Pompilius and Sextus Hostilius and Dick were all gone," although he does not mention abolition. Instead, he explains that the young man, his father, migrated to New York.

> He didn't make much of a fortune, but he *did* meet my mother. . . .
> So they were married. They worked hard and were strong and good. They had many children and one of them happened to be ME.
> I am proud of my mother and my father and of their mothers and fathers. I am proud of the country that they helped to build.

In *They Were Strong and Good*, members of a privileged class attain success through a combination of sweat and destiny. They marry happily and have "many

FIGURE 4.11. Robert Lawson, overviewing the industrial history of Paterson, New Jersey, provides images of its 1940s factories and its nineteenth-century farms in his family history, *They Were Strong and Good* (1940).

children" who grow up to be the writers of history. This text orients its child subject toward the past and toward a narrow version of American history rather than directing the reader toward an understanding of contemporary events and uncertainty. It ostensibly recuperates the ancestral past, yet exists firmly in its 1940 context.

*They Were Strong and Good* was by no means extraordinary in its time. What is extraordinary, to readers today, is the evident acceptability of the ideas expressed. Lawson's notoriety and skill as an artist helped him reach a wider audience than most picture-book creators, but otherwise *They Were Strong and Good* is an ordinary expression of American nationalism for its day, which makes its racism and ethnic slurs all the more striking now. Another problematic example comes from the well-known children's creators Maud and Miska Petersham, whose *An American ABC* (1941) likewise appeals to a nation on the brink of, and then officially involved in, the Second World War. If Lawson's *They Were Strong and Good* inspires nationalism with specific stories of immigrant grandparents, a slaveholding father, and a mother acquainted with

impolite Indians, the Petershams' ABC provides a more generalized account
of U.S. history, using blue or red display type to identify each letter of the
alphabet. According to a survey of U.S. children's literature, the Petershams'
"most distinguished work was very American: *An American ABC* (1941) and
*The Rooster Crows: A Book of American Rhymes and Jingles* (Caldecott Medal,
1946)."[47] Yet this praise of the couple's "distinguished . . . very American" work
neglects the brand of national identity the texts promote. *The Rooster Crows*
was altered in the 1950s to remove a stereotypical image of an African American child, and *An American ABC* primarily celebrates the Pilgrims and a Revolutionary War–era America while erasing or essentializing people of color
(Figure 4.12).

On the opening page, "A is for AMERICA / The land I love," a boy in blue
denim overalls and a red-striped shirt naps comfortably on a flowery hillside,
backed by a fantasy image of a bald eagle and vertical red stripes suggestive of the
flag. This is bookended by the closing spread, "Z is for Zeal / An American trait,"

FIGURE 4.12. Proclaiming "This is America," Maud and Miska Petersham picture
a globe featuring the Americas for *An American ABC* (1941), published when U.S.
involvement in World War II was imminent. The book, which opens and closes with
blond children of the 1940s, salutes colonists, heroes of the American Revolution,
frontiersmen, and European immigrants.

A is for AMERICA
The land I love

Z is for ZEAL
An American trait

It was zeal which made navigators of old voyage over dangerous seas and find this New World.

It was zeal that gave the early settlers the strength and the courage to build their homes in the great wilderness of a strange new land.

It was zeal that kept the colonies together and won for them their independence.

It is this same zeal that will keep America a great land and a land of liberty and freedom.

and a full-page image of the boy leading a girl by the hand across a meadow, while a guardian eagle spreads its wings overhead. Zeal, claims the text, "will keep America a great land and a land of liberty and freedom." Most spreads between *A* and *Z* concern the founding and colonization of America, larded with images of the star-spangled banner ("N is for National Anthem," "O is for Old Glory"), and a few make reference to religion (including "F is for Freedom," which promotes "the right to worship God in one's own way" but pictures only one option: a Christian girl kneeling to say her prayers). Some pages attest to iconic figures. Predictably, "D is for Daniel Boone," among "the bravest and strongest of the white men" and bold enough to challenge "tribes of redskins with tomahawks and war paint"; a less expected spread, "S is for South America / and for Simon Bolivar," pictures a uniformed Bolívar, on a white horse, greeted by two barefoot South Americans in woven ponchos. This image of the Venezuela-born Bolívar allows the Petershams to note that the United States and South America "have now come together in an All-American Union, a Pan American union for peace and friendship and to help one another." Bolívar, who modeled his vicious battles against colonial Spain on the American Revolution, thus amplifies the patriotic values of *An American ABC* and underscores modern political treaties. Ethnic diversity, too, is acknowledged in the spread "E is for Emigrants," which pictures an Eastern European father, mother, and three children on the deck of a ship. The text implies the importance of patrilineal descent while recommending an unexamined "goodness" among neophyte citizens: "Our great-great-grandfathers, our grandfathers, even perhaps our fathers, were all emigrants to America. . . . They came to America because this country stood for Freedom. . . . Good emigrants make true Americans."

If *An American ABC* nods to forties internationalism and a spirit of revolution, its notable omissions and misrepresentations are indicative of forties ideology, too. The lone African American child illustrated in the book sits on a rail fence and gapes in amazement as another boy ("G is for George Washington / The Father of his country") rides bareback on a colt. The only other mention of African Americans appears in the context of "L is for Lincoln / Honest Abe Lincoln," who "worked, and finally died, for two great causes—to free the Negroes from slavery, and to keep this country a united nation."

The book includes comparatively numerous representations of Native Americans, but in a troubling manner. In a spread dated 1621 and headlined "R is for Redskins, the first Americans," a Native man identified as "Squanto . . . one of the friendly redskins," teaches a white boy to catch eels in a brook. The Petershams picture the man wearing a loincloth and a feather, exoticizing him in relation to the boy, who wears rolled-up pants and has left his hat, shoes, and shirt on the riverbank. The Native man towers over the boy and hands him an eel, effectively passing on knowledge for the colonists' use in the story of how America came to be. The text tautologically repeats, "The redskins or Indians of North and South America were the first real Americans," without qualifying the equation of "redskins" to "Indians" or saying what "real Americans" (as opposed, perhaps, to "true Americans," on the Emigrants spread) might imply. This superficially inclusive story verbally and visually marginalizes Native Americans in its national origin myth, relegating them to the past, as in Walter Cole's 1932 *ABC*

*Book of People.* Elsewhere, "T is for Thanksgiving," where Pilgrims serve plates of food to obliging, quiet Natives; and "J is for Jamestown," which pictures Captain John Smith persuading one of "the unfriendly Indians," who sullenly dips his chin and crosses his arms, to take a blue blanket in trade for two woven baskets full of corn. *An American ABC* likely could not appear in an updated edition, because of offensive Native American caricatures that easily passed muster for educators in the forties, yet it makes a potent analogue to new patriotic texts that appear in a flag-fueled twenty-first century context.

*An American ABC* largely situates nationhood in a pre-twentieth-century space, bypassing time-sensitive U.S. and world affairs in favor of a textbook, pictorial American past. For comparison, Ingri and Edgar Parin d'Aulaire wrote and illustrated the popular biographies *George Washington* (1936), which un-critically depicts the first U.S. president as a fighter of "Indians" and a slave owner, and *Abraham Lincoln* (1939), which treats the protagonist as a hero to the slaves. These books, too, present appealing visual representations of iconic men of history. Bader writes, in reference to how the Petershams' and d'Aulaires' pic-ture books inform American citizens and international readers alike, "It is not accidental that colonial and frontier America was put into picturebooks for [and by] 'foreigners'; for them it was as much a picturebook place as old Hungary or snowbound Norway was to Americans."[48] Bader notes the d'Aulaires' and Miska Petersham's immigration, their attainment of "the American dream," and their urge to represent American history for a young audience. Bader also allows that picture-book creators who were lifelong American citizens, such as Daugh-erty and Lawson, had political reasons for writing about the United States in the late thirties and early forties: "From looking abroad for local color and exotic customs, Americans took to looking around. The impetus was partly socio-political—the specter of fascism in Europe compelled attention to the practice of democracy and appreciation of differences at home—and partly it stemmed from the schools and the displacement of history and geography by a broader, more people-oriented social studies."[49] Yet, in many instances where picture-book "social studies" are produced, nationalist ideologies go underexplored. *Daniel Boone, Ben and Me, They Were Strong and Good,* and *An American ABC* define citizenship as implicitly Anglo- and European American while maintain-ing restrictive origin myths for the United States around Boone and other fight-ers, who remained popular well past midcentury. In these cases, the fairy tale of modernity exists in service to state power, aligning revolutionary rhetoric with the patriotic fervor of 1776 and, despite nods to immigration, naturalizing the pictured white subject as the dominant and rightful heir to the nation.

# The Picture Book after 1942

In 1941, the American Institute of Graphic Arts (AIGA), which since 1923 had compiled an annual "Fifty Best Books" list, presented "An Exhibition of Books Made for Children." The exhibition, held in New York City, included picture books and illustrated texts published between 1937 and 1941. Reviewing the show, and speaking from the formalist point of view of production experts, Evelyn Harter wrote, "It is almost incredible that an exhibition of this sort devoted to children's books from the angle of format should not have been done before. It would seem that from now on this show might usefully become an annual institution, serving as an inventory of progress and change."[1] Publishers provided an initial set of books for consideration, and AIGA's four-person jury (New York Public Library stalwart Anne Carroll Moore, artist Boris Artzybasheff, Macmillan editor Louise Seaman Bechtel, and printing professional Larry June) whittled the list to ninety-four selections, operating under the provision that they not "select more than ten books of any one publisher."[2] June attested that in these books for young readers, "the general level of bindery work is quite high. Papers used are good. The type faces are not stodgy. The various methods shown of combining art work with plate making are amazing. Jackets are gay and attractive." He noticed, however, "a general tendency to overstrain in the use of color and superficial decoration," and he criticized "uneven" printing registrations, dust jackets that were "a separate piece of art not contained in the book," and "uncomplementary colors . . . for cloth and ink stamping," presumably under the jackets.[3]

The 1941 picture-book category contains a who's who of creators whose work remains popular or at least known among scholars to the present day. Despite Artzybasheff's place on the jury, his own book *Seven Simeons* makes the list, with four-color line engravings from his drawings. Also listed are Ludwig Bemelmans's *Madeline*; Robert McCloskey's *Make Way for Ducklings*; and two books by Wanda Gág, *Nothing at All* and the Caldecott Honoree *Snow White and the Seven Dwarfs*. Quite a few entries, including Thomas Handforth's Caldecott-winning *Mei-Li*, Evelyn Young's *Wu and Lu and Li*, and Claire Hutchet Bishop and Kurt Wiese's *The Five Chinese Brothers*, address China and

Asian topics generally, attesting to Americans' continuing curiosity about Asian people; Lucy Herndon Crockett's *Lucio and His Nuong*, whose brown, green, and red palette still stands out in printer's art, is among these selections. Others include Hardie Gramatky's *Little Toot*, Munro Leaf and Robert Lawson's *Wee Gillis*, E-Yeh-Shure's *I Am a Pueblo Indian Girl*, and Henry B. Kane's information book *The Tale of the Whitefoot Mouse*, whose close-up black-and-white photos follow a field mouse from birth through its everyday activities. Harter remarks upon the innovative and costly techniques on display, all in the service of amusing a juvenile demographic: "The free use of color and of various special processes was considered too expensive for adults' books, but if children liked color, and their parents were willing to buy it in sufficient quantities, they were to get it." Harter also asserts a preference for educational over fanciful books, which—given that she was writing for the *Horn Book Magazine*, an industry organ—signals that the fairy tale debate of the thirties was concluding and the tendency to personify obsolete machines had become shopworn. "In general we [in publishing houses and production departments] are for more informational books and less whimsy . . .," she writes. "I think all of us would rather work on more books about our physical world—our bodies, birds, beasts, planets, flowers, maps. It seems to most of us more important that a child in the 1940's should know how the pistons of a car work rather than what happened to little Honk because he had an inferiority complex."[4] Although not necessarily indicative of the majority opinion across the United States, Harter's statements imply a practical-minded spirit transforming the engineering- and alienated-labor-based books of the thirties to the science and informational texts shared with cold war–era youth.

AIGA's 1941 exhibition signals a mainstream willingness to accept the picture book as a sequential example of the printer's art, and identifies a point of completion in the development of picture-book content and design conventions. After years of avant-garde and mainstream experimentation between the wars—having to do with tastes in art, production costs and risks, and movements in education reform and age-grading—picture-book conventions stabilized into the shorter, more fixed format preferred today, even if picture-book content remained unpredictable and open to innovation.

The year 1942 ushered in Virginia Lee Burton's *The Little House*, a memorable book done in a style Burton had mastered; Margaret Wise Brown and Clement Hurd's *The Runaway Bunny*, a reassuring call-and-response conversation between a mother and child rabbit, illustrated in a surprising fauvist style; and other inventive blends of nostalgic content and modernist fabrication.

After 1942, effectively coterminous with the United States' entry into World War II and with the limits this imposed on daily life for Americans, a postwar picture-book era began. Certainly Burton had new work in progress, including her comics-based *Calico the Wonder Horse* (1943), printed on tissue-thin paper in a time of rationing. Brown added to the Noisy Book series and turned her onomatopoeic poems and repetition-based stories, perfected in the lab environment of the Bank Street School, into quintessential midcentury children's reading. Lawson had yet to publish some memorable (if still problematic) work such as *Rabbit Hill* (1944), which introduces an animal population threatened by the mechanical inventions, not to mention the cats and dogs, of human beings. McCloskey was established as a commentator on quaint rural life, as in *Homer Price* (1943), and would develop into an artist more concerned with the natural world in *Blueberries for Sal* (1948), *One Morning in Maine* (1952), and *Time of Wonder* (1957). The children's picture-book career of graphic illustrator and op-ed cartoonist Dr. Seuss, which auspiciously began with *And to Think That I Saw It on Mulberry Street* (1937) and prose stories satirizing fascist authority (*The 500 Hats of Bartholomew Cubbins* [1938] and *The King's Stilts* [1939]), would ignite with additional, subversive critiques of power in *Horton Hatches the Egg* (1940) and *Horton Hears a Who!* (1954), among other memorable books. These and other picture-book makers' career trajectories were well under way in 1942. This study omits influential post-1942 texts because these inaugurate the picture book's next generation.

The American publishing industry, and thus the picture-book landscape, changed significantly during and after the World War II years. Socioeconomic restrictions altered book production and shifted the workforce. Developing international attitudes, educational theories, and child psychology movements influenced picture-book content; graphic illustration and modern art affected book design and visual appeal, despite sticking to the lithographic techniques developed in the previous half century. Not that the war brought stagnancy to the industry—quite the contrary. "While the havoc created by the war almost brought children's book publication in Europe to an end, in America it flourished, and it was here that refugees came to join those from the first war . . . ," writes Tessa Rose Chester. "The work of Artzybasheff, the Petershams and the d'Aulaires was joined by that of a host of others from Russia, Hungary, Poland, Italy, Germany and France."[5] Further, as a result of the later cold war and baby boom, the political content of educational materials was monitored, and new families perceived picture books as ideal, and safe, children's reading. Although picture books like filmmaker Frank Tashlin's *The Bear That Wasn't* (1946), which mocks a conformist corporate workforce, and Margaret Wise Brown and Clement Hurd's celebrated *Goodnight, Moon* (1947) appeared not long after the period covered in this study, these texts built upon the innovations of 1919 through 1942. The period from 1942 to 1963—starting with the wartime climate and ending with Maurice Sendak's *Where the Wild Things Are*, along the way covering watershed moments in civil rights, communist witch hunts, and multimedia art—is a topic for another picture-book survey.

Picture books of the 1910s through 1940s have a quaint retro look now, especially compared to their high-gloss, digitally enhanced descendants. But they once sat crisp and new on school, library, bookstore, and home shelves. Less than a century ago in the United States, picture books were colorful novelties, a newly affordable mode of production aimed at young people with time on their hands, and commentaries on changing American society. Like the children for whom they were created, these texts circulated in a revved-up marketplace of multimedia spectacles such as experimental painting, commercial photography, billboards, and blinking neon shop signs. They developed alongside cinema and radio. They grew up alongside print and advertising media. They celebrated the noisy new forms of transportation, the factory products, and the domestic technologies competing for public attention. They presented machines and commodities as friendly to children who were leaving the labor force and the street for the safer school, library, and playground. Unsurprisingly, many picture books of the teens through the forties pursue a national myth of American progress, fetishizing mechanical force, human labor, and the skyscraper-studded city. Others forgo industrial change to focus instead on mythology, heraldry, fairy tales, and nursery rhymes. Still others imply population change and metropolitan growth, acknowledging racial, ethnic, and class diversity while stubbornly prescribing a normative white, middle-class reader. Today, the familiar material format and the anachronistic content of such texts signify childhood and suspended leisure time, and simultaneously give evidence of how those born in the 1910s to 1940s enjoyed picture books, then grew up to pass those texts (and the ideologies within) to their own children, grandchildren, and great-grandchildren. A contemporary reader may yet be surprised by the sophisticated imagery, typography, layouts, and written composition of these ostensibly outmoded texts.

# Acknowledgments

Since beginning this project, I have visited numerous libraries, museums, galleries, and historical societies, and have borrowed material from far-flung sources. My first expression of gratitude goes to all the interlibrary loan and museum personnel who indulged my whims and requests. Among the specialists who shared their expertise and enthusiasm, I especially thank Laura Wasowicz of the American Antiquarian Society; Gabrielle Fulton at the Free Library of Philadelphia; Mary Beth Dunhouse at the Boston Public Library; Donna Webber at the Horn Book Archive, Simmons College; Andrea Immel at the Cotsen Collection, Princeton University; librarians in the Donnell Library Center and the Humanities and Social Sciences Library of the New York Public Library; Lynne Thomas and Angela Schroeder in Founders Memorial Library, Northern Illinois University; Kathy Nichol at Leslie F. Malpass Library, Western Illinois University; and Julie Derden and Maureen Brunsdale at Milner Library, Illinois State University. The College of Arts and Sciences, the Department of English, and the Office of Research and Sponsored Programs at Illinois State University provided me with initiative grants, extra funding for permissions and travel, and an environment congenial to interdisciplinary research.

Many people contributed to my scholarship in recent years by providing forums for critical collaboration, writing on my behalf, offering encouragement, and discussing academic commitments. I benefited immeasurably from the good will of Beverly Lyon Clark, Margaret Higonnet, William Moebius, Judith Plotz, John Stilgoe, Elizabeth Goodenough, the anonymous readers at the University of Minnesota Press, Richard Morrison, Julie Pfeiffer, Christine Doyle, Julia Mickenberg, Philip Nel, Karin Westman, Richard Flynn, Kenneth Kidd, Mark I. West, Mike Cadden, Lynn Vallone, Troy Boone, Nancy Condee, Lucy Fischer, Nancy Tolson, Lynn Worsham, and Gary Olson. I appreciate those faculty members, graduate students, and undergraduates at Illinois State University and Pacific Lutheran University who discussed historic picture books and concepts of childhood as I pursued this project. I extend particular thanks and warm wishes to my friends and associates Diane Roback, Elizabeth Devereaux, Kass Fleisher, Joe Amato, Heather Jordon, Alison Bailey, Rebecca Saunders,

Lois Steinberg and the Iyengar yoga community of YICU, Melissa Johnson, Andrea Lapin, Chris Horvath, Greg Rose, Kirstin and Thomas Zona and their family, John Poole, Ben Buja and his family, and Joe Wezorek and his family. For her dear friendship and heartfelt counsel since we met in 1996, Valerie Krips deserves special mention.

My closing words of appreciation go to my family. I am fortunate for the affection and affirmation of my mother, Carol, and her husband, Paul, as well as the kindness of my brother Christopher, my niece Sydney, and my father, Ludo. The generosity and positive attitudes of Don A. and Christel Lacey always make me feel at home. Ivy and Fern are cats and will not be reading this, but writing would be a lonely endeavor without their companionship. And of course Don and Oona provide stability and surprises, remind me to cultivate humor and compassion, and keep me curious about what life has to offer. Love to you all.

# Notes

## INTRODUCTION

1. H. A. and Margret Rey, *Curious George* (Boston: Houghton Mifflin, 1941), n.p.

2. Daniel Hade, "Curious George Gets Branded: Reading as Consuming," *Theory into Practice* 40, no. 3 (Summer 2001).

3. Louise Borden, *The Journey That Saved Curious George: The Wartime Escape of Margret and H. A. Rey*, illus. Allan Drummond (Boston: Houghton Mifflin, 2005).

4. Anthony L. Manna, "Robert McCloskey's *Make Way for Ducklings*: The Art of Regional Storytelling," in *Touchstones: Reflections on the Best in Children's Literature*, vol. 3, *Picture Books*, ed. Perry Nodelman (West Lafayette, Ind.: Children's Literature Association, 1989), 91. Manna places McCloskey "among a number of children's book writers and illustrators in the forties [e.g., Ellis Credle, Glen Rounds, and James Daugherty] who, taking their cue from the American Scene artists of the thirties, particularly Grant Wood, Boardman Robinson, and T. H. Benton, turned their attention to things indigenous; they were filled with a strong sense of region that emanated from their personal experience with a section of the country rather than a conscious study of it" (93).

5. See, for instance, "Children's Literature and Modernism," a special edition of *Children's Literature Association Quarterly* (vol. 32, no. 4 [Winter 2007]), edited by Karin Westman.

6. David Lewis, "The Picture Book: A Form Awaiting Its History," *Signal* 77 (May 1995): 108.

7. Joseph Schwarcz, *Ways of the Illustrator: Visual Communication in Children's Literature* (Chicago: American Library Association, 1982), 4.

8. Anonymous, *What Baby Sees*, illus. Eulalie Wilson (New York: Platt and Munk, 1937), n.p.

9. Perry Nodelman, *Words about Pictures: The Narrative Art of Picture Books* (Athens: University of Georgia Press, 1988), 199.

10. Ibid., 8.

11. According to Walter Benjamin, nothing "commends a story to memory more effectively than that chaste compactness which precludes psychological analysis. And the more natural the process by which the storyteller forgoes psychological shading, the greater becomes the story's claim to a place in the memory of the listener; the more completely the story is integrated into the latter's own experience, the greater will be his inclination to repeat it to someone else someday, sooner or later. This process of assimilation . . . requires a state of relaxation which is becoming rarer and rarer. . . .

Boredom is the dream bird that hatches the egg of experience." Walter Benjamin, "The Storyteller: Observations on the Works of Nikolai Leskov" (1936), *Walter Benjamin: Selected Writings*, vol. 3, *1935–1938*, trans. Harry Zohn (Cambridge: Harvard University Press, Belknap Press, 2002), 149. See also Walter Benjamin, *Illuminations*, trans. Harry Zohn (New York: Schocken, 1969), 91. For Benjamin, storytelling is "an artisanal form of communication," meaningful in ways that are vanishing with modernity, and his observation recommends consideration of oral stories and "compact," memorable, read-aloud texts such as picture books.

12. Juliet Dusinberre, *Alice to the Lighthouse: Children's Literature and Radical Experiments in Art* (New York: St. Martin's, 1999), 49.

13. Ibid., 44. Dusinberre writes, "The work will only reach the child in the first place if it wins adult applause. . . . The unlearning of pride and prejudice is the concern of the adult reader, not of the child, who learns them from the adult world with the air he breathes" (12).

14. Peter Hollindale argues that the child is never a blank slate but the already interpellated subject of semiotics and symbolic language: "Ideology is not something which is transferred to children as if they were empty receptacles. It is something which they already possess, having drawn it from a mass of experiences far more powerful than literature." "Ideology and the Children's Book," in *Literature for Children: Contemporary Criticism*, ed. Peter Hunt (New York: Routledge, 1993), 35. See also Louis Althusser, "Ideology and Ideological State Apparatuses (Notes towards an Investigation)," in *Lenin and Philosophy and Other Essays*, trans. Ben Brewster (New York: Monthly Review Press, 1972).

15. Beverly Lyon Clark, *Kiddie Lit: The Cultural Construction of Children's Literature in America* (Baltimore: The Johns Hopkins University Press, 2003), 5.

16. Katharine White, *New Yorker*, November 1939, quoted in Jill Lepore, "The Lion and the Mouse," *New Yorker*, July 21, 2008, 70.

17. Jacqueline Rose opens *The Case of Peter Pan; or, The Impossibility of Children's Fiction* (Philadelphia: University of Pennsylvania Press, 1984) by pointing out, "Children's fiction rests on the idea that there is a child who is simply there to be addressed and that speaking to it might be simple. It is an idea whose innocent generality covers up a multitude of sins" (1). Rose's study of *Peter Pan* as theatrical piece, novel, and social phenomenon; her doubling of the terms "simply" and "simple"; and her accounts of innocence and concepts of childhood inform my account of the misrecognition of picture books.

18. Maurice Sendak, *Caldecott and Co.: Notes on Books and Pictures* (New York: Farrar, Straus and Giroux, 1988), 186.

19. Ibid., 21.

20. Lynd Ward, "Contemporary Book Illustration," in *Contemporary Illustrators of Children's Books*, ed. Bertha E. Mahony and Elinor Whitney (Boston: Bookshop for Boys and Girls / Women's Educational and Industrial Union, 1930; repr., Detroit: Gale, 1978), 2.

21. Ibid.

22. Rémy Charlip's phrase is cited in William Moebius, "Introduction to Picture-

book Codes," in *Children's Literature: The Development of Criticism*, ed. Peter Hunt (New York: Routledge, 1990), 132. Moebius's essay first appeared in *Word and Image* 2 no. 2 (April–June 1986): 141–51ff.

23. Ibid., 132.

24. Erwin Panofsky explains, "Every historical phenomenon . . . must necessarily belong to a multitude of frames of reference. The human beings who created it lived through a particular number of years and not only left a series of older generations behind them but also witnessed a series of younger generations growing up beside them. They entered into new spheres of influence through their own journeys and through contact with traveling artists or works of art. Thus each of their creations in a sense represents the intersection of numerous frames of reference that confront each other as products of different spaces and times and whose interaction in each instance leads to a unique result." "Reflections on Historical Time" (1927), trans. Johanna Bauman, *Critical Inquiry* 30 (Summer 2004): 700.

25. According to Selma G. Lanes, *Down the Rabbit Hole: Adventures and Misadventures in the Realm of Children's Literature* (New York: Atheneum, 1971), "To be a young child is to be locked in an ever-advancing present. . . . When parents tell children of events from the parents' own childhoods, the recollections already have, to the small listeners, the character of romance and myth." To children, "beyond the next few hours, the future has no real meaning and the past is entirely personal, inextricably entwined in the developing self. This perhaps explains in part why so many of the most memorable children's books take place outside of any specifically identifiable time or place and have about them an air of the everlasting now. . . . They have about them, as childhood does, an aura of the immortal" (179–80).

26. Every child is a new presence in the world, an interruption of chronological time, and a rupture in historical consciousness. Therefore, every child is a political creature and a potentially revolutionary subject, according to Walter Benjamin. Ariel Dorfman and Armand Mattelart sound a cautionary note on utopian and revolutionary claims, however: "In his children's reading, man stages and performs over and over again the supposedly unproblematical scenes of his inner refuge. . . . The future (the child) reaffirms the present (the adult), which, in turn, transmits the past. . . . Thus, *the imagination of the child is conceived as the past and future utopia of the adult.*" *How to Read Donald Duck: Imperialist Ideology in the Disney Comic* (1970; repr., Oakland, Calif.: AK Press, 2003), 30–31; emphasis in original.

27. Jonathan Crary, *Suspensions of Perception: Attention, Spectacle, and Modern Culture* (Cambridge, Mass.: MIT Press, 1999).

28. Picture books constitute figurative and literal *lieux de mémoire* (sites of memory) and points of collective reference, as detailed in Pierre Nora, *Realms of Memory: Rethinking the French Past (Les lieux de mémoire)*, vols. 1–3, trans. Arthur Goldhammer (New York: Columbia University Press, 1996–98); and Maurice Halbwachs, *On Collective Memory*, trans. Francis J. Ditter Jr. and Vita Yadzi Ditter (New York: Harper and Row, 1980). On children's texts and objects as sites of memory, see Valerie Krips, *The Presence of the Past: Memory, Heritage, and Childhood in Postwar Britain* (New York: Garland, 2000).

29. Picture books are not only narratives but signifying *things*. Bill Brown writes that "the gap between the function of objects and the desires congealed there became clear only when those objects became outmoded. . . . History is exactly the currency that things trade in and . . . obsolescence as an accusation, whenever it represses its own history, is utterly passé." Charges of obsolescence challenge critics to reinvestigate once-popular things and narratives, such as the fairy tales of modernity. "Thing Theory," introduction to *Things*, ed. Bill Brown (Chicago: University of Chicago Press, 2004), 13.

30. "The reading of the book on the attaining of success is itself the symbolic attaining of that success. It is while they read that these readers are 'succeeding.' . . . The lure of the book resides in the fact that the reader, while reading it, is then living in the aura of success." Kenneth Burke, "Literature as Equipment for Living," in *The Philosophy of Literary Form: Studies in Symbolic Action* (1941; repr., Berkeley and Los Angeles: University of California Press, 1973,), 299; emphasis in original. The picture book may be viewed as sanctioned equipment for the flourishing of new generations.

31. Though associated with children, picture books express adult desires and adult beliefs about childhood. Jacqueline Rose argues, "There is no child behind the category 'children's fiction,' other than the one which the category itself sets in place, the one which it needs to believe is there for its own purposes. . . . Talking to the child is . . . an act of love, but it is also a claim on the child, a demand made on the child as a means of holding it fast" (*Case of Peter Pan*, 10, 23).

32. Gillian Avery, *Behold the Child: American Children and Their Books, 1621–1922* (London: Bodley Head, 1994), 213.

33. In 1922, May Massee began her editing career with a job at Doubleday, and the American Library Association established the annual Newbery Medal to honor the best writing for children.

## I. HERE-AND-NOW FAIRY TALES

1. David A. Beroná's *Wordless Books: The Original Graphic Novels* (New York: Abrams, 2008) critically examines a variety of woodcut novels and wordless books from 1918 through 1951.

2. Barbara Bader, *American Picture Books from "Noah's Ark" to "The Beast Within"* (New York: Macmillan, 1976), 31.

3. Ibid., 61.

4. Moebius describes "a kind of 'plate tectonics' of the picturebook, where word and image constitute separate plates sliding and scraping along against each other. . . . What Roland Barthes has called the 'reference code' is probably also active here, as we attempt to cross this buffer zone." William Moebius, "Introduction to Picturebook Codes," in *Children's Literature: The Development of Criticism*, ed. Peter Hunt (New York: Routledge, 1990), 135.

5. Joyce Irene Whalley and Tessa Rose Chester, *A History of Children's Book Illustration* (London: John Murray / Victoria and Albert Museum, 1988), 180–81.

6. Thomas Mann, introduction to Frans Masereel's *Passionate Journey: A Novel in 165 Woodcuts*, trans. Joseph M. Bernstein (San Francisco: City Lights Books, 1994), 2.

7. Ibid., 5–6.

8. Ibid., 7.

9. E. Boyd Smith's *The Farm Book* (1910), *The Seashore Book* (1912), and *The Rail-road Book* (1913) were republished by Houghton Mifflin in the 1980s. All exemplify picture-book sequence with an exposition-heavy format adapted from illustrated newspapers. Smith provides detailed information on fading ways of life (e.g., the building and rigging of an ocean sailboat, soon to be replaced by transatlantic steamers).

10. Bertha E. Mahony and Elinor Whitney, eds., *Realms of Gold in Children's Books* (Garden City, N.Y.: Doubleday, Doran, 1929), 149.

11. A advertisement for *The Slant Book* (New York: Harper and Bros., 1910), printed on *The Rocket Book*'s rear cover, confidently assures buyers, "The truth is, this new book is even funnier than 'The Hole Book,' which made everybody laugh." The ad signals Peter Newell's popularity as a series creator without asserting that picture books are for children alone.

12. Anne Carroll Moore, "The Creative Spirit in America," in *My Roads to Childhood: Views and Reviews of Children's Books* (Boston: Horn Book Inc., 1970), 193–94. Moore's book was originally published in 1923 as *New Roads to Childhood*.

13. Bertha E. Mahony, Louise P. Latimer, and Beulah Folmsbee, eds., *Illustrators of Children's Books, 1744–1945* (1947; repr., Boston: Horn Book Inc., 1970), describe C. B. Falls as "self-taught" and broadly skilled: "His posters have won him high rank and he has fared widely in the field of art, illustrating books, designing silks, making lithographs and etchings, designing stage sets and costumes, and painting murals" for the American Radiator Building, the Players' Club in New York City, and the State Office Building in Albany (307).

14. With Alfred Stieglitz, Edward Steichen (1879–1973) founded the Little Galleries of the Photo Succession in 1905, promoting the concept of photography as an art form. In the 1920s and 1930s, he worked as a commercial and fashion photographer for *Life* and Condé Nast publications such as *Vogue* and *Vanity Fair*. The austere photographs in *The First Picture Book* evidence his pared-down, uncluttered visual style at this time.

15. Mary Steichen Martin and Edward Steichen, *The First Picture Book: Everyday Things for Babies* (New York: Harcourt, Brace and Co., 1930), n.p. A new edition, with an introduction by John Updike, was published in 1991 by Fotofolio, in association with the Whitney Museum of American Art, New York. The 1991 edition identifies Mary Steichen Martin as Mary Steichen Calderone.

16. Through the camera eye, *The First Picture Book* reconceives the still life for a child audience. The full-bleed pages suggest a crossover between the page plane and the three-dimensional world. On still life as a domestic mode, see Norman Bryson, *Looking at the Overlooked: Four Essays on Still Life Painting* (London: Reaktion, 1990), and Meyer Schapiro, "The Apples of Cézanne: An Essay on the Meaning of Still-Life" (1968), in *Modern Art, Nineteenth and Twentieth Centuries: Selected Papers* (New York: Braziller, 1982), 1–38. Svetlana Alpers, *The Art of Describing* (Chicago: University of Chicago Press, 1983), explores still life as an optical illusion and a test of the eye's capabilities.

17. Bader compares Lois Lenski's *The Choosing Book* (1932) to *The First Picture Book*: "One can't *not* participate in *The Choosing Book*; it puts hard questions like which of four nice houses Mother and Father and Teddy and Ruth select, which of four dogs Teddy favors (they all like him), which of four cats will be Ruth's. . . . 'The pictures are of the type one finds in department store advertising,' a reviewer noted, and it was from a like source, the Sears-Roebuck catalog, that Mary Steichen Martin got the idea for one of the most characteristic of the preschool books, *The First Picture Book*." (*American Picture Books*, 79–80, qtg. a review by Helen Hammett Owen, *New York Herald Tribune Books*, July 3, 1932).

18. Advertisement for Mary Steichen Martin and Edward Steichen, *The Second Picture Book* (New York: Harcourt, Brace and Co., 1931), in *Horn Book Magazine*, November 1931, 345.

19. Anne MacLeod, "Literary and Social Aspects of Children's Books of the Twenties and Thirties," in *Stepping Away from Tradition: Children's Books of the Twenties and Thirties*, ed. Sybille A. Jagusch (Washington, D.C.: Library of Congress, 1988), 51.

20. Ibid., 52.

21. Gillian Avery, "Children's Literature in America, 1870–1945," in *Children's Literature: An Illustrated History*, ed. Peter Hunt (Oxford: Oxford University Press, 1995), 241–42.

22. "New inventions, conceived out of the fantasy of one generation, are received within the cultural experience of another. . . . At the intersection between collective history and personal history, between society's dream and childhood dream, the contents of the collective unconscious are transmitted." Susan Buck-Morss, *The Dialectics of Seeing: Walter Benjamin and the Arcades Project* (Cambridge, Mass.: MIT Press, 1991), 273.

23. David Lewis, "Pop-Ups and Fingle-Fangles: The History of the Picture Book," in *Talking Pictures: Pictorial Texts and Young Readers*, ed. Morag Styles and Victor Watson (London: Hodder and Stoughton, 1996), 11–12.

24. Ibid., 20.

25. See Maurice Sendak, *Caldecott and Co.: Notes on Books and Pictures* (New York: Farrar, Straus and Giroux, 1988); Anne Lundin, *Victorian Horizons: The Reception of the Picture Books of Walter Crane, Randolph Caldecott, and Kate Greenaway* (Lanham, Md.: Scarecrow, 2001); and Brian Alderson, *Sing a Song for Sixpence: The English Picture Book Tradition and Randolph Caldecott* (Cambridge: Cambridge University Press; London: British Library, 1986).

26. Moebius, "Introduction to Picturebook Codes," 133.

27. See Michael Patrick Hearn, *McLoughlin Brothers, Publishers: 1828–1978* (New York: Schiller, 1980), n.p.

28. *One Hundred Years of Children's Books, 1828–1928: And a Presentation of Modern Style Trends in Juvenile Literature* (Springfield, Mass.: McLoughlin Bros., 1928), 9.

29. Fewer than one in six seventeen-year-olds graduated from high school circa 1920, but "from 1930 to 1932, high school enrollment jumped 17 percent, and over the next two years enrollment rose another 10 percent. By 1939 three-quarters of fourteen- to seventeen-year-olds were high school students, and by 1940 half the nation's

seventeen-year-olds were high school graduates—twice as many as in 1929." Stephen Mintz, *Huck's Raft: A History of American Childhood* (Cambridge: Harvard University Press, Belknap Press, 2004), 197, 239. Race, immigrant or native-born status, and socioeconomic class influenced access to secondary school. On southern and northern states, white and African American students, and working-class and white-collar families, see David Macleod, *The Age of the Child: Children in America, 1890–1920* (New York: Twayne, 1998), 149.

30. Daniel Thomas Cook explains, in *The Commodification of Childhood: The Children's Clothing Industry and the Rise of the Child Consumer* (Durham: Duke University Press, 2004), "There was little children's merchandising (the physical grouping of goods) to speak of until after the First World War, toys and toy departments aside." Cook studies how children went from being "customers" to "consumers" (70), how brands such as Cracker Jack were marketed to a young crowd (74–76), and how the term "toddler" evolved as a marketing category distinct from "child," around 1936 (85–89): "It is no longer useful, after the toddler, to think of a commodity as 'an object outside us,' as Marx famously remarked, for commodification becomes increasingly inseparable from the very journey through the early life course" (85).

31. Viviana Zelizer, *Pricing the Priceless Child: The Changing Social Value of Children* (New York: Basic Books, 1985), 65, 97–98. Zelizer details the shift from "child labor" to "child work" from 1870 to 1930, in factory, agricultural, and home-based labor. She investigates child life insurance as a response to urban danger and as a controversial economic valuation of the child's "priceless" existence. Labor trends described by Zelizer closely parallel picture books' American development.

32. Garth S. Jowett, Ian C. Jarvie, and Kathryn H. Fuller, *Children and the Movies* (Cambridge: Cambridge University Press, 1996), 12. For statistics and observations on child attendance at nickelodeons and variety features, all-ages entertainment, and new subjectivities forged by the cinema, see Charles Musser, *The Emergence of Cinema: The American Screen to 1907*; and Elizabeth Bowser, *The Transformation of Cinema, 1907–1915* (both Berkeley and Los Angeles: University of California Press, 1994).

33. "Newspapers, cheap literature, magazines, movies and eventually radio and television . . . constituted a threat because they were not under the control of the 'guardians of the culture' and were the source of information and ideas that often ran counter to the prevailing (Protestant) mores." Jowett, Jarvie, and Fuller, *Children and the Movies*, 23.

34. On consumer desire, see Lisa Jacobson, *Raising Consumers: Children and the American Mass Market in the Early Twentieth Century* (New York: Columbia University Press, 2004); Nicholas Sammond, *Babes in Tomorrowland: Walt Disney and the Making of the American Child, 1930–1960* (Durham: Duke University Press, 2005); and Gary Cross, *Kids' Stuff: Toys and the Changing World of American Childhood* (Cambridge: Harvard University Press, 1997) and *An All-Consuming Century: Why Commercialism Won in Modern America* (New York: Columbia University Press, 2000), especially "Setting the Course: 1900–1930" (17–66). As age-targeted consumerism took root in the United States, Georg Lukács wrote that "the reified mind has come to regard [forms of capital] as the true representatives of his societal existence." See Georg Lukács, "Reification and the Consciousness of the Proletariat," in *History and*

*Class Consciousness: Studies in Marxist Dialectics*, trans. Rodney Livingstone (1922; repr., Cambridge: MIT Press, 1999), 93.

35. See Michael Denning, *The Cultural Front: The Laboring of American Culture in the Twentieth Century* (New York: Verso, 1997), on books as a "relatively inert commodity" in comparison to new modes such as cinema, synchronized sound, and radio (40).

36. See Lawrence Levine, *Highbrow/Lowbrow: The Emergence of Cultural Hierarchy in America* (Cambridge, Mass.: Harvard University Press, 1988), on the threat to "elites," on the challenge to "many of the new industrialists as well as many members of the new middle classes" from the changing mainstream, and on acceptable tastes in popular culture (176–77).

37. Franklin S. Hoyt, qtd. in John Tebbel, "For Children, with Love and Profit: Two Decades of Book Publishing for Children," in Jagusch, *Stepping Away from Tradition*, 15–16.

38. Lucy Sprague Mitchell, *Here and Now Story Book* (New York: Dutton, 1921), 41.

39. On the transition from workforce to public school and leisure, see Macleod, *Age of the Child*; Mintz, *Huck's Raft*; Zelizer, *Pricing the Priceless Child*; and Gail Schmunk Murray, *American Children's Literature and the Construction of Childhood* (New York: Twayne, 1998).

40. Tebbel, "For Children, with Love and Profit," 21–22.

41. This necessarily brief history only touches upon the rich developments in children's publishing. For insider accounts and biographies of key editors, booksellers, and librarians, see, e.g., Leonard S. Marcus, *Seventy-Five Years of Children's Book Week Posters: Celebrating Great Illustrators of American Children's Books* (New York: Knopf, 1994).

42. On the politics of prizing and the ALA's consecration of texts, see Kenneth Kidd, "Prizing Children's Literature: The Case of Newbery Gold," *Children's Literature* 35 (2007): 166–90.

43. Bertha E. Mahony, "The First Children's Department in Book Publishing," *Horn Book Magazine* 4, no. 3 (August 1928): 4–5.

44. Anne Carroll Moore, "Reviewing Children's Books," in *The Three Owls: Contemporary Criticism of Children's Books, 1927–1930*, bk. 3 (New York: Coward-McCann, 1931), 2–4. Moore writes, "Children's books published in the decade between 1920 and 1930 reveal more new forms, both outward and inward, than at any other period of their history" (7).

45. According to the U.S. Bureau of the Census, from 1900 through 1920, "Americans were growing more prosperous, accumulating resources essential if parents and reformers were to invest more in children. In 1900 dollars, Gross National Product per capita stood at $203 in 1890, $246 in 1900, $316 in 1910, and $320 in 1920. These average incomes looked large, both by world standards and by those of the American past" (Macleod, *Age of the Child*, 6). By the mid-1930s, "native-born white families" earned about $1,580 annually, in stark contrast to the "average annual income of $728"—less than half the middle-class white income—for an African American family in Chicago (Mintz, *Huck's Raft*, 240).

46. The Saalfield rhyme appears on various anonymous volumes, including *Mother*

*Goose Jingles* (ca. 1904). Dean Rag Books such as *ABC* (ca. 1900) include large and small images of the dogs.

47. See Avery et al.,"Children's Literature in America," 225–51. For a concise history of children's publishing economics and details on editors and retailers who shaped the industry, see Leonard S. Marcus, "Make Way for Marketing," *Publishers Weekly*, September 17, 2001, 30–34.

48. Alice Payne Hackett, *Sixty Years of Bestsellers, 1895–1955* (New York: Bowker, 1956), 11.

49. Ibid., 62–69.

50. Mahony and Whitney, *Realms of Gold*, 71.

51. Age groupings set rules of thumb for acceptable child labor, despite resistance among working-class and ethnic groups that needed children's incomes and among those who exploited child labor: "Between 1879 and 1909, the number of states with age limit provisions (for any occupation except dangerous employments and mining) increased from seven to forty-four. The legal age limit was first raised from ten to twelve and then to fourteen. After the 1920s, child labor organizations fought to raise the age limit from fourteen to sixteen" (Zelizer, *Pricing the Priceless Child*, 75–76). On age and legal restrictions, see James Kincaid, *Child-Loving: The Erotic Child and Victorian Culture* (New York: Routledge, 1992), 68.

52. J. H. Plumb, "The Great Change in Children," in *Rethinking Childhood: Perspectives on Development and Society*, ed. Arlene Skolnick (Boston: Little, Brown, 1976), 206. Philippe Ariès, likewise, links age grading and developmental stages to class distinctions, changing definitions of labor, and consumer markets, rather than any agreed-upon theory of physical and mental development. Ariès's examples relate social class to school class, with less-advantaged children graduating from primary school to apprenticeships, trade schools, or the workplace. Philippe Ariès, *Centuries of Childhood*, trans. Robert Baldick (1960; repr., New York: Vintage, 1962), 239–40.

53. If children are defined as an undifferentiated class, then class membership is predetermined by a dominant culture. Raymond Williams writes, "A new class is always a source of emergent cultural practice, but . . . is still, as a class, relatively subordinate. . . . This can be seen . . . in the emergence and incorporation of working-class writing . . . an incorporation, so to say, which already conditions and limits the emergence." Raymond Williams, *Marxism and Literature* (Oxford: Oxford University Press, 1977), 124.

54. "Only 36 percent of the population lived in cities as late as 1920. Meanwhile, the proportion of people living on farms remained stubbornly large: about 42 percent in 1900 and 30 percent in 1920. No one setting predominated: cities large and small, towns and villages, and the open countryside all were home to large numbers of people" (Macleod, *Age of the Child*, 2–3).

55. Leonard Marcus, *Minders of Make-Believe: Idealists, Entrepreneurs, and the Shaping of American Children's Literature* (Boston: Houghton Mifflin, 2008), 74. Mathiews's aligning the Boy Scouts with U.S. national defense parallels Robert Baden-Powell's founding of the British Boy Scouts as a protomilitary organization. See also Mintz, *Huck's Raft*, 193.

56. Humphrey Carpenter, *Secret Gardens: The Golden Age of Children's Literature* (Boston: Houghton Mifflin, 1985), 210.

57. Whalley and Chester, *History of Children's Book Illustration*, 177. Chester calls Edward Ardizzone's *Little Tim and the Brave Sea Captain* (London: Oxford University Press, 1936) "the greatest visual triumph of the '30s" in English picture books and attributes its success partly to Jean de Brunhoff's fashionable lithographs for *Babar*. (Kathleen Hale's 1938 *Orlando the Marmalade Cat* and its sequels also saw international success.) *Little Tim and the Brave Sea Captain* upholds the trend against Arcadian fantasy, placing its characters in mortal peril on the high seas without the supernatural, expressionist quality of *Millions of Cats* or the fairy tale structure and anthropomorphism of *Mike Mulligan and His Steam Shovel*, American picture books that became popular in Britain, too. Chester adds, "The recent development of photo-offset litho meant that it was now possible to reproduce delicate crayon and wash drawings. *Little Tim* was one of the first books to be printed by this method, though initial drying problems in the hot, humid summer of New York in 1935 meant that the resulting 64-page folio had both the hand-lettered text and colour pictures printed on one side only of each leaf, so that, like the [Beatrix] Potter books, there were blank pages at regular intervals. . . . [Ardizzone] uses the turn of the page to create question and answer, suspense and resolution, with the utmost skill" (189).

58. Malcolm Cowley, introduction to *Exile's Return: A Literary Odyssey of the 1920s*, rev. ed. (New York: Viking, 1951), 9. The first edition of *Exile's Return* was published in 1934.

59. Ibid., 5.

60. A structure of feeling emerges in connection with "the rise of a class . . . [or] to contradiction, fracture, or mutation within a class." An avant-garde or counterculture must stay alert to an active "pre-emergence, active and pressing but not fully articulate," given that the unarticulated structure of feeling may become the dominant social formation. The future depends on the narratives that are told (including past and present narratives of childhood). Williams, *Marxism and Literature*, 134, 125–26.

61. In "The Storyteller: Observations on the Works of Nikolai Leskov" (1936), *Walter Benjamin: Selected Writings*, vol. 3, *1935–1938*, trans. Harry Zohn (Cambridge: Harvard University Press, Belknap Press, 2002), Walter Benjamin describes modern people's inability to communicate the bizarre variety of new experiences to one another and argues that this explains the common deployment of old narratives and storytelling devices in contemporary contexts.

62. Mahony and Whitney, *Realms of Gold*, 175, qtg. Rachel M. Fleming, *Round the World in Folk Tales* (New York: Harcourt, Brace, 1924). *Realms of Gold* lists illustrated folk- and fairy tale collections, such as those edited by librarian Frances Jenkins Olcott of the Carnegie Library of Pittsburgh. Olcott's books include several Arabian Nights collections; *The Book of Elves and Fairies*; *Tales of the Persian Genii*, illustrated by Willy Pogány; *Wonder Tales from China Seas*; *Wonder Tales from Pirate Isles*; *Wonder Tales from Windmill Lands*; and *The Red Indian Fairy Book*.

63. Bader, *American Picture Books*, 113. On "the fairy tale wars," see Jacalyn Eddy,

*Bookwomen: Creating an Empire in Children's Book Publishing, 1919–1939* (Madison: University of Wisconsin Press, 2006), 110–14.

64. The years of the fairy tale debate correspond to Paul Faucher and Lila Durdik-ova Faucher's founding of Flammarion's Père Castor series, in December 1931. Based on child psychology and educational theory, these French texts, like Mitchell's here-and-now stories, "aimed at developing systematically the imagination, skills, artistic taste, reading ability, and manual dexterity of children," and covered informational and mythological topics alike. A. L. de Saint-Rat, "Children's Books by Russian Émigré Artists, 1921–1940," *Journal of Decorative and Propaganda Arts* 11 (Winter 1989): 101.

65. Mitchell, *Here and Now Story Book*, 5, 15–16.

66. Lucy Sprague Mitchell, foreword to *Another Here and Now Story Book* (New York: Dutton, 1937), xv–xviii.

67. Beverly Lyon Clark, *Kiddie Lit: The Cultural Construction of Children's Literature in America* (Baltimore: The Johns Hopkins University Press, 2003), 6.

68. Ibid., 57.

69. Ibid., 73.

70. Anne Carroll Moore, "Picture Storybooks," in *My Roads to Childhood: Views and Reviews of Children's Books* (Boston: Horn Book Inc., 1961), 261.

71. Moore, *Three Owls*, bk. 2, 24. Eddy writes that Moore "paradoxically gave voice to [children] *and* silenced them since hers was ultimately the opinion that mattered. . . . Children, in a sense, served as grist for bookwomen's metaphor mill, nostalgically representative of innocence and simplicity—qualities the nation no longer seemed to demonstrate" (*Bookwomen*, 117, 126).

72. Moore, *Three Owls*, bk. 2, 25.

73. Marguerite MacKellar Mitchell, "The New Picture Books," *Horn Book Magazine*, November 1933, 175. Mitchell's quotation of Vox indicates the degree to which Americans sought European ideals for children's literature. Averill alerted Mitchell to Paul Hazard's meditation on children's reading titled *Les livres, les enfants, et les hommes* (1932). After wartime delays, Mitchell's translation of Hazard appeared as *Books, Children, and Men* (1944; repr., Boston: Horn Book Inc., 1982), 175. Both Hazard and Vox defended the importance of imaginative children's literature and quiet spaces for reading in a period of restrictive far-right politics that a younger generation stood to inherit. Hazard stresses democracy to counteract nationalist tendencies in international literature: "Yes, children's books keep alive a sense of nationality; but they also keep alive a sense of humanity. They describe their native land lovingly, but they also describe faraway lands where unknown brothers live. . . . Every country gives and every country receives—innumerable are the exchanges—and so it comes about that in our first impressionable years the universal republic of childhood is born" (*Books, Children, and Men*, 146).

74. Mitchell, "New Picture Books," 175–76. Notably, Walter Benjamin argued that aestheticizing the political is a symptom of fascism, and called instead for a political art, a critique of aesthetic pleasure, and cautious contemplation of perceived beauty. Picture books, so invested in visual pleasure, can serve as pretty propaganda or can provide a radical political lens of the sort Benjamin sought. On socialist children's texts

and radical ideology, see Paul C. Mishler, *Raising Reds: The Young Pioneers, Radical Summer Camps, and Communist Political Culture in the United States* (New York: Columbia University Press, 1999); Julia L. Mickenberg, *Learning from the Left: Children's Literature, the Cold War, and Radical Politics in the United States* (New York: Oxford University Press, 2005); and Evgeny Steiner, *Stories for Little Comrades: Revolutionary Artists and the Making of Early Soviet Children's Books* (Seattle: University of Washington Press, 1999).

75. Mitchell, "New Picture Books," 175–76.

76. Wanda Gág, "I Like Fairy Tales," *Horn Book Magazine*, March 1939, 75–77. Gág read Maria Shedlock's *The Art of Storytelling* on the advice of the NYPL's Moore, and Moore regularly called upon Shedlock to teach storytelling and to reinforce oral traditions for teachers and youth librarians.

77. Harold Darling, *From Mother Goose to Dr. Seuss: Children's Book Covers, 1860–1960* (San Francisco: Chronicle, 1999), 71.

78. Anne Carroll Moore, *The Creation and Criticism of Children's Books: A Retrospect and a Prospect* (pamphlet, Horn Book records, Simmons College Archives, "reprinted from the proceedings of the American Library Association conference, Montreal, June 1934"), 6.

79. Moore's anxiety around graphic narrative suggests that the rise of the picture book is a symptom of avant-garde abstraction in mass culture. Later in the century, sociologist David Riesman took comics to task in *The Lonely Crowd: A Study of the Changing American Character* (New Haven: Yale University Press, 1950).

80. Ruth Hill Viguers, "1920–1950: The Golden Age," in *A Critical History of Children's Literature: A Survey of Children's Books in English*, ed. Cornelia Meigs, rev. ed. (New York: Macmillan, 1964), 435–36.

81. Like Viguers, Lynd Ward recognizes a "vitality" in 1920s design that he places "practically in revolutionary relation to" fin-de-siècle book arts: "The day of the pretty drawing, the careful, uninspired and pretty penwork, the large and literal oil painting, is over. . . . Instead of asking 'How far can I go and still get the stuff between book covers by means of complex reproduction?' [today's illustrator] demands of himself, 'What modern processes have been developed that are logically suited to the creation of work that is pure book?' " Ward asserts that improved printing processes enable the book artist to reject baroque flourishes and unify compositions. See Lynd Ward, "Contemporary Book Illustration," in *Contemporary Illustrators of Children's Books*, ed. Bertha E. Mahony and Elinor Whitney (Boston: Bookshop for Boys and Girls / Women's Educational and Industrial Union, 1930; repr., Detroit: Gale, 1978), 1.

82. Ernestine Evans made international sojourns in search of novelties and publishable material. Bader calls her "a journalist by trade, an initiator by inclination. Variously a correspondent during the Russian Revolution, feature editor of the *Christian Science Monitor*, author of the first American study of Diego Rivera, she had a range of acquaintances as broad as her interests. Her reputation as an expert on children's books was based on the year-end roundups she edited for *The New Republic* in 1926 and 1927, where Bertrand Russell and Charles Beard led off and the top librarian-reviewers mopped up" (*American Picture Books*, 31).

83. Mary Kissell, "Wanda Gág's *Millions of Cats*: Unity through Repetition," in *Touchstones: Reflections on the Best in Children's Literature*, vol. 3, *Picture Books*, ed. Perry Nodelman (West Lafayette, Ind.: Children's Literature Association, 1989), 54–62.

84. The horizontal, meandering journey from the left to the right margin of a spread popped up in American picture books that followed. Bader marks a similar spread in Virginia Lee Burton's *Mike Mulligan and His Steam Shovel* (whose cozy rocking-chair-and-pipe conclusion pays homage to Gág, too). A similar countryside layout appears in Ellis Credle's *Across the Cotton Patch* (1935), showing the rolling hills between a grand plantation house and a group of log cabins.

85. The repeating, time-lapse kitten image, often misread by young readers as ten separate kittens, exemplifies what Joseph Schwarcz calls "continuous narrative" illustration, which implies the passage of time and relies on the reader's understanding that the images are related and mobile: "The continuous narrative causes the visual text to become linear to some extent, which means that there is one logical direction in which the eye must follow the imaginary movements of the recurring figure, if the picture's meaning is to be revealed." Joseph Schwarcz, *Ways of the Illustrator: Visual Communication in Children's Literature* (Chicago: American Library Association, 1982), 30.

86. Richard Cox, qtd. in Kissell, "Wanda Gág's *Millions of Cats*," 60. Kissell feels Cox "go[es] too far . . . when he asserts that Gág's folktales 'were partly allegories of modern problems,'" and when he links the cats' battle to World War I. Kissell argues instead that a scene like the cats' "battle is clean and bloodless, described simply and generally" and is thus a generic "archetypal conflict" rather than a commentary (61). Actually, Kissell here refuses the usefulness and flexibility of a folktale rather than admitting that Gág's work has relevance to violent early-century events. Folk retellings and newly invented tales derive from and critique modern concerns, providing counsel for listeners and readers in contemporary life.

87. This haunting image of a farmhouse, shadowed by skyscrapers, predates Virginia Lee Burton's *The Little House* (1942) and its similar image of a rundown home.

88. Lucy Fischer, *Sunrise: A Song of Two Humans* (London: British Film Institute, 1998), 30.

89. Erwin Panofsky, "Style and Medium in the Motion Pictures" (1934, revised 1947), in *Film Theory and Criticism: Introductory Readings*, 4th ed., ed. Gerald Mast, Marshall Cohen, and Leo Braudy (London: Oxford University Press, 1998), 240–41.

90. Karal Ann Marling, *Wall-to-Wall America: A Cultural History of Post-Office Murals in the Great Depression* (Minneapolis: University of Minnesota Press, 1982), 15.

91. Reyner Banham, *Theory and Design in the First Machine Age*, 2d ed. (Cambridge, Mass.: MIT Press, 1980), 98–105, describes futurism's beginnings.

92. Gág abandoned initialing in *The ABC Bunny*. Children's illustrators took many approaches to signing work, some (e.g., Dorothy Lathrop, Robert Lawson) doing so consistently.

93. Zoltan Haraszti, "Printing Art in the New Children's Books," *Horn Book Magazine*, November 1927, 5.

94. Moore, *Three Owls*, bk. 3, 111–13.

95. Ibid., 113.

96. Wanda Gág, introduction to *Tales from Grimm* (New York: Coward-McCann, 1936), viii.

97. Sigmund Freud, "The Uncanny" (1919), in *Standard Edition of the Complete Psychological Works of Sigmund Freud*, vol. 17, trans. and ed. James Strachey (London: Hogarth, 1955), 246. For his part, Schwarcz believes Hans Christian Andersen, in his fairy tales, "called forth the 'industrial revolution' in children's literature, the animism in modern fantasy" (*Ways of the Illustrator*, 152).

98. Gág's project recalls that of a fond antiquarian who "seeks to both distance and appropriate the past" and "is nostalgic for use value, for objects that characterized the preindustrial village economy." Old objects such as the enchanted spindle (or the cottage in *Millions of Cats*) "simultaneously transform nature into art as they mourn the loss of 'pure nature' at a point of origin." Susan Stewart, *On Longing: Narratives of the Miniature, the Gigantic, the Souvenir, the Collection* (1984; repr., Durham: Duke University Press, 1993), 142–44.

99. See *The Complete Fairy Tales of the Brothers Grimm*, trans. Jack Zipes (New York: Bantam, 1992).

100. Murray Pemberton, *New Yorker*, January 25, 1930, qtd. in Audur Helgadottir Winnan, "Wanda Gág: A Lifetime of Drawing," in *Wanda Gág: A Catalogue Raisonné of the Prints* (Washington: Smithsonian Institution Press, 1993).

101. Winnan, "Wanda Gág," 11–12.

102. Ibid., 57–58.

103. Jean Baudrillard, *The System of Objects*, trans. James Benedict (London: Verso, 1996), 73, 75, 80.

104. "The antique object no longer has any practical application, its role being merely to *signify* . . . namely the signifying of time" (ibid., 74).

105. On the found object and the readymade, see Maurice Nadeau, *The History of Surrealism*, trans. Richard Howard (Cambridge: Harvard University Press, Belknap Press, 1989), 185.

106. "Within contemporary consumer society, the collection takes the place of crafts as the prevailing form of social pastime. Ironically, such collecting combines a preindustrial aesthetic of the handmade and singular object with a postindustrial mode of acquisition/production: the readymade" (Stewart, *On Longing*, 166).

107. *Junket Is Nice* echoes Gág's *The Funny Thing* (New York: Coward-McCann, 1929), n.p., which likewise features naive imagery, a handmade aesthetic, a food theme, and long-bearded "Bobo, the good little man of the mountains." Bobo makes daily treats for woodland animals. When he meets the Funny Thing, a haughty "aminal" with a giraffe's neck, blue points down its spine, and a disturbing hunger for dolls, Bobo cannot bear the thought that children's toys might be eaten. He hurries to his kitchen and creates a new dish he names "jum-jills." He convinces the Funny Thing that jum-jills "make blue points more beautiful, and little tails grow into big ones." The Funny Thing's repeated admission, "And very good they are—jum-jills," prefigures Kunhardt's "oh my oh my but junket is nice!"

108. Gertrude Stein, *The Autobiography of Alice B. Toklas* (1933; repr., New York: Vintage, 1990), 132. For remarks on "servile" commas and other overused punctuation

marks, see Gertrude Stein, "Poetry and Grammar," *Lectures in America* (1935; repr., Boston: Beacon, 1957), 219. Stein and Kunhardt might have admired one another's work.

109. Five years later, William R. Scott Company debated whether to print Gertrude Stein's *The World Is Round* (1939) on rose-colored paper, since stock would have to be tinted pink especially. This proved not to be cost effective, despite Margaret Wise Brown's advocacy of Stein. See Leonard Marcus, *Margaret Wise Brown: Awakened by the Moon* (Boston: Beacon, 1992), 108–14. On *The World Is Round*, see, e.g., Barbara Will, "'And Then One Day There Was a War': Gertrude Stein, Children's Literature, and World War II," *Children's Literature Association Quarterly* 32, no. 4 (Winter 2007): 340–53; and Jan Susina, "Children's Reading, Repetition, and Rereading: Gertrude Stein, Margaret Wise Brown, and *Goodnight Moon*," in *Second Thoughts: A Focus on Rereading*, ed. David Galef (Detroit: Wayne State University Press, 1998), 115–25.

110. Experimental shapes and sizes did not please booksellers and librarians, because tiny or unusual books were hard to shelve and easy to steal. "Many put them down as simply exotic private press productions. Sizes changed as time went on, to meet the demands of the market.... [Nevertheless, the company] Ives and Helen Gentry continued to do such imaginative things as sprinkling oil of cloves into the binding of *Spice on the Wind*, by Irmengarde Eberle, and binding *Lumbercamp*, by Glen Rounds, in wood" (Tebbel, "For Children, with Love and Profit," 33). A reviewer noted Eberle's gimmick, too: "[*Spice on the Wind*] gives off a smell of clove when the pages are opening. This is an amusing touch, but the book will be quite as good in years to come when the odor is gone." Evelyn Harter, "An Exhibition of Books Made for Children," *Horn Book Magazine*, March 1942, 99. Extant copies, indeed, no longer smell like cloves.

111. Esther Averill, "Feodor Rojankovsky," in *Five Years of Children's Books*, ed. Bertha E. Mahony and Elinor Whitney (Garden City, N.Y.: Doubleday, Doran, 1936), 25.

112. Margery Clark, *The Poppy Seed Cakes*, illus. Maud and Miska Petersham (Garden City, N.Y.: Doubleday, 1924), n.p. Margery Clark is the pseudonym of coauthors Mary Clark and Margery Quigley.

113. Abe Lerner, "Designing Children's Books," in Jagusch, *Stepping Away from Tradition*, 38. Lerner worked with May Massee at Viking and designed *Make Way for Ducklings*, among many famous books.

114. Ibid., 39–41.

115. Grace W. Allen, "Color Printing in Books for Children," *Horn Book Magazine*, January–February 1936, 8–9.

116. Ibid., 12.

117. Ibid., 15.

## 2. PICTURE-BOOK ETHNOGRAPHY

1. On the Fordist eight-hour workday (1914), the forty-hour workweek, minimum wage laws, and the establishment of child labor laws (1938), see Michael Denning, *The Cultural Front: The Laboring of American Culture in the Twentieth Century* (New York:

Verso, 1997), 28; and Howard Zinn, *A People's History of the United States, 1492–Present* (New York: HarperPerennial, 1995), 393–94.

2. Denning attributes a growing sense of international laborers' solidarity to "proletarian globe-hopping" among American agricultural workers and immigrants who moved to the industrial centers of the United States (*Cultural Front*, 7).

3. Marchal E. Landgren, *Years of Art: The Story of the Art Students League of New York* (New York: McBride, 1940); Raymond J. Steiner, *The Art Students League of New York: A History* (Saugerties, N.Y.: CSS Publications, 1999).

4. *Life*, March 11, 1926, 7. This issue appeared ten years before *Life*'s 1936 reinvention as an oversize photo-magazine.

5. John L. Fell, *A History of Films* (New York: Holt, Rinehart and Winston, 1979), 25.

6. Donald Crafton, *Before Mickey: The Animated Film, 1898–1928* (Cambridge, Mass.: MIT Press, 1982), 55–57.

7. Miriam Hansen, *Babel and Babylon: Spectatorship in American Silent Film* (Cambridge, Mass.: Harvard University Press, 1991), 34.

8. Tom Gunning, "The Cinema of Attraction: Early Film, Its Spectator, and the Avant-Garde," *Wide Angle* 8, nos. 3–4 (1986): 63–70.

9. Hansen, *Babel and Babylon*, 111–12.

10. Karl F. Cohen, *Forbidden Animation: Blacklisted Cartoons and Blacklisted Animators in America* (Jefferson, N.C.: McFarland, 1997), 22.

11. On Geisel's 1941–42 contributions to *PM*, see Richard H. Minear, *Dr. Seuss Goes to War: The World War II Editorial Cartoons of Theodor Seuss Geisel* (New York: New Press, 1999).

12. On the "third meaning," see, e.g., the essay so named in Roland Barthes, *Image Music Text*, trans. Stephen Heath (New York: Hill and Wang, 1977).

13. Ronald Takaki, *A Different Mirror: A History of Multicultural America* (Boston: Little, Brown, 1993), 307.

14. William E. Vickery and Stewart G. Cole, *Intercultural Education in American Schools: Proposed Objectives and Methods* (New York: Harper, 1943), 89.

15. *Little Annie Rooney*, DVD, directed by William Beaudine (1925; Terra, 2003). On Pickford's peculiar performances of childhood, see Gaylyn Studlar, "Oh, 'Doll Divine': Mary Pickford, Masquerade, and the Pedophilic Gaze," *Camera Obscura* 16, no. 3 (2001): 197–227.

16. Crane famously despised sugary depictions of urban children and opened his devastating *Maggie, a Girl of the Streets* (1893) with a vicious battle among very young boys.

17. Barbara Bader, *American Picture Books from "Noah's Ark" to "The Beast Within"* (New York: Macmillan, 1976), 38.

18. Joseph Schwarcz, *Ways of the Illustrator: Visual Communication in Children's Literature* (Chicago: American Library Association, 1982), 6.

19. *Horn Book Magazine* issues of 1937 list international bibliographies and books.

20. Bader 39, quoting Helen Hammett Owen and May Massee.

21. In *Ola and Blakken and Line, Sine, Trine* (New York: Doubleday, 1933), Ingri and Edgar Parin d'Aulaire explain that the three sisters' names, "Line, Sine, Trine, should be pronounced to rhyme with 'seen-a.'" In this Norwegian folk narrative, Ola, the sisters, and their horse, Blakken, confront an enormous, multicolored "troll-cock," which Ola bravely shoots with a "blunderbuss." Ten horses cannot budge the bird, so the children rally all the farm animals to drag it to the farm. "From the troll-cock's feathers they made the softest of cushions and feather beds; from the claws they made pitchforks; from the skin, twelve pairs of shoes, and the finest pair was for Mother. / From the huge beak they made a sturdy boat. Then they built a big fire in a grove close to the farm and above the fire they put the cock to roast." All their neighbors come to the feast, including animals (a moose, bear, wolf, and rabbit form a conga line), "gnomes," and mysterious young women who, "though they looked like real girls . . . were Huldermaidens and lived on farms inside the hill" (n.p.).

22. Henry C. Pitz, "The Art of Illustration" (October 1962), in *Horn Book Reflections on Children's Books and Reading*, ed. Elinor Whitney Field (Boston: Horn Book Inc., 1968), 78.

23. Bertha E. Mahony and Elinor Whitney, eds., *Realms of Gold in Children's Books* (Garden City, N.Y.: Doubleday, Doran, 1929), 215.

24. Wallace Stegner and the editors of *LOOK*, *One Nation*, Life-in-America Prize Books (Boston: Houghton Mifflin, Riverside Press, 1945). This text, considered antisegregationist in its day, includes captioned black-and-white photos of diverse U.S. residents, a forbidding overview called "The Unaccepted," chapters on ethnoracial groups and regions, and an examination of Catholicism and Judaism. Yet the language maintains us-and-them divisions. For example, a four-photo spread on Filipino Americans notes a 14:1 ratio of male to female immigrants from the Philippines, adding that state miscegenation laws "prevent the marriage of Filipinos to women of the Caucasian race. . . . They are the most starved and dispossessed of our racial groups . . . and the loneliest. Ardent and extremely social, the typical Filipino is a lover of gay times. If he is lucky, his Saturday night will involve a visit to a Filipino barber, whose skill is much admired . . . a new suit, a pretty Filipina, and an orchid to accent her rarity" (31). The text promotes an ethnographic, objectifying "look" rather than genuine empathy.

25. Bertha E. Mahony, Louise P. Latimer, and Beulah Folmsbee, eds., *Illustrators of Children's Books, 1744–1945* (1947; repr., Boston: Horn Book Inc., 1970), 126.

26. Maria Cimino, "Foreign Picture Books in a Children's Library," in ibid., 129.

27. "The Polish people who visited the room continually throughout the exhibition found in it a reaffirmation of their cultural heritage," Cimino writes, linking childhood's books and nationalist yearning (ibid., 141).

28. Ibid., 130.

29. Grace and Carl Moon's illustrated novels and story collections include *Nadita (Little Nothing)* (1927), *Solita* (1938), *Chi-Weé: The Adventures of a Little Indian Girl* (1925; repr., 1946), and *Chi-Weé and Loki of the Desert* (1926; repr., 1945), as well as *The Runaway Papoose*, *The Magic Trail*, *The Missing Katchina*, *The Arrow of Tee-May*, *Far-Away Desert*, *The Book of Nah-wee*, *Singing Sands*, and *White Indian*.

30. Abe Lerner, "Designing Children's Books," in *Stepping Away from Tradition: Children's Books of the Twenties and Thirties*, ed. Sybille A. Jagusch (Washington, D.C.: Library of Congress, 1988), 39–41.

31. After Anne Carroll Moore returned from visiting publishers overseas, she learned from a bookseller friend "that while I had been gliding over the polished surfaces of French publishing houses in Paris he had been further afield and had brought back genuine treasures from other countries, notably from Italy and Czechoslovakia." Anne Carroll Moore, "Visits to French and English Publishers," in *My Roads to Childhood: Views and Reviews of Children's Books* (Boston: Horn Book Inc., 1970), 188–89.

32. Moore exemplified Francophilia, reporting "that every Anglo-Saxon must rediscover for himself this miracle of the continuing tradition of children and childish play in the everyday life of France which makes Paris, above all other cities, a children's paradise." Moore spent three months in France yet seems to have based her understanding of the nation on representations that were several decades out of date: "Since I do not speak the French language I was more than ever grateful for [Maurice] Boutet de Monvel's accurate pictorial interpretation of the daily life of French children in village and town." Anne Carroll Moore, "The Children of France," in *My Roads to Childhood*, 174.

33. A. L. de Saint-Rat, "Children's Books by Russian Émigré Artists, 1921–1940," *Journal of Decorative and Propaganda Arts* (Winter 1989): 92, 97. See also Michael Patrick Hearn, "The Picture Book Revolution," in *From the Silver Age to Stalin: Russian Children's Book Illustration in the Sasha Lurie Collection* (Amherst, Mass.: Eric Carle Museum of Picture Book Art, 2003), an exhibition catalog.

34. May Massee, "Developments of the Twentieth Century," in Mahony, Latimer, and Folmsbee, *Illustrators of Children's Books*, 234. On the Story Book series, see chapter 3.

35. Cimino, "Foreign Picture Books," 144.

36. Bader links Harnoncourt's 1931 *The Hole in the Wall* to comics and muralism: "Taking up the pictorial devices of [Germany's Wilhelm] Busch and his comic-strip confederates (the sort-of speech balloons, the growing man, the buckling stool), d'Harnoncourt goes further and makes the whole page his field of action . . . [so] we take it in at once as design, in sequence as story. Murals work in a similar fashion, and also combine deep perspective with emphasis on the picture plane, and altogether these picture-filled white pages—only eight in number—might be walls that d'Harnoncourt . . . painted on" (*American Picture Books*, 70). Bader links Harnoncourt to a Continental comics artist, yet might as easily link him to Mexican painters whose aesthetic he freely borrowed.

37. Ibid., 47. Bader adds that World War II "turned American attention briefly southward, a phenomenon reflected in children's books generally" (47), although the U.S. market saw few Central American or South American picture books by people native to those regions.

38. Lucy Herndon Crockett, biographical note, in Mahony, Latimer, and Folmsbee, *Illustrators of Children's Books*, 295.

39. *Aladdin and the Wonderful Lamp*, illus. Elizabeth MacKinstry (New York: Macmillan, 1935).

40. Bertha E. Mahony and Elinor Whitney, eds., *Five Years of Children's Books* (Garden City, N.Y.: Doubleday, Doran, 1936), 22.

41. Margery Williams Bianco, introduction to *Marcos: A Mountain Boy of Mexico*, by Melicent Humason Lee, illus. Berta and Elmer Hader (Chicago: Whitman, 1937), n.p. (The accent in Márcos's name does not appear in the title but is in the text itself.)

42. Arna Bontemps and Langston Hughes, *Popo and Fifina: Children of Haiti* (1932; repr., New York: Oxford University Press, 2000). Hughes spent April to July 1931 in Haiti on funds he received from the Harmon Gold Award for Literature. Upon his return, he and Bontemps wrote this novel.

43. On the problematic and romanticized historical content of Bontemps' solo novel, written in the context of the 1935 Haitian constitution and the authoritarian rule of president Sténio Vincent, see Mark Christian Thompson, "Voodoo Fascism: Fascist Ideology in Arna Bontemps's *Drums at Dusk*," *MELUS* 30, no. 3 (Fall 2005): 155–77.

44. J. Michael Dash, *Haiti and the United States: National Stereotypes and the Literary Imagination* (New York: St. Martin's, 1988), 46.

45. Ibid., 46–47. "Neither respectfully historical nor wildly sensationalist, this plaintive and understated children's book concentrates on the quiet endurance of the Haitian peasantry," writes Dash. ". . . The text is not overtly political but the children sense that something is amiss in a factory where black workers can pineapples for shipment to the United States" (53).

46. Alain Locke, *Opportunity* (Jan. 1933), qtd. in *The Collected Works of Langston Hughes: Essays on Art, Race, Politics, and World Affairs*, vol. 9, ed. Christopher C. De Santis (Columbia: University of Missouri Press, 2001), 17.

47. Violet J. Harris, "From Little Black Sambo to Popo and Fifina," *The Lion and the Unicorn* 14 (1990): 119. "Haiti is not depicted as an exotic, teeming island populated by uncivilized people," Harris writes. "This is not a literary travelogue. These people, the reader learns, want decent housing, food, and education" (118).

48. In an afterword, Arnold Rampersad writes, "Many of Hughes's radical ideas about Haiti are simply unexpressed in this book. There is no attack on the mulatto leadership class—indeed, no mention of this class at all . . . [and] only a single reference to the foreign soldiers [U.S. Marines]." Bontemps and Hughes, *Popo and Fifina* (2000), 106. Original flap copy found in *Popo and Fifina: Children of Haiti* (New York: Macmillan, 1932).

49. Drewey W. Gunn, in *American and British Writers in Mexico* (1974), qtd. in Edward J. Mullen, "The Literary Reputation of Langston Hughes in the Hispanic World and Haiti," in *Langston Hughes in the Hispanic World and Haiti* (Hamden, Conn.: Archon, 1977), 15–46.

50. Mullen, "Literary Reputation of Langston Hughes," 34.

51. Langston Hughes, "People without Shoes" (1931), qtd. in ibid., 34.

52. In *Popo and Fifina*, Papa Jean goes "barefooted" and is identified, nonjudgmentally, as a peasant (2). By comparison, in the editorial "People without Shoes," *New Masses*, October 1931, Hughes acidly observes, "Haiti is a land of people without shoes—black people, whose bare feet tread the dusty roads to market in the early morning, or pat softly on the bare floors of hotels, serving foreign guests. . . . All of the work that keeps Haiti alive, pays for the American Occupation, and enriches foreign traders—that vast and basic work—is done by Negroes without shoes. . . . To be seen in the streets barefooted marks one as a low-caste person of no standing in the community." In De Santis, *Collected Works of Langston Hughes*, 46–48.

53. In addition to *Marcos* and *Children of Banana Land*, Melicent Humason Lee catered to a fascination with international children in *Pablo and Petra: A Boy and Girl of Mexico* (1934); *At the Jungle's Edge: A Boy and Girl of Costa Rica* (1938); and *Volcanoes in the Sun: A Boy and Girl of Guatemala* (undated in advertisement).

54. See Katharine Capshaw Smith, *Children's Literature of the Harlem Renaissance* (Bloomington: Indiana University Press, 2005); and Diane Johnson-Feelings, *The Best of "The Brownies' Book"* (New York: Oxford University Press, 1996), for debates among 1920s African American critics on how best to inform children about the inequities of racism and create social activists for the future without making children too pessimistic.

55. Julia Mickenberg writes that *Popo* "showed the real potential of American children's books to be popular yet politically engaged . . . . [despite] only one scene in the book that uses explicitly revolutionary imagery. . . . Papa Jean stays up late one night after work, and the children awaken to find a red kite with yellow and green trimmings (red, of course, is associated with revolutionary strength, while yellow and green are associated with Pan-Africanism)." Julia L. Mickenberg, *Learning from the Left: Children's Literature, the Cold War, and Radical Politics in the United States* (New York: Oxford University Press, 2005), 79–81. When the children fly the kite, it tangles with a "dull brown" kite flown by a challenger, but their kite emerges victorious.

56. Langston Hughes, "Books and the Negro Child" (from *Children's Library Yearbook*), in *Collected Works*, 49–50. In a way that seems heavy-handed now but is common to 1930s rhetoric, Bontemps and Hughes celebrate blackness, repeatedly referencing the characters' "black" skin, and they allude to Haiti's colonial history by mentioning how "the wind went through [Papa Jean's] ragged shirt, flapping it like a bullet-torn flag" (57).

57. For a discussion of little magazines and texts, including children's books that represented African American subjects, see Caroline Goeser, *Picturing the New Negro: Harlem Renaissance Print Culture and Modern Black Identity* (Lawrence: University of Kansas Press, 2007).

58. Silhouette imagery features in Pierre Pinsard's primitivist woodcuts for Blaise Cendrars's collection of African folktales, *Little Black Stories for Little White Children*, trans. Margery Bianco (1929); originally published as *Petits contes nègres pour les enfants des blancs*. Unlike Campbell, Pinsard pictures opaque masks and wild animal shapes rather than people. Such images do not enable eye contact between readers—the presumed "little white children"—and the nonwhite sources whose tales Cendrars retells.

Pinsard's silhouette art, although in a style popular among Harlem Renaissance artists, operates to place "black stories" in a primeval wilderness, remote from the urbanized, industrialized space of the 1920s United States.

59. Elizabeth Willis De Huff, *Taytay's Memories* (New York: Harcourt, Brace, 1924), n.p.

60. Allan Houser, biographical entry, in Mahony, Latimer, and Folmsbee, *Illustrators of Children's Books*, 321.

61. Unusual names (e.g., Ping, Ferdinand, Babar, and Nanook [from the film *Nanook of the North* (1921)] are a prologue to ethnographic accounts of cultural difference. Armstrong Sperry made a cottage industry of the practice in his "One Day with" books of the mid-1930s. Maynard Dixon's storybook *Injun Babies* (1923) mimics vaudeville-Indian diction in its slangy use of "Injun" and chapters that include "A-Wáy-She-Go: The Runaway Girl," "He-Wánts-Tu-Kwit: The Old Tired Horse," and "Me-Nó-Can: The Boy Who Learned How." About Jack Roberts's *The Wonderful Adventures of Ludo, the Little Green Duck*, reviewers averred, "We see in bold and bright pictures Ludo's trip around the world from his little farm in Normandy through the land of the Chin-Chin Chinamen to the cannibals of the South Seas and the Indians of North America" (Mahony and Whitney, *Realms of Gold*, 65). Rhea Wells introduced international locales in illustrated novels with exotic page borders, including *Peppi the Duck* (the Alps), *Ali the Camel* (the Middle East), and *Beppo the Donkey* (Italy), each of which matches an ethnic origin to a zoological specimen.

62. China and its evocative names were also subjects of fascination in *Shen of the Sea* (1925), *The Pigtail of Ah Lee Ben Loo* (1928), *Little Pear* (1931), and *Ching-Li and the Dragons* (1931), among numerous other children's titles.

63. Chinese laborers were imported to the United States for railroad work in the nineteenth-century West, but exclusion laws prohibited their becoming citizens. "In 1943, Congress repealed the Chinese exclusion laws and allowed a quota for Chinese immigration . . . [yet] this new policy permitted just a tiny trickle of Chinese immigrants, only 105 annually. . . . Between 1944 and 1952, only 1,428 Chinese were naturalized" (Takaki, *Different Mirror*, 387). See also Iris Chang, *The Chinese in America: A Narrative History* (New York: Viking, 2003); and Moon-Ho Jung, *Coolies and Cane: Race, Labor, and Sugar Production in the Age of Emancipation* (Baltimore: The Johns Hopkins University Press, 2006). Jung calls the term "coolie" "a racialized and racializing figure that denied Asian migrants the liberal subjectivity that 'immigrants' presumably possessed." Moon-Ho Jung, "Coolie," in *Keywords for American Cultural Studies*, ed. Bruce Burgett and Glenn Hendler (New York: NYU Press, 2007), 65.

64. This memorable repeated phrasing, "just quietly," resonates with Ernest Hemingway's signature sentences, as in *The Sun Also Rises* (1926; repr., New York: Scribner, 1954): "Romero's bull-fighting gave real emotion, because he kept the absolute purity of line in his movements and always quietly and calmly let the horns pass him each time" (168). If Leaf and Lawson read *Death in the Afternoon* (1932) and other Hemingway endeavors, Hemingway certainly knew about *Ferdinand*, and answered it with a 1951 short story called "The Faithful Bull" (*Holiday* 9, no. 3): "One time there was a bull and his name was not Ferdinand and he cared nothing for flowers. He loved to fight and

he fought with all the other bulls of his own age, or any age, and he was a champion" (51). Hemingway's faithful bull, who fights for pure pleasure, is a failure as a stud because he remains sexually faithful to just one cow. He is sent to the bullring, where he dies, according to Hemingway, with the matador's respect (as Ferdinand does not). On intersections of Hemingway and Leaf and Lawson, see Jean Streufert Patrick, "Robert Lawson's *The Story of Ferdinand*: Death in the Afternoon or Life under the Cork Tree?" in *Touchstones: Reflections on the Best in Children's Literature*, vol. 3, *Picture Books*, ed. Perry Nodelman (West Lafayette, Ind.: Children's Literature Association, 1989), 74–84.

65. Gary D. Schmidt, *Robert Lawson* (New York: Twayne, 1997), 8–9.

66. Ibid., 10.

67. Michael Steig views *The Story of Ferdinand* as "a plea for peace" and a satire of machismo, reading Ferdinand alternately as a "conscientious objector" and as a role model combining manly muscle with pacifist calm. Less convincingly, Steig relates the story to Rudyard Kipling's "The Bull That Thought" (1926), which describes a strategic-minded, murderous bull whose keen intellect, untroubled by sweetness, helps him escape the bullring alive. Michael Steig, "Ferdinand and Wee Gillis at Half Century," *Children's Literature Association Quarterly* 14, no. 3 (1989): 118–23.

68. Schmidt, *Robert Lawson*, 10, paraphrasing Michael Patrick Hearn, "Ferdinand the Bull's Fiftieth Anniversary," *Washington Post Book World*, November 9, 1986, 22.

69. Joseph H. Schwarcz and Chava Schwarcz, *The Picture Book Comes of Age: Looking at Childhood through the Art of Illustration* (Chicago: American Library Association, 1991), 168.

70. Hearn, "Ferdinand the Bull's Fiftieth Anniversary," 22.

71. Perry Nodelman, *The Pleasures of Children's Literature* (White Plains, N.Y.: Longman, 1996), 18.

72. H. A. and Margret Rey began composing *Curious George* (Boston: Houghton Mifflin, 1941), then titled "The Adventures of Fifi," in 1939. Hans Augusto and Margret Rey, German Jews from Hamburg, acquired Brazilian citizenship while living in Rio de Janeiro in the mid-thirties. They spent four years in Paris until, in the 1940 evacuation, they fled to Spain, Portugal, Brazil, and the United States, carrying their manuscript all the way. See Louise Borden, *The Journey That Saved Curious George: The Wartime Escape of Margret and H. A. Rey*, illus. Allan Drummond (Boston: Houghton Mifflin, 2005). Their monkey tale aligns with depictions of the irrepressible Other under lock and key, yet the Reys themselves were immigrants who created the text over several years and locations. The zoo depicted in *Curious George* is European rather than American, suggesting nostalgia for childhood pastimes ruined by war. *Curious George* operates on several intriguing levels, as animal tale, comedy, and artifact of longing.

73. Jean Perrot, "The French Avant-Garde Revisited: or, Why We Shouldn't Burn Mickey Mouse," in *Critical Perspectives on Postcolonial African Children's and Young Adult Literature*, ed. Meena Khorana (Westport, Conn.: Greenwood, 1998), 81. Perrot flays Herbert Kohl's "Should We Burn Babar?" in *Should We Burn Babar? Essays on Children's Literature and the Power of Stories* (New York: New Press, 1995), 3–29. Whereas Kohl wonders, "Who has been uninvited to Babar's world?" (25), quizzes a

"Black South African from Capetown" (27) on *Babar's* contemporary value, and frets about colonial literature's threat to children, Perrot argues for critical literacy and for teaching children "to read these books properly" without the "aggressiveness of the adult critic" (80–81).

74. Adam Gopnik, "Freeing the Elephants," *New Yorker*, September 22, 2008, 47. Gopnik views the Babar books as fairy tales of French modernity: "Far more than an allegory of colonialism, the Babar books are a fable of the difficulties of a bourgeois life" (50). He also links the series to the avant-garde, the Fauves in particular (48). See also Edmund Leach, "Babar's Civilization Analyzed," *New Society*, December 20, 1962, 16–17; Patrick Richardson, "Teach Your Baby to Rule," in *Suitable for Children? Controversies in Children's Literature* (Berkeley and Los Angeles: University of California Press, 1976), 179–83; and Claire-Lise Malarte-Feldman and Jack Yeager, "Babar and the French Connection: Teaching the Politics of Superiority and Exclusion," in Khorana, *Critical Perspectives*, 69–77.

75. Varying accounts of Sperry's itinerant life may be found in Ruth Hill Viguers, "1920–1950: The Golden Age," in *A Critical History of Children's Literature: A Survey of Children's Books in English*, ed. Cornelia Meigs, rev. ed. (New York: Macmillan, 1964), 486–87; and in Bertha Mahony Miller and Elinor Whitney Field, eds., *Newbery Medal Books, 1922–1955* (Boston: Horn Book, Inc., 1955), 192–207.

76. Miller and Field, *Newbery Medal Books*, 204.

77. Ibid., 200–201.

78. "Native American pupils entering day school faced abrupt shocks intended to strip them of identity: short haircuts, traditional garb confiscated, and a new moniker imposed at random. . . . Students lost the 'warm blanket' of attentive kinfolk, lived alongside members of different tribes, and learned to speak English all the time on pain of punishment." David Macleod, *The Age of the Child: Children in America, 1890–1920* (New York: Twayne, 1998), 90. On day and boarding schools for Native American youth, see, e.g., Frederick E. Hoxie, *A Final Promise: The Campaign to Assimilate the Indians, 1880–1920* (Cambridge: Cambridge University Press, 1989); Robert A. Trennert Jr., *The Phoenix Indian School: Forced Assimilation in Arizona, 1891–1935* (Norman: University of Oklahoma Press, 1988); Michael C. Coleman, *American Indian Children at School, 1850–1930* (Jackson: University Press of Mississippi, 1993); and Wallace Adams, *Education for Extinction: American Indians and the Boarding School Experience, 1875–1928* (Lawrence: University Press of Kansas, 1995).

79. Mahony and Whitney, *Realms of Gold*, 116.

80. On the marginalization of African Americans as producers and consumers of children's texts, see Donnarae MacCann and Gloria Woodard, *The Black American in Books for Children: Readings in Racism* (Metuchen, N.J.: Scarecrow, 1985); Donnarae MacCann, *White Supremacy in Children's Literature* (New York: Routledge, 2000); Osayimwense Osa, ed., *The All-White World of Children's Books and African American Children's Literature* (Trenton, N.J.: Africa World, 1995); Michelle H. Martin, *Brown Gold: Milestones of African-American Children's Picture Books, 1845–2002* (New York: Routledge, 2004); and Smith, *Children's Literature of the Harlem Renaissance*.

81. Ellis Credle, biographical entry, in Mahony, Latimer, and Folmsbee, *Illustrators of Children's Books*, 295.

82. Roland Barthes, "The Death of the Author," in *Image Music Text*, 145–48.

## 3. SENTIENT MACHINES

1. See Siegfried Kracauer, "Farewell to the Linden Arcade" (1930), in *The Mass Ornament: Weimar Essays*, ed. and trans. Thomas Y. Levin (Cambridge, Mass.: Harvard University Press, 1995), 337–42; and Walter Benjamin, *The Arcades Project*, trans. Howard Eiland and Kevin McLaughlin (Cambridge, Mass.: Harvard University Press, Belknap Press, 1999), on the change of the urban space and the outmoded arcades as a shopping and strolling area.

2. Leonore St. John Power, "Jig-Saws and Steam Shovels in Literature: *Little Machinery*," in *The Three Owls*, bk. 2, ed. Anne Carroll Moore (New York: Coward-McCann, 1928), 32.

3. Ibid., 33.

4. Marshall Berman, *All That Is Solid Melts into Air: The Experience of Modernity* (New York: Simon and Schuster, 1982), 25. Berman argues that twentieth-century modernity is characterized by a loss of empathy that had been active in earlier critiques of industrialism, and wishes to revive nineteenth-century modes of thinking. Although I agree that a prior understanding of empathy was lost, picture books and illustrated texts instructed their readers in modern modes of empathy and perception, in nostalgia, and in a definition of empire acceptable to the mainstream.

5. Donna Haraway, *Simians, Cyborgs, and Women: The Reinvention of Nature* (New York: Routledge, 1991), 152.

6. Guy Debord, *The Society of the Spectacle*, trans. Donald Nicholson-Smith (New York: Zone, 1995), 12.

7. Jonathan Crary, *Suspensions of Perception: Attention, Spectacle, and Modern Culture* (Cambridge, Mass.: MIT Press, 1999), 73–74.

8. Hal Foster writes, "In *Mechanization Takes Command: A Contribution to Anonymous History* (London, 1948), Sigfried Giedion, a friend of the surrealists, dates 'the time of full mechanization' to 1919–1939, a period that surrealism spans; 'around 1920, mechanization involves the "domestic sphere" as well' (42). This says nothing of the culture of spectacle that Guy Debord also dates to this period (e.g., the profusion of radio and advertising, the development of sound film and advertising)." Hal Foster, *Compulsive Beauty* (Cambridge, Mass.: MIT Press, 1993), 273n48.

9. American picture books on machines from this period mirror Soviet priorities along the same lines and were influenced by communication with Russia and immigrants from that country following the 1917 revolution. See A. L. de Saint-Rat, "Children's Books by Russian Émigré Artists," and Evgeny Steiner, *Stories for Little Comrades: Revolutionary Artists and the Making of Early Soviet Children's Books* (Seattle: University of Washington Press, 1999).

10. C. B. Falls, *Modern ABC* (New York: Day, 1923); Elizabeth King, *Today's ABC Book* (New York: McBride, 1929), unpaginated.

11. Harper and Brothers' City and Country series includes *The Story of Transportation*, by Jeanette Eaton, illus. Maurice Day, 1927; *The Story of Books Up through the Ages*, by Marjorie Maxwell, illus. Max Schwartz, 1928; *The Story of Light*, by Jeanette Eaton, illus. Max Schwartz, 1928; *The Story of Water Supply*, by Hope Halway, illus. Elmer Hader, 1929; *The Story of Athletics*, by Marian King, illus. Bernard Westmacott, 1931; *The Story of Mining*, by Martha Gruening, illus. A. A. Klinke, 1931; *The Story of Music*, by Theodore Stearns, illus. Alexander Kahn, 1931; and *The Story of Printed Pictures*, by Katherine Stanley-Brown, illus. Rudolph Stanley-Brown, 1931.

12. Advertisement in Eaton's *The Story of Transportation*, 53. Additional page references in text. Other Harper series books focused on children's nutrition, given that vitamins and packaged grocery goods were being marketed to parents and in schools. In an effort to demystify milk production, urban children were taught about cows, dairies, and factories.

13. Berta and Elmer Hader, *The Picture Book of Travel: The Story of Transportation* (New York: Macmillan, 1928), 24–25. Additional page references in text.

14. Maud and Miska Petersham, *The Story Book of Iron and Steel* (Chicago: Winston, 1935).

15. Alice Payne Hackett, *Sixty Years of Bestsellers, 1895–1955* (New York: Bowker, 1956), 65.

16. Hildegarde Hoyt Swift, *Little Blacknose: The Story of a Pioneer*, illus. Lynd Ward (New York: Harcourt, Brace, 1929), 4–5. Additional page references in text.

17. Swift and Ward, both prolific creators in children's literature, later worked together on *The Little Red Lighthouse and the Great Gray Bridge* (1942). In a 2006 conference presentation, "Anxieties of the Inanimate: Zamacois's *Memoirs of a Railway Car*," Robert A. Davidson described a 1922 Spanish avant-garde novel, published in Madrid and told from the point of view of a luxury railcar. Davidson aptly associates the creation and use of the railway car (purchased in France, sent to Spain) with the growth of the capitalist marketplace and the state. The railcar, like Blacknose, is frightened at the thought of being junked; it witnesses two train wrecks, "split[s] the skull of a suicide victim," and shudders at "old dead" railcars like itself. Davidson attributes this fear to a social anxiety around the cessation of dynamic modern motion. Modernist Studies Association conference, October 20, 2006.

18. Dorothy Walter Baruch, *Big Fellow*, illus. Jay Van Everen (Eau Claire, Wisc.: Cadmus, 1929), n.p. Additional page references in text.

19. Troy Boone details a tendency in British literature to grant scopic power to a middle-class overseer and to deny specular ability to the working-class subject: "[Henry] Mayhew [in *London Labour and the London Poor*] constructs a scale by which to measure a Londoner's visual power as urban observer, a scale in which the poor street-sellers see and know little of the city. . . . Mayhew's depiction of the working classes as deprived of visual power, like his depiction of them as a juvenile group, moves freely between figurative and literal expression." *Youth of Darkest England: Working-Class Children at the Heart of Victorian Empire* (New York: Routledge, 2005), 28. Mayhew's London is a far cry from 1920s America, yet a similar scopic regime is manifest in American picture books that imply the loitering observer's superior perspective.

20. For details on paving and highway building in the period 1910–39, see *ARBA Pictorial History of Roadbuilding* (Washington, D.C.: American Road Builders' Association, 1975); Daniel L. Schodek, *Landmarks in American Civil Engineering* (Cambridge, Mass.: MIT Press, 1987); and Clay McShane, *Down the Asphalt Path: The Automobile and the American City* (New York: Columbia University Press, 1994), and "Transforming the Use of Urban Space: A Look at the Revolution in Street Pavements, 1880–1924," *Journal of Urban History* 5 (May 1979). According to McShane, "The metropolis held the nation's highest concentration of cars, and the *Times* claimed that residents of the Greater New York area owned nearly half the cars registered in the U.S. as late as 1905. It was the site of the first motor vehicle accidents, pedestrian-auto conflicts, and traffic jams. New York built the first limited access suburban roads in the world. As late as 1928, when highway engineers built the world's first cloverleaf intersection in suburban New Jersey [the same year Newark International Airport opened], New York area highway engineers led developments in that discipline. Traffic police, one-way streets, and traffic lights all appeared first in Gotham" (*Down the Asphalt Path*, xiii–xiv).

21. Mike Gold, Notes of the Month, *New Masses* 5 (Jan 1930), qtd. in Barbara Foley, *Radical Representations: Politics and Form in U.S. Proletarian Fiction, 1929–1941* (Durham, N.C.: Duke University Press, 1993), 66, and Julia L. Mickenberg, *Learning from the Left: Children's Literature, the Cold War, and Radical Politics in the United States* (New York: Oxford University Press, 2005), 61.

22. These oversize, sentient machines differ from automata and small-scale figurative toys such as dolls and stuffed animals. Winnie-the-Pooh and the Velveteen Rabbit were 1920s store-bought commodities, not the metal tools of industry. Endowing the fictive plaything with soulful life is distinct from anthropomorphizing the unplayful, hardworking machine. See Lois Kuznets, *When Toys Come Alive* (New Haven, Conn.: Yale University Press, 1984), especially 136–56; and Mary V. Jackson, *Engines of Instruction, Mischief, and Magic: Children's Literature in England from Its Beginnings to 1839* (Lincoln: University of Nebraska Press, 1989).

23. Joseph Schwarcz, *Ways of the Illustrator: Visual Communication in Children's Literature* (Chicago: American Library Association, 1982), 153 and 166.

24. Ibid., 154.

25. Walter Benjamin, "The Storyteller: Observations on the Work of Nikolai Leskov" (1936), trans. Harry Zohn, in *Walter Benjamin: Selected Writings*, vol. 3, *1935–1938*, ed. Howard Eiland and Michael W. Jennings (Cambridge, Mass.: Harvard University Press, Belknap Press, 2002), 144.

26. Stephen Crane, "New York's Bicycle Speedway," in *Maggie, a Girl of the Streets, and other New York Writings*, ed. Luc Sante (New York: Modern Library, 2001), 219. See also "New York Journalism," in *The Works of Stephen Crane*, vol. 8, ed. Frederick Bowers (Charlottesville: University Press of Virginia, 1973).

27. Crane, "New York's Bicycle Speedway," 220.

28. Ibid., 221.

29. *Steamboat Willie*, DVD, directed by Ub Iwerks and Walt Disney (1928; Walt Disney Productions, 2005). Cartoon metamorphoses also feature in animation such

as Max and Dave Fleischer's 1930s Betty Boop cartoons. See Donald Crafton, *Before Mickey: The Animated Film, 1898–1928* (Cambridge, Mass.: MIT Press, 1982), 59–67. Schwarcz, considering mechanized liveliness in picture books and animation, comments: "One day, probably, Walt Disney's animated cartoons will be recognized as a major symbol of this process of mutual interchangeability [between machines and humans]: are those jerky creatures not both mechanical men and hominoid mechanisms?" (*Ways of the Illustrator*, 162).

30. Erwin Panofsky, "Style and Medium in the Motion Pictures" (1934, revised 1947), in *Film Theory and Criticism: Introductory Readings*, 4th ed. Gerald Mast, Marshall Cohen, and Leo Braudy (New York: Oxford University Press, 1998), 240.

31. For instance, Émile Cohl's stop-motion film *Mobilier fidele* (*The Automatic Moving Company*, 1910) shows furniture wiggling out of one apartment, onto a waiting truck, and into another building.

32. Walter Benjamin, "On Some Motifs in Baudelaire" (1940), in *Selected Writings*, vol. 4, 328.

33. Wolfgang Schivelbusch, *The Railway Journey: Trains and Travel in the Nineteenth Century*, trans. Anselm Hollo (New York: Urizen, 1979); John R. Stilgoe, *Metropolitan Corridor: Railroads and the American Scene* (New Haven, Conn.: Yale University Press, 1983); and Lynne Kirby, *Parallel Tracks: The Railroad and Silent Cinema* (Durham, N.C.: Duke University Press, 1997).

34. Alice Jenkins, "Getting to Utopia: Railways and Heterotopia in Children's Literature," in *Utopian and Dystopian Writing for Children and Young Adults*, ed. Carrie Hintz and Elaine Ostry (New York: Routledge, 2003), 23.

35. Ibid., 27–28.

36. Louise H. Seaman, " 'Berta and Elmer' and Their Picture Books," *Horn Book Magazine*, August 1928, 56–57.

37. Camaraderie among locomotives and engineers pervades short film and cinematic comedy. D. W. Griffith's early experiment in cross-cutting and stunts, *The Lonedale Operator* (1911), details an attempted rail-station robbery and the bold young woman who telegraphs a warning to an engineer, who rushes his train to the rescue. Buster Keaton's comfort with the speeding locomotive in *The General* (1927) similarly depicts human-machine collaboration. Keaton's Civil War–era engineer, Johnny Gray, adores his engine, the General. His framed image of the General is much larger than a portrait of his human beloved, and his own body is in perfect harmony with the fast-moving machine. When Yankees kidnap the heroine, Johnny drives to her rescue, securing a Confederate victory in battle and winning the chance to become a soldier himself. Johnny's mechanical ingenuity and physical pliability signify his own technologization, reveal his bravery, and prove his masculinity, despite his small stature and prior failure as a soldier.

38. Jacalyn Eddy notes that although library budgets suffered and book purchasing declined, "only two small houses went bankrupt" and "book circulation in many cities rose by as much as 40 percent, partly because, unlike other activities, reading could be free." *Bookwomen: Creating an Empire in Children's Book Publishing, 1919–1939* (Madison: University of Wisconsin Press, 2006), 139.

39. "The skills developed in the twenties for making the most tasteful and fullest use of typography and color were now brought to bear on the new problems with striking effect. . . . By the end of 1935, the output of titles had definitely turned upward again." John Tebbel, "For Children, with Love and Profit: Two Decades of Book Publishing for Children," in *Stepping Away from Tradition: Children's Books of the Twenties and Thirties*, ed. Sybille A. Jagusch (Washington, D.C.: Library of Congress, 1988), 27.

40. Anne MacLeod, "Literary and Social Aspects of Children's Books of the Twenties and Thirties," in Jagusch, *Stepping Away from Tradition*, 67–68. MacLeod—who discusses class but not race or ethnic heritage—finds thirties children's fiction "consistently upbeat. . . . The stream ran clear and steady, with no fearful undercurrents. . . . There is truth as well as wish in these stories" (66–67). These texts are reassuring, yet I contend there is a discernable anxiety in these fairy tales of modernity, whose construction of idyllic domestic and public spaces so clearly contradicts lived reality.

41. For an account of Henry Ford's abhorrence of waste and obsolescence, the challenge to Ford Motor Company in 1926–27 from General Motors, and Ford's grudging design and production of the new Model A in 1927, see Susan Strasser, *Waste and Want: A Social History of Trash* (New York: Holt, Metropolitan, 1999). On literary representations of waste and efficiency, see Cecelia Tichi, *Shifting Gears: Technology, Literature, Culture in Modernist America* (Chapel Hill: University of North Carolina Press, 1987).

42. E. B. White, "Farewell, My Lovely! (An Aging Male Kisses an Old Flame Good-Bye, circa 1936)," in *Essays of E. B. White* (New York: Harper and Row, 1977), 162.

43. Ibid., 164–65.

44. Lynd Ward's dramatic wordless novels, which lack written text other than occasional chapter titles, influenced early 1930s comics sequences. *Mad Man's Drum* (1930) features a three-word primitivist title and sequence of high-contrast, scratchboard-style wood engravings. The visual story implies shock, criminal insanity, religious fervor, and murder brought on by ownership of a magical drum or, more subtly, by colonialist complicity in the slave trade.

45. Schwarcz, *Ways of the Illustrator*, 80–81.

46. Judith Richardson, *Possessions: The History and Uses of Haunting in the Hudson Valley* (Cambridge, Mass.: Harvard University Press, 2003), 64.

47. Ibid., 3.

48. Wilfred Jones, *How the Derrick Works* (New York: Day, 1930). Mickenberg groups *How the Derrick Works* with Henry Lent's *Diggers and Builders* (New York: Macmillan, 1931) and writer Vera Edelstadt and illustrator Romano's *A Steam Shovel for Me!* (New York: Stokes, 1933). See Mickenberg, *Learning from the Left*, 44, 295n58.

49. Bertha E. Mahony and Elinor Whitney, eds., *Contemporary Illustrators of Children's Books* (Boston: Bookshop for Boys and Girls / Women's Educational and Industrial Union, 1930; repr., Detroit: Gale, 1978), 42.

50. Howard Zinn notes the "simplified unskilled jobs" assigned under a Taylorist assembly-line system, often to the populous immigrant labor force. Howard Zinn, *A People's History of the United States, 1492–Present* (New York: HarperPerennial, 1995), 317.

51. "Modernist architecture and planning created a modernized version of pastoral:

a spatially and socially segmented world—people here, traffic there; work here, homes there; rich here, poor there; barriers of grass and concrete in between." Berman, *All That Is Solid*, 168.

52. Lewis Hine, *Men at Work: Photographic Studies of Modern Men and Machines* (New York: Macmillan, 1932; 2d ed., New York: Dover, 1977). Alan Trachtenberg, *Reading American Photographs: Images as History; Matthew Brady to Walker Evans* (New York: Hill and Wang, 1989), compares Hine's social criticism of the laboring body to Alfred Stieglitz's formalist attention to the skyscraper's ultramodern shape.

53. Trachtenberg, *Reading American Photographs*, 218.

54. Ibid., 224.

55. Lucy Sprague Mitchell, Elsa H. Naumburg, and Clara Lambert, Skyscraper (New York: Junior Literary Guild / Day, 1933). Page references in text.

56. Michael Denning, *The Cultural Front: The Laboring of American Culture in the Twentieth Century* (New York: Verso, 1997), 239.

57. Tichi, *Shifting Gears*, 34. Tichi says the efficiency movement influenced style and form in literature and industrial design alike. Taylorism's "ethos of synchronized design, abundance, and functionalism, its kinetics, its utilitarian motivation and method of spatial and temporal reformulation all came to have a significant impact on American literature in the twentieth century" (90). This ethos characterizes picture books about skyscrapers and equipment, which compare fit bodies to firm structures stabilized with girders and rivets.

58. Foster, *Compulsive Beauty*, 129.

59. Jessica Riskin's "The Defecating Duck; or, The Ambiguous Origins of Artificial Life" and Jonathan Lamb's "Modern Metamorphoses and Disgraceful Tales," in *Things*, ed. Bill Brown (Chicago: University of Chicago Press, 2004), compellingly investigate Brown's "thing theory" via mechanical minds, automatons, the autobiographies of objects, and fictive sentience.

60. On changes in perception from the nineteenth to the twentieth century, see Crary, *Suspensions of Perception* and *Techniques of the Observer: On Vision and Modernity in the Nineteenth Century* (Cambridge, Mass.: MIT Press, 1990).

61. Walter Benjamin, "The Work of Art in the Age of Its Technological Reproducibility (Third Version)" (1939), trans. Harry Zohn and Edmund Jephcott, in *Selected Writings*, vol. 4, 255 (emphasis in original). See also *Illuminations*, trans. Harry Zohn (New York: Schocken, 1969), 222–24.

62. Margaret Wise Brown trained as an elementary school instructor with Lucy Sprague Mitchell, and Brown's early work appears in *Another Here and Now Story Book*, focusing on sensory experience in the urban space. Brown also edited children's books for William R. Scott, Inc., and wrote poetry based on Gertrude Stein's aesthetic. In her picture books, Brown toys with nonlinearity and voiced sound, and chooses avant-garde artists to illustrate her aural compositions. See Leonard Marcus, *Awakened by the Moon: Margaret Wise Brown* (Boston: Beacon Press, 1992).

63. Schwarcz refers to picture-book creators' use of "visible sound . . . [as] a mainstay of the comics code[,] . . . . ubiquitous in the lower arts [e.g., animation, advertising], and frequently used in modern art altogether" (*Ways of the Illustrator*, 77).

64. Walter Benjamin, "On Some Motifs in Baudelaire," 338. See also *Illuminations*, 186–88.

65. Barthes refers to this as the "madness" inherent in the photograph, which cannot look back. Art theorist James Elkins explores this phenomenon in *The Object Stares Back: On the Nature of Seeing* (New York: Simon and Schuster, 1996).

## 4. MURALS IN MINIATURE

1. Mary Liddell, *Little Machinery: A Critical Facsimile Edition*, foreword by John Stilgoe and critical essay by Nathalie op de Beeck (Detroit: Wayne State University Press, 2009). *Little Machinery* belongs to what Anne Thaxter Eaton calls the "steam-shovel school of literature" in *Reading with Children* (New York: Viking, 1947), 27, qtd. in Jacalyn Eddy, *Bookwomen: Creating an Empire in Children's Book Publishing, 1919–1939* (Madison: University of Wisconsin Press, 2006), 112. This "steam-shovel school" belonged to the here-and-now category, carrying the fairy tale debate from the twenties well into the thirties.

2. Mark Seltzer, *Bodies and Machines* (New York: Routledge, 1992), 63.

3. The Streamliner trains and routes fell into disuse within twenty years, and the original Pioneer Zephyr is now displayed in Chicago's Museum of Science and Industry. See, e.g., the PBS *American Experience* documentary *Streamliners: America's Lost Trains*, directed by Thomas Ott (2001); and the 1934 film *The Silver Streak*, directed by Thomas Atkins.

4. Jeanette Eaton's *Story of Transportation* (New York: Harper, 1927) comments on the use of steam shovels to dig cellars. Burton, who graduated from Sonora High School in California in 1927 and moved to Boston in 1928, grew up cognizant of the changes in the vast U.S. landscape. See Barbara Elleman, *Virginia Lee Burton: A Life in Art* (Boston: Houghton Mifflin, 2002), 10–13.

5. Barbara Bader, *American Picture Books from "Noah's Ark" to "The Beast Within"* (New York: Macmillan, 1976), 202.

6. Gillian Avery et al., "Children's Literature in America, 1870–1945, *Children's Literature: An Illustrated History*, ed. Peter Hunt (Oxford: Oxford University Press, 1995), 248.

7. Maria Nikolajeva and Carole Scott, *How Picturebooks Work* (New York: Routledge, 2006), 14.

8. Ibid., 15.

9. Ibid., 26.

10. Ibid.

11. Marjorie Flack's poignant *Humphrey: One Hundred Years along the Wayside with a Box Turtle* (Garden City, N.Y.: Doubleday, Doran, 1934) considers the same issues from a living thing's perspective. Humphrey is an aging tortoise who meets various children, observes changes in architecture, and witnesses shifts from stagecoaches to railroads to automobiles between 1834 and 1934. *Humphrey* parallels Field and Lathrop's *Hitty* and similar tales of wooden dolls and rusty mechanisms, yet it involves a

sentient creature that is ignored or forgotten as humans change the land at an ever more hectic pace.

12. "The curving lines and rhythmic patterns found throughout Burton's artwork surely emanated from her love of dance," Elleman writes (*Virginia Lee Burton*, 39–40). Dance was one of many art forms Burton practiced with astonishing intensity. A tireless reviser of manuscripts and prints, she observed small details with an energy bordering on the obsessive.

13. Ibid., 39.

14. Ibid., 40.

15. Jon C. Stott and Teresa Krier, "Virginia Lee Burton's *The Little House*: Technological Change and Fundamental Verities," in *Touchstones: Reflections on the Best in Children's Literature*, vol. 3, *Picture Books*, ed. Perry Nodelman (West Lafayette, Ind.: Children's Literature Association, 1989), 35–37.

16. Virginia Lee Burton, autobiographical note in *Illustrators of Children's Books, 1744–1945*, ed. Bertha E. Mahony, Louise P. Latimer, and Beulah Folmsbee (1947; repr., Boston: Horn Book Inc., 1970), 287.

17. Edith Thatcher Hurd and Clement Hurd unapologetically imitate Burton and Gramatky in their coauthored book series of 1940–56, but their mechanical protagonists lack cartoonish faces and consequently demand less sympathy. Their early 1940s titles include *Engine, Engine, No. 9* (New York: Lothrop, Lee and Shepard, 1940); *The Annie Moran* (New York: Lothrop, 1942), an obsolete-equipment story, like *Mike Mulligan*, about a tugboat like *Little Toot*; and *Speedy the Hook and Ladder Truck* (New York: Lothrop, 1942), similar to *Hercules*.

18. Attesting to the continued currency of 1930s and 1940s picture-book artists, the Eric Carle Museum of Picture Book Art, in Amherst, Massachusetts, organized the exhibits "Toot and Re-Toot: The Return of Hardie Gramatky" (December 21, 2007– May 4, 2008) and "Those Telling Lines: The Art of Virginia Lee Burton" (March 24–June 21, 2009).

19. Robert D. Feild, *The Art of Walt Disney*, qtd. in Bader, *American Picture Books*, 203.

20. Bader, *American Picture Books*, 204.

21. Julia L. Mickenberg writes that *Tootle*, illustrated by Hungarian communist and artist Tibor Gergely, "is arguably more about the subversive pleasures of resisting pressures to conform" and that "going *off* the tracks . . . might be a more memorable message than 'staying on the tracks no matter what.'" *Learning from the Left: Children's Literature, the Cold War, and Radical Politics in the United States* (New York: Oxford University Press, 2005), 7–8. Considering how strongly Gergely's book parallels *Choo Choo*, readers must assess the machine-human analogy explicit in the misbehaving locomotive-child. The mechanical object's acquiescence to control after a stimulating vacation or a wild weekend is analogous to the necessity of wage labor for the average worker. In picture books, closure typically arrives when mischief is brought under social control.

22. "In the 1920s, monotony became an issue as psychologists like [Berlin's Otto]

Lipmann began to recognize that the [American] standardization of movements à la Taylor could inhibit efficiency if the worker's 'bio-psychological' interests were not considered. Lipmann also acknowledged the pleasure that a well-organized pattern of work could evoke." Anson Rabinbach, *The Human Motor: Energy, Fatigue, and the Origins of Modernity* (New York: Basic Books, 1990), 282. Despite proposed solutions to monotony and fatigue, "these nostalgic alloys of modern industry and preindustrial community were rarely adopted" unless one counts the European turn to Fordist production (282). Picture books about bored machines address this issue, with the typical solution being workers' adaptation to conditions.

23. James Daugherty, *Daniel Boone* (New York: Viking, 1940). In the same vein, Daugherty later illustrated Irwin Shapiro's *Yankee Thunder: The Legendary Life of Davy Crockett* (New York: Messner, 1944).

24. Mickenberg, *Learning from the Left*, 36.

25. "Unlike a published reproduction of a mural or a frieze, upon which the eye can wander, scanning a wide field for pattern, signs of unity, the picturebook opening allows only limited exposures." William Moebius, "Introduction to Picturebook Codes," in *Children's Literature: The Development of Criticism*, ed. Peter Hunt (New York: Routledge, 1990), 132.

26. Lynd Ward, "A Note on James Daugherty," *Horn Book Magazine*, July 1940, 240. As far back as 1930, Ward saluted Daugherty's interdependent word-image texts: "Consider Elizabeth MacKinstry and James Daugherty. . . . Are not the drawings in, say, 'The White Cat' and 'Abe Lincoln Grows Up' as much a part of their books as the stories themselves?" Lynd Ward, "Contemporary Book Illustration," in *Contemporary Illustrators of Children's Books*, ed. Bertha E. Mahony and Elinor Whitney (Boston: Bookshop for Boys and Girls / Women's Educational and Industrial Union, 1930; repr., Detroit: Gale, 1978), 2.

27. Ward, "Note on James Daugherty," 242.

28. "The Iron Horse," "Steamboat around the Bend," and "The Model-T Decade," in *Life*, October 25, 1937.

29. Ward, "Note on James Daugherty," 240.

30. Ibid., 245.

31. Ward implies similarities between composing a pictorial sequence such as his *Mad Man's Drum*, with its racialized overtones of injustice, and composing an intertwined set of murals, which also require socially and historically conscious reading strategies. See David A. Beronä, *Wordless Books: The Original Graphic Novels* (New York: Abrams, 2008); and Beronä, introduction to *Mad Man's Drum: A Novel in Woodcuts*, by Lynd Ward (New York: Dover, 2005).

32. Levin, "Note on James Daugherty," 25.

33. Ibid., 26.

34. Stein made this attribution in 1938. See Patrick Wright, "Cubist Slugs," *London Review of Books*, June 23, 2005, 16–20. Wright reviews *Strategic Camouflage*, by Solomon J. Solomon (London: Murray, 1920), a book touting the notion that "art alone could screen men and intentions where natural color failed."

35. Rebecca Lawton, introduction to *Heroic America: James Daugherty's Mural Drawings of the 1930s*, 58. This exhibition catalog, based on a limited 1998 show of sketches and drawings at the Frances Lehman Loeb Art Center at Vassar, concerns Daugherty's avant-garde training and the mixed reception of his mural proposals and projects.

36. Josiah Titzell, "James Daugherty, American: A Painter of Oils and Murals Who Has Entered into the New Spirit of Bookmaking," *Publishers Weekly*, October 26, 1929, 2073.

37. Ibid.

38. Ibid., 2076.

39. James Daugherty, "Children's Books in a Democracy," *Horn Book Magazine*, July 1940, 233.

40. Ward, "Note on James Daugherty," 239–41.

41. "Daugherty's images of African Americans—for instance, his portrait of John Henry's powerful wife [in Irwin Shapiro's *John Henry and the Double-Jointed Steam Drill* (1945)]—were clearly intended to be sympathetic, but in some instances his representations of African Americans veer dangerously close to caricature" (Mickenberg, *Learning from the Left*, 249). Mickenberg also details Daugherty's antifascist activism (130, 315–52n43).

42. Daugherty, "Children's Books in a Democracy," 235.

43. Karal Ann Marling, *Wall to Wall America* (Minneapolis: University of Minnesota Press, 1984), 91. Marling details public taste and consensus building around mural projects of the New Deal.

44. Warren French, ed., *A Companion to "The Grapes of Wrath"* (New York: Viking, 1963), includes the full text of *Their Blood Is Strong*.

45. Caroline Levander, *Cradle of Liberty: Race, the Child, and National Belonging from Thomas Jefferson to W. E. B. Du Bois* (Durham, N.C.: Duke University Press, 2006), 34. Levander notes racially biased nineteenth-century texts in which people tout Anglo-Saxon heritage and their "great and glorious Ancestors" (36).

46. Gary D. Schmidt discusses a revision to this passage in subsequent editions of *They Were Strong and Good*. The revision "seeks to eliminate the sleight of hand about slavery, but . . . retains the sense of ownership: 'When my father was very young he had a Negro slave and two dogs. The dogs were named Sextus Hostilius and Numa Pompilius. The Negro boy was just my father's age and his name was Dick.' The ready acceptance of slavery, the refusal to question, is most problematic, especially in a book focusing on the strong and good people that grew a country. One can hardly imagine such a text being written today, and perhaps this explains why this Caldecott-winning work is so rarely on the shelves of bookstores." *Robert Lawson* (New York: Twayne, 1997), ix–x. Schmidt details similar offensive representations of African Americans in Lawson's other books but says nothing of the painful and ugly representations of thieving Native Americans in *They Were Strong and Good*.

47. Avery, "Children's Literature in America," 247.

48. Bader, *American Picture Books*, 45.

49. Ibid., 58.

## POSTSCRIPT

1. Evelyn Harter, "An Exhibition of Books Made for Children," *Horn Book Magazine*, March 1942, 101.

2. "Rules Governing the Selection of Books," in *An Exhibition of Books Made for Children* (New York: American Institute of Graphic Arts, 1941), 2.

3. Larry June, "A Word from the Jury," in *Exhibition of Books*, 4.

4. Harter, "Exhibition of Books," 95.

5. Tessa Rose Chester, "The Economies of the '40s and '50s," in *A History of Children's Book Illustration*, ed. Joyce Irene Whalley and Tessa Rose Chester (London: John Murray / Victoria and Albert Museum, 1988), 209.

# Permissions

Every effort has been made to obtain permission to reproduce previously published material in this book. If any proper acknowledgment has not been made, we encourage copyright holders to contact the publisher.

Figure 1.1. Photographs from *The First Picture Book* by Mary S. Steichen, illustrated by Edward Steichen, copyright 1930 by Harcourt, Brace and Company, Inc., and renewed 1958 by Mary Steichen Martin and Edward Steichen. Reproduced by permission of Houghton Mifflin Harcourt Publishing Company.

Figure 1.2. From *The ABC Bunny* by Wanda Gág, copyright 1933 by Wanda Gág, renewed 1961 by Robert Janssen. Used by permission of Coward-McCann, a division of Penguin Young Readers Group (USA) Inc., 345 Hudson Street, New York, NY 10014. All rights reserved.

Figure 1.3. From *Millions of Cats* by Wanda Gág, copyright 1928 by Wanda Gág, renewed 1956 by Robert Janssen. Used by permission of Coward-McCann, a division of Penguin Young Readers Group, a member of Penguin Group (USA) Inc., 345 Hudson Street, New York, NY 10014. All rights reserved.

Figure 1.4. From *Junket Is Nice* by Dorothy Kunhardt, published in 1933 by Harcourt, Brace.

Figure 1.5. From *Now Open the Box* by Dorothy Kunhardt, published in 1934 by Harcourt, Brace.

Figure 1.6. From *The Poppy Seed Cakes* by Margery Clark, copyright 1924 by Doubleday, a division of Random House, Inc. Used by permission of Doubleday, a division of Random House, Inc.

Figure 2.1. From *Miki: The Book of Maud and Miska Petersham*, by Maud and Miska Petersham. Used by permission of Doubleday, a division of Random House, Inc.

Figure 2.2. From *Kees and Kleintje* by Marian King, illustrated by Elizabeth Enright, published in 1934 by Albert Whitman and Company.

Figure 2.3. From *Aladdin and the Wonderful Lamp* by Elizabeth MacKinstry, published in 1935 by The Macmillan Company.

Figure 2.4. From *Pancho and the Bull with the Crooked Tail* by Berta and Elmer Hader, published in 1942 by The Macmillan Company. Reprinted with permission from Simon and Schuster Children's Publishing Division. Hader Connection, Ltd., a nonprofit organization dedicated to reintroducing the art and writings of Berta and Elmer Hader, grants permission to reprint the Hader images in this book; www.haderconnection.com. Signed copy used with permission from Illinois State University's Special Collections, Milner Library.

Figures 2.5 and 2.6. From *Jamaica Johnny* by Berta and Elmer Hader, published in 1935 by The Macmillan Company. Hader Connection, Ltd., a nonprofit organization dedicated to reintroducing the art and writings of Berta and Elmer Hader, grants permission to reprint the Hader images in this book; www.haderconnection.com.

Figures 2.7 and 2.8. From *Green and Gold: The Story of the Banana* by Berta and Elmer Hader, published in 1936 by The Macmillan Company. Hader Connection, Ltd., a nonprofit organization dedicated to reintroducing the art and writings of Berta and Elmer Hader, grants permission to reprint the Hader images in this book; www.haderconnection.com.

Figure 2.9. From *I Am a Pueblo Indian Girl* by E-Yeh Shure', published in 1939 by William Morrow and Company.

Figure 2.10. From *The Story about Ping* by Marjorie Flack, illustrated by Kurt Wiese, copyright 1933 by Marjorie Flack and Kurt Wiese, renewed 1961 by Hilma L. Barnum and Kurt Wiese. Used by permission of Viking Penguin, a division of Penguin Young Readers Group, a member of Penguin Group (USA) Inc., 345 Hudson Street, New York, NY 10014. All rights reserved.

Figure 2.11. From *The Story of Ferdinand* by Munro Leaf, illustrated by Robert Lawson, copyright 1936 by Munro Leaf and Robert Lawson, renewed 1964 by Munro Leaf and John W. Boyd. Used by permission of Viking Penguin, a division of Penguin Young Readers Group, a member of Penguin Group (USA) Inc., 345 Hudson Street, New York, NY 10014. All rights reserved.

Figure 2.12. From *One Day with Jambi in Sumatra* by Armstrong Sperry, published in 1934 by The John C. Winston Company.

Figure 2.13. From *One Day with Tuktu, an Eskimo Boy* by Armstrong Sperry, published in 1935 by The John C. Winston Company.

Figure 2.14. From *Little Eagle, a Navajo Boy* by Armstrong Sperry, published in 1938 by The John C. Winston Company.

Figure 2.15. From *Across the Cotton Patch* by Ellis Credle, published in 1935 by Thomas Nelson and Sons.

Figure 2.16. From *Down, Down the Mountain* by Ellis Credle, published in 1934 by Thomas Nelson and Sons.

Figure 2.17. From *Pepe and the Parrot* by Ellis Credle, published in 1937 by Thomas Nelson and Sons.

Figure 3.1. From *Today's ABC Book* by Elizabeth King, published in 1929 by Robert M. McBride and Company.

Figure 3.2. From *What Makes the Wheels Go Round* by George E. Bock, published in 1931 by The Macmillan Company.

Figure 3.3. From *The Picture Book of Travel* by Berta and Elmer Hader, published in 1928 by The Macmillan Company. Copyright the Estate of Berta and Elmer Hader. Hader Connection, Ltd., a nonprofit organization dedicated to reintroducing the art and writings of Berta and Elmer Hader, grants permission to reprint the Hader images in this book; www.haderconnection.com.

Figure 3.4. From *Diggers and Builders* by Henry B. Lent, copyright 1931 Macmillan Publishing Company; copyright renewed 1959 by Henry B. Lent. Reprinted with permission from Simon and Schuster Children's Publishing Division.

Figure 3.5. From *Clear Track Ahead!* by Henry B. Lent, copyright 1932 Macmillan Publishing Company; copyright renewed 1960 by Henry B. Lent. Reprinted with permission from Simon and Schuster Children's Publishing Division.

Figure 3.6. From *The Wonderful Locomotive* by Cornelia Meigs, illustrated by Berta and Elmer Hader, published in 1928 by The Macmillan Company. Hader Connection, Ltd., a nonprofit organization dedicated to reintroducing the art and writings of Berta and Elmer Hader, grants permission to use the Hader images in this book; www.haderconnection.com.

Figure 3.7. From *Stop Tim! The Tale of a Car* by May Yonge McNeer, illustrated by Lynd Ward, published in 1930 by Farrar and Rinehart.

Figure 3.8. From *How the Derrick Works* by Wilfred Jones, published in 1930 by The Macmillan Company.

Figure 3.9. From *The Noisy Book* by Margaret Wise Brown, illustrated by Leonard Weisgard, published in 1939 by Harper and Row.

Figure 4.1. Illustration from *Choo Choo* by Virginia Lee Burton, copyright 1937 by Virginia Lee Burton; copyright renewed 1964 by Aristides Burton Demetrios and Michael Burton Demetrios. Reprinted by permission of Houghton Mifflin Harcourt Publishing Company. All rights reserved.

Figure 4.2. Illustrations from *Mike Mulligan and His Steam Shovel* by Virginia Lee Burton, copyright 1939 by Virginia Lee Burton, copyright renewed 1967 by Aristides Burton Demetrios and Michael Burton Demetrios. Reprinted by permission of Houghton Mifflin Harcourt Publishing Company. All rights reserved.

Figure 4.3. Illustrations from *The Little House* by Virginia Lee Burton, copyright 1942 by Virginia Lee Burton, copyright renewed 1969 by Aristides Burton Demetrios and Michael Burton Demetrios. Reprinted by permission of Houghton Mifflin Harcourt Publishing Company. All rights reserved.

Figure 4.4. Illustrations from *The Little Red Lighthouse and the Great Gray Bridge* by Hildegarde H. Swift and Lynd Ward, copyright 1942 by Harcourt, Inc.; copyright renewed 1970 by Hildegarde H. Swift and Lynd Ward. Reprinted by permission of Houghton Mifflin Harcourt Publishing Company. All rights reserved.

Figure 4.5. From *Little Toot* by Hardie Gramatky, copyright 1939, renewed 1967 by Hardie Gramatky. Used by permission of G. P. Putnam's Sons, a division of Penguin Young Readers Group, a member of Penguin (USA) Inc., 345 Hudson Street, New York, NY 10014. All rights reserved.

Figure 4.6. From *Hercules* by Hardie Gramatky, published in 1940 by G. P. Putnam's Sons. Used by permission of Linda Gramatky Smith and Sterling Lord Literistic, Inc.

Figure 4.7. From *Loopy* by Hardie Gramatky, published in 1941 by G. P. Putnam's Sons. Used by permission of Linda Gramatky Smith and Sterling Lord Literistic, Inc.

Figure 4.8. From *Daniel Boone* by James Daugherty, copyright 1939, renewed 1967 by James Daugherty. Used by permission of Viking Penguin, a division of Penguin Young Readers Group, a member of Penguin (USA) Inc., 345 Hudson Street, New York, NY 10014. All rights reserved.

Figure 4.9. From *Andy and the Lion* by James Daugherty, copyright 1938, renewed 1966 by James Daugherty. Used by permission of Viking Penguin, a division of Penguin Young Readers Group, a member of Penguin (USA) Inc., 345 Hudson Street, New York, NY 10014. All rights reserved.

Figure 4.10. From James Daugherty's mural sequence at Fairfield Court in Stamford, Connecticut, 1937. Used by permission of the Charles M. Daugherty Testamentary Trust.

Figure 4.11. From *They Were Strong and Good* by Robert Lawson, copyright 1940 by Robert Lawson, renewed 1968 by John W. Boyd. Used by permission of Viking Penguin, a division of Penguin Young Readers Group, a member of Penguin (USA) Inc., 345 Hudson Street, New York, NY 10014. All rights reserved.

Figure 4.12. From *An American ABC* by Maud and Miska Petersham, copyright 1941 Macmillan Publishing Company; copyright renewed 1968 by Mrs. Maud Petersham and Miska Fuller Petersham. Reprinted with permission from Simon and Schuster Books for Young Readers, an imprint of Simon and Schuster Children's Publishing Division.

Plates 1 and 2. From *The Little Book about God* by Lauren Ford, copyright 1934 by Lauren Ford. Used by permission of Doubleday, a division of Random House, Inc.

Plates 3 and 4. From *ABC Book Designed and Cut on Wood* by Charles B. Falls, copyright 1923 by Doubleday, a division of Random House, Inc. Used by permission of Doubleday, a division of Random House, Inc.

Plates 5 and 6. From *The Modern ABC Book* by C. B. Falls, published in 1930 by the John Day Company. Used by permission of HarperCollins Publishers.

Plate 7. From *Miki: The Book of Maud and Miska Petersham* by Maud and Miska Petersham. Used by permission of Doubleday, a division of Random House, Inc.

Plates 8 and 9. From *The ABC Book of People* by Walter Cole, published in 1932 by Minton Balch.

Plate 10. From *Lucio and His Nuong* by Lucy Herndon Crockett, published in 1939 by Henry Holt and Company.

Plate 11. From *Aladdin and the Wonderful Lamp* by Elizabeth MacKinstry, published in 1935 by The Macmillan Company.

Plate 12. From *One Day with Manu* by Armstrong Sperry, published in 1933 by The John C. Winston Company.

Plate 13. From *One Day with Jambi in Sumatra* by Armstrong Sperry, published in 1934 by The John C. Winston Company.

Plate 14. From *What Makes the Wheels Go Round* by George E. Bock, published in 1931 by The Macmillan Company.

Plate 15. From *The Picture Book of Travel* by Berta and Elmer Hader, published in 1928 by The Macmillan Company. Hader Connection, Ltd., a nonprofit organization dedicated to reintroducing the art and writings of Berta and Elmer Hader, grants permission to use the Hader images in this book; www.hader connection.com.

Plate 16. From *Runaway Balboa* by Enid Johnson, illustrated by Anne Merriman Peck, published in 1938 by Harper and Brothers.

# Index

**Nathalie op de Beeck** is associate professor of English at Pacific Lutheran University. Her scholarly projects include *Little Machinery: A Critical Facsimile Edition.*